*COMPARATIVE*
*AND INTERNATIONAL*
*LIBRARIANSHIP*

# Comparative and International Librarianship

*ESSAYS ON THEMES AND PROBLEMS*
*MILES M. JACKSON, Jr.*
EDITOR

GREENWOOD PUBLISHING CORPORATION
WESTPORT, CONNECTICUT

*To my wife, Bernice*

*Library of Congress Catalog Card Number: 77-98710*

*SBN: 8371-3327-0*

*Greenwood Publishing Corporation*
*51 Riverside Avenue, Westport, Connecticut 06880*

*Greenwood Publishers Ltd.*
*42 Hanway Street, London, W.1., England*

*Designed by Winston Potter*

*Printed in the United States of America*

# Contents

# Introduction

In this decade, professionals in the field of librarianship and the information sciences will continue to be faced with most of the problems that have haunted libraries for generations, problems that can be best summed up as the attempt to reduce the anonymity of information. There will also be many new problems. Some of these are already becoming apparent, while others are still unknown. But librarians need not despair; the past record is clear. Through the use of sophisticated electronic machines, we have begun to master the bibliographical control and retrieval of information, we have improved the communication between librarians and the consumers of information on a national and international basis, and we have refined the many problems concerned with cataloging and classifying information. In addition, library education has been on the front line in trying to educate people to understand the complexities of organizing and disseminating information of all types.

The purpose of bringing together this volume of original essays was to give to both students and practitioners of librarianship and the related sciences a composite view of the problems, progress, and prospects for librarianship. Although it is impossible to give a comprehensive coverage of subjects and countries, this work provides an assessment of recent and historical developments that have taken place on a worldwide basis. By using the comparative method, we can at once view the alternatives that face us in a world that is rapidly changing. As Louis Shores so aptly states, "We must begin by comparing ourselves with each other; individually as librarians, collectively as librarians, in our own community, our state, region, nation [and] world . . . on equal footing."

The problems related to making libraries a viable force in the community, whether it be academic or village, will no doubt present increasing challenges. Meeting these challenges will require reevaluation of the philosophy of library and information science. In looking at our cities we find that, by and large, libraries have been slow in helping to close the gap between the "haves" and the "have nots." Although there have been successful attempts to serve the poor areas of cities, with funds that year by year seem to diminish, as Milton Byam points out, even with the most innovative programs ever attempted by library systems "nothing has happened."

Our traditional school, public, and academic libraries received repeated salvos during the 1960s from librarians and educators alike. School libraries have been faced with the necessity of coping with the new media and new concepts about the learning process. The concern for poverty and its effects on learning have received high priority in the United States and promises to be one of the major educational challenges during this decade. Project Headstart, a facet of the war on poverty, instituted story hours for pre-schoolers. Libraries have been started for members of the Job Corps. These were bold ideas and certainly not luxuries. We must not allow this healthy movement to fade away; there is ample proof that the mixture of books and poverty has stimulated interesting results.

In her essay, Carolyn Whitenack reminds us that the "medium is the message." She points out that the new professional school media specialist will be neither a librarian nor an audiovisual specialist, but a new type of leader who utilizes the best of both fields and combines them with psychology, management, and communication.

If some of our more established programs in the United States have had what might be considered only modest success while others have begun to blaze new trails in organization and service, perhaps Western Australia can serve as an example of what is possible in developing a new program of public library service. F. A. Sharr attributes the success in Western Australia to the utilization of lessons learned in England, the philosophical approach found in Scandinavia, and the early foundation óf library services of the United States. Local support in Western Australia is based on the fact that resources and services are directly related to the economic, technological, and educational development of the population.

The growing tendency during the last three or four years on the part of public officials to demand more creative use of personnel and resources and tighter control of funds has presented serious operational problems for academic libraries. The demand for more efficient computer equipment to· solve many of the problems of acquisitions, processing, and cataloging of materials will continue during the 1970s. Yet, the diminishing funds from the United States government and shrinking institutional appropriations have required academic institutions to move with greater caution and stricter guidelines in automating libraries. A system that requires hundreds of dollars per hour to operate must have extensive planning. Despite some fumbling in the past decade, it appears that through the use of electronic data-processing equipment and modern management techniques the future of the academic library will be safely built on the accomplishments of the past few years.

The question of to what extent academic libraries utilize research in determining needs is a logical one. In J. P. Wilkinson's essay, we have a report of a recent study he made of Canadian academic libraries' use of research in establishing the rationale used in determining the relationship between need and response. His conclusions point out that the pragmatic approach in academic library administration predominates in Canada. This revelation should be of great interest to academic librarians throughout the world. A. J. E. Dean suggests that in English-speaking West Africa academic libraries have had the same uneven development as academic libraries in most parts of the world. The future, however, will demand that if these countries are going to continue to educate men and women to solve the social, economic, and technical problems facing them, considerable attention will have to be given to supporting and accepting the educational potential of academic libraries and librarianship.

In a symposium sponsored by the United Nations' Educational, Social and Cultural Organization in 1958, it was unanimously agreed that one of the most important duties of a national library is to insure the organization and publication of current national bibliography. Ideally, the national library should attempt to have complete bibliographical coverage, irrespective of language. In this sense "complete" means that all types of media are included—monographs, pamphlets, official documents, newspapers and periodicals, maps, atlases, music scores, phonograph recordings, and microforms. Three contributors, Ivan Kaldor, Arthur Gropp, and Hans Panofsky discuss the bibliographical responsibilities of the national libraries of the Soviet Union, Latin America, and Africa. In the U.S.S.R., bibliography is looked upon by leaders of the country as a highly developed function of the Lenin Library and the All-Union Book Chamber. Kaldor, who has done extensive research on the historical development of libraries in the Soviet Union, points out that contrary to many previously published reports, the early development of librarianship in that country was influenced by library practices in the United States, Great Britain, and Switzerland. In Latin America, national libraries go beyond the usual bibliographical function and extend their programs to "generate popular interest and pride in national culture by organizing lecture series, radio programs, and exhibitions." A considerable amount of the cultural work involves publications. In Africa, the national library, in many cases, is the only link between libraries within the nation and abroad. Panofsky presents the interesting proposal that instead of a number of smaller libraries, one well-organized and strong library could very well suffice. A strong national library could also serve as both a public library and the repository of government archives.

If there is to be continued and sustained progress in the fields of information storage and retrieval and classification, the testing ground will no doubt be Europe. Robert L. Collison assesses the problems in these fields and concludes that because of Europe's great diversity, contributions are likely to come from Paris, Berlin, London, and Moscow on an equal basis.

Library development, particularly in the special libraries of Southwest Asia, has had only sparse and scattered treatment in the literature. John F. Harvey presents here a survey of the current status of special libraries and information centers in this region of the world. In contrast to some of the earlier reports made on the status of libraries in the developing nations of Southwest Asia, we learn from this current comparative assessment that many of the special libraries and information centers in these twelve nations are giving modern services and are experiencing, in many cases, successful intercountry cooperation.

Finally, the editor wishes to express his sincere gratitude to all of the contributors for taking time from their busy schedules to prepare the essays included in this work.

MILES M. JACKSON, JR.

*State University of New York*
*College of Arts and Science at Geneseo*
*December 1969*

# PART ONE

# Perspective

# 1/ Comparative Librarianship: A Theoretical Approach

LOUIS SHORES

*Florida State University*

In retrospect, the next generation may most dissent with our lack of comparatives.

"To know thyself," Goethe once wrote, "compare thyself to others." As 1999 looks back three decades, the younger generation will unquestionably make comparisons with its parents. It will ask the older generation to account for its "establishment," to apologize for presenting its children with problems, to make good on its promises for a better society. The youngsters who emerge as citizens on the eve of the new century may even undertake some comparisons that their protesting parents of the sixties overlooked.

For example, was the 1969 establishment in the United States worse than any other 1969 establishment elsewhere? Or, in the long record of civilization, was there ever an establishment more deserving of violent protest than the order of things against which demonstrators marched "non-violently" in the seventh decade of this century?

Inevitably, they will conclude that no young generation ever compared itself less to other young generations of other places and of other times than the protesting youngsters of the 1960s. Possibly because none of us (regardless of our age, color, politics, religion, and almost any other of the artificial measures we use these days to separate humans) is willing to compare ourselves with others before protesting injustices perpetrated by others, society appears to be more frustrating than ever.

Although the proximate thesis here is that librarianship as a profession can best improve itself by comparative study, the ultimate thesis is that our professional destiny is to lead this troubled world out of its current dilemmas by teaching people everywhere to compare their ideals and their societies.

## Some Proximates

Librarianship is even now a distinguished profession among the occupations the world recognizes. Despite the protesters in our own ranks, our profession is based on a substantive discipline, as substantive as any in our customary curricula. If we will but compare our journal writings with those found in the journals of other disciplines, some of us who disparage our writings will discover that indeed librarians write literature. And if, before the neophyte writes his letter to the editor about "what's wrong with library school," he will look at the revolt in school and on campus in general, perhaps he will discover that library education is relatively relevant. Like the rest of the world, we librarians suffer from the same malady that has afflicted all mankind: a lack of significant comparisons.

Librarianship is a distinguished profession, based on a substantive discipline. But our profession and its discipline can never reach their high destiny until they begin to compare more significantly. Librarians the world over can never assume their decisive role until librarianship becomes comparative.

Since the key word is *comparative*, the dictionary definition chosen to represent best a vital element in my theoretical approach to Comparative Librarianship is that found in Webster's Seventh New Collegiate: "Comparative, n.1 one that compares with another especially on equal footing . . . " We must begin by comparing ourselves with each other, individually as librarians, collectively as libraries, in our own community, in our state, region, nation, world—and who knows, as space opens to us, in the universe—*on equal footing*. This is the basic approach in all comparative study. It is the essence of Comparative Librarianship and its theoretical approach.

Once again I offer this definition of Comparative Librarianship:

Study and comparison of library theory and practice in all of the different countries of the world for the purpose of broadening and deepening our understanding of professional problems and solutions.[1]

Although the emphasis appears to be on international librarianship, it is most important to the approach here sponsored that comparisons begin at home.

If we begin here, then we will have to admit that Comparative Librarianship has always loomed large, despite the omission of a separate entry under this heading in our American current bibliography, *Library Literature*[2] (although the British *Library Science Abstracts* does have this subject indexed).[3] All of our library standards are efforts at comparative evaluations. We report library statistics of all kinds—accessions, circulation, finances, and so on—comparatively. We even undertake some qualitative comparisons in service, personnel, and instruction. Our comparisons are by type of library—academic, public, school, special—and by size categories in each type and so on. But this is only a beginning. It is not the approach that will bring librarianship to its role of destiny.

To this point, librarianship in general, and in the United States in particular, has had to be entirely too pragmatic. It has concerned itself, disproportionately, with technique, things, and tangibles. When it has made surveys, as it has most frequently of late, it has done so quantitatively more often than otherwise. Its standards, despite repeated efforts to eschew figures, have returned again and again to statistics as a base for measures. As evidence, review the whole series of ACRL standards for academic libraries, beginning with the first in 1940, developed by an ALA committee which I chaired.[4] Review the public library series and the standards for school libraries, even through the joint AASL-DAVI current set for media centers.[5] Let it be clear: these have all been signal comparative efforts. They have spurred libraries and librarians toward excellence. But these standards, perhaps necessarily in a society committed overwhelmingly to the material, have had to accentuate tangibles.


*Acquisitions*

For illustration, let us begin with acquisitions, the first of the big four divisions of librarianship. Our principal items of comparison at present are still the *number of accessions* and the *amount of money*. Academic librarianship likes to point to the libraries that can boast of over a million volumes in the collection. Perhaps there is some correlation between the size of a collection and the quality of higher education, as has been pointed out on a number of occasions. There is, however, some argument for very much smaller collections to make undergraduate learning more effective. Public and school libraries also compare themselves on the basis of quantitative standards, on the minimum and average size of collections, and, of course, all types measure themselves on per capita appropriations. These are good bases for making comparisons, tangible and essential, if libraries are to flourish and even survive.

Where librarianship has become qualitatively comparative in *acquisition* it has been, most dramatically, in selection. Here, the negative aspect of "censorship" has provided a qualitative element vital to the profession's highest role. Through its library bills of rights (school, as well as general), librarianship in the United States has declared boldly to the world, on both sides of what we have called the "Iron Curtain," our intention to protect the freedom of people to read what they like. We have maintained our vigilance against invasions and infiltrations of our freedom ramparts through a national Committee on Intellectual Freedom and many state committees. With conviction we have insisted that selection is always positive, and censorship is always negative. And with equal assurance we have almost always assumed that *we* select; *others* censor. But Comparative Librarianship, the qualitative type being here espoused, compels us to look critically at our position. A good case could be made for American intellectual freedom as compared with other national brands today, although one might doubt that in the face of current protests. Certainly, our ALA Intellectual Freedom Committee has devoted itself passionately to ferreting out violations of the freedom to read. I know this firsthand, both from serving on the ALA Committee for six years and from starting, during my presidency of the Florida Library Association, what was probably the first state committee on intellectual freedom. From this background, and from my involvement in black-white relations going back to the beginning of my Fisk librarianship in 1928, I am confident that no country I have lived in or visited, in any part of the world, more earnestly strives to protect the freedom to read, to speak, to write, to worship, to think, than does the United States. Nevertheless, there is just a possibility we are not as free as we think. The intellectual freedom our American librarianship currently defends may be based on a questionable foundation.

Comparative Librarianship offers a qualitative measure of our contemporary brand of intellectual freedom. We cannot dismiss the dissent of some librarians abroad. Certainly, the librarians of the Soviet Union, to say nothing of the librarians of the People's Republic of China, do not agree with our perspective on reading. Indeed, even the point of view of some colleagues in the more independent socialist nation of Czechoslovakia suggests that they are not in full accord, as hinted by Jaroslav Drtina.[6] Something more than a hint is contained in the "Soviet View of American Libraries."[7]

From many conferences and conversations with librarians abroad I have been forced to scrutinize our "intellectual freedom" stance, even as colleagues over there frequently do. For example, is there really an element of censorship in our book selection aids? The power of accrediting agencies from without, and the desire of the librarian and his library to conform to "good practice," may not these be a kind of force that is more totalitarian than any that might be exerted by a politburo in a socialist country? (Let not the question mark be overlooked, however.) In London and in Cape-town, in Sydney and in Tokyo, in Manila and in Mexico City, I have entered into dialogue with librarians about the concept of censor-ship. I have insisted politely that we do not mean to sound smug or trite when we declare self-righteously that "selection is positive; censorship negative." Most American librarians are aware of the fact that any time we do not select a book, for whatever cause—inade-quate budget, intellectual preference, interpretation of community interest profile, or whatever—we may be accused of censorship by someone who considers the unpurchased book preferable to one purchased.

But beyond the political consideration, sharpened by the current struggle between the communist world and the other half, there is a philosophical and ethical element. Today, this issue can be best illustrated by the other of the two subjects that keep our Committee on Intellectual Freedom busiest. If library censorship arises on any issue more than on communism, it is on the controversy over sex. To the "liberal," whoever he may now be, or let us say to the "liberated," sex is here to stay and we may as well make the most of it in all of the media of communication. Consequently, any attempt to limit the free expression in print of this natural function is considered to be censorship.

There is still, however, something in mankind to which the liberated refer rather contemptuously as the "Puritan Ethic." It is equated with "Victorianism" as an antiquated and hypocritical position of reactionaries. Any effort to limit language that is symbolized by the four-letter word is branded as censorship by those who crusade for intellectual freedom today. If the Puritan does not want to read what he calls pornography, that is his choice. But if one who is liberated wants to read Frank Harris' *Autobiography* or *Candy* or *Fanny Hill* (which accomplishes the same without four-letter words) for whatever reason—science, social science, research, or even as Tom Lehrer puts it, "Because dirty books are fun"—that is his right and his freedom.[8]

Here, Comparative Librarianship may enter. As we look at the contemporary literary scene, are we comparatively free or comparatively censored? There were periods when novels like *Tropic of Cancer* had to be published in France and imported into the United States surreptitiously. Now, fiction published in this country makes *Tropic* almost Victorian by comparison. Anything goes—almost—in print; and on the screen all the producer has to do is indicate "for mature audiences" in order to be permitted to have actors perform publicly what Bob Hope jokingly admitted "I don't dare to do in bed." Comparatively, the permissive pendulum has swung so far that it is possible that the freedom of those who want to write or read about sex, for whatever purpose, is far less threatened than that of those who do not.

It is Comparative Librarianship that must call us back to perspective on the current crusade for intellectual freedom. In a climate where "anything goes" is it not tilting with windmills to crusade for sex freedom? In the gold rush of publishing, which rewards authors of "frankness" with unprecedented royalties, and lush movie and television contracts, is it not a bit unnecessary to "protect" freedom to write? Might not the profession better concern itself with intellectual responsibility? And this is another approach for Comparative Librarianship: to help us relate to the climate. If the intellectual state is totalitarian, then the struggle for intellectual freedom becomes paramount. But when the conditions are as extremely permissive as they are today, when the media compete with each other to communicate the cause of protest, then I suggest that librarianship, through its comparative vision, must offer the balance.

One more issue in the book selection division of the acquisitions area: review. Pick up any paperback of a current bestseller that lures readers by means of a salacious picture on its cover, and you will find inside the cover excerpts from some of our best literary reviews extolling the talents of the book's author in adjectives which reduce Shakespeare to a second-rate hack. Sophisticated reviewers may feel free to express uncritical admiration of sheer "frankness," but Librarianship, especially if it is comparative, must not abdicate its literary judgment, no matter how celebrated the name of the reviewer who extols the book under consideration.

I venture the opinion that librarian evaluation, uninfluenced by well-known critics, is more wholesome than sophisticated literary criticism. Of course, I recognize the fact that "wholesomeness" is obnoxious to the realist school of literary criticism. But if the realist will not walk out, as is the custom of the neo-liberal today, when the time comes for the opposition's turn at bat, he can hear a case for reality over realism that will have considerable philosophical as well as literary foundation. Only Comparative Librarianship can fortify the librarian to confront the litterateur as peer, to call back reading to some eternal values.

### Comparative Preparations

The second of the four major divisions of librarianship—preparations—has also always been quantitatively comparative, on numbers of volumes cataloged, sent to the binder, and so forth. When preparations has been most qualitatively comparative it has usually been in its bibliographic descriptive efforts and in its attempts to classify knowledge. Bibliographically, catalogers and bibliographers have compared styles of entry sequences, as developed by the British-American code committees, with entry forms adopted by other national libraries, and by learned societies, here and abroad. Under UNESCO and other agencies' sponsorships, some attempts at standardization have been made. All of these efforts can be considered an important part of Comparative Librarianship.

Even more significant have been librarians' efforts to classify man's knowledge. There will be, of course, some ancillary detractors in our professional ranks who will scoff at these classifiers' claims to contributions in the philosophical division of epistemology. But if a librarian is able to make truly comparative judgments, he will proudly compare Melvil Dewey (even now when it is a mark of professional sophistication to belittle Dewey Classification) with Linnaeus and Mendeleev, as well as with others who have worked to classify all that man knows. Today, some revolutionary thinking is taking place in the field of library classification. But there is too little comparative thinking going on.

Academic librarians in the United States, for example, are moving irresistibly toward reclassification from DC to LC. The professional literature, currently, is overwhelmingly in favor of Library of Congress classification. Led by the large university and some special library leaders, smaller senior and junior colleges are accepting now Library of Congress Classification initially or through conversion of their present Dewey arrangement. Even some public libraries have succumbed to this trend, but apparently no school libraries of any significant number. Perhaps the arguments for DC over LC are overwhelming.

Comparative Librarianship, however, reveals no such conviction abroad. DC, or UDC, seems still to be the most frequently adopted library classification system. Public libraries in the United Kingdom overwhelmingly favor Dewey, and many larger libraries have adopted Universal Decimal Classification; LC is almost nonexistent. DC is found in libraries on the Continent, in Africa, Asia, Australia, the Philippines, and Japan, to follow the route of my last tour round the library world.[9]

Without Comparative Librarianship, it would be easier to conclude that librarians abroad lack our classification sophistication. Library visitations in the United Kingdom, in Australia, in Germany, in South Africa, in the Philippines, in Japan, and elsewhere and conferences with library leaders, followed by readings in their library journals and monographs, make new insights into knowledge classification and library arrangement inevitable. For example, United States library schools have taught the principle that the larger the library, the closer the classification. If we accept the "equal footing" part of the definition for the word *comparative*, we will have to ponder the basis for the opposite theory advanced by some of our classification experts abroad.

The larger the library, the broader the classification of the *physical book*, some of them advocate. Once a book is placed on a shelf in relation to other books, the more closely it is classified the more it tends to establish a relationship more favorable to one subject than another and the more closely it is related to one specialization than to other possible specializations. This violates the professional principle of impartiality toward all disciplines. By classifying the physical book broadly, librarianship commits itself as little as possible to favoring any one discipline over another. But librarianship does undertake to serve the individual subjects with tailored bibliographies which are closely classified to serve the specialization for which the bibliography has been compiled.

Comparative Librarianship also alerts us to contemporary developments that may put in hazard expensive conversions to LC. The innovation of computerized printout book catalogs, still in its early technical stages, may render all enumerative classification obsolete for library cataloging. Computer programmers tell us that the simple ID number computes far more easily than the complex notation of LC or any other classification system which uses a combination of letters, figures, and perhaps other symbols as well.

## *Comparative Circulation*

The third major area of librarianship—circulation—is probably the most tempting area in which to make quantitative comparisons. It is particularly an American weakness to celebrate progress through boasts of increased book circulation. If per capita loans reveal above average circulation or a highest decile for a region or state or even the nation, this is seen as evidence of successful administration. There is no intention of discounting these comparisons. On the contrary, they must be continued, refined, and ever more critically analyzed.

Qualitative analysis of these figures can be said to approach the mission of Comparative Librarianship. Such analyses have assumed different dimensions as professional stresses have shifted. For example, Louis Round Wilson in his *Geography of Reading*[10] considers reading interests from an approach somewhat different from that of Douglas Waples, a member of his faculty some years earlier, in *What People Want to Read About.* Dr. Waples compiled his subject lists from the topics most frequently treated in American popular magazines.[11]

There have been other comparative approaches to library circulation with exciting qualitative potential. Of significance now would be one related to the issues for which protesters currently march. An ulterior motive might point to converting the contemporary *physical* activism to a kind of *intellectual* action that would result in a higher record of reform accomplishment than the march, for all the claims made by protesters of all generations. If libraries could anticipate issues that stimulate violence, lure potential marchers off the streets and into reading rooms to document problems, and identify solutions so superior that their adoption would irresistibly overcome current social evils, then Comparative Librarianship would be approaching its own high role.[12]

## Comparative References

For at least as long as the American term for the library's major area of information service has existed, Reference has been defined as the interpretation of the collection to the user. In the first of the American Library Association series of published textbooks, the late distinguished Reference leader James Ingersoll Wyer undertook to differentiate among three philosophies of library Reference.[13] In the conservative school of thought, the librarian must do nothing for the user that the user can do for himself. The liberal Reference philosophy, however, advocates the opposite. Give unlimited information service to the reader. In between these two extreme philosophies of service, Dr. Wyer described a moderate school, which attempts the golden mean of encouraging user independence by assisting only as long as necessary. In all three schools, it must be pointed out, Reference is an ancillary function of the library. In every case, the inquirer is expected to initiate the information process by requesting assistance in the location of answers to questions or sources for investigation of a problem.

Since World War II, at least, a less traditional approach to information has paralleled the efforts of Reference librarians in public and school libraries particularly, and to some extent in academic and special libraries. The newer approach, now called *Information Science*, may have had its origin, as Dr. Bradford indicated at the turn of this century in the work of Otlet, Fontaine, and others.[14] But in my opinion, Dr. Bradford himself has as good a claim to fatherhood of this information movement as any because of his little classic on documentation. In it he gave the definition of documentation as "the process of collecting and subject classifying all the records of new observations and making them available, at need, to the discoverer or the inventor."[15] Since 1960, especially, the movement has become more closely identified with terms like *Information Science* and *information retrieval*. Indeed, the learned society in the United States most concerned with this information movement changed its name recently from American Documentation Institute to the American Society for Information Science.

A definition of Information Science universally acceptable to all concerned is still wanting. As one of the information scientists wrote some time back, Information Science is "an expression of hope or a slogan to rally around . . . ."[16] Perhaps this delay is a result of the duel between the pure and the applied, between information theory and information application or engineering, the schism duplicated in so many newer disciplines, occasionally as a show, I sometimes suspect, of establishing a substantive new discipline in the blue book of sciences.

Despite this debate within the ranks of information scientists (to say nothing of the duel between Reference and Information Science), some rather good approaches to definition can be found in Robert Taylor's effort,[17] in the writings of Gerald Jahoda, and even in an occasional abridged college dictionary of the English language, like Funk & Wagnalls *Standard* (1963). Although the entry in the last is under "Information Theory," the definition constitutes a start:

A branch of communication theory concerned with the quantitative study of communication processes and in particular with the encoding and decoding of messages through randomly disturbed channels.

Confronting traditional library Reference with contemporary Information Science reveals nothing so much as that the profession has neglected making comparisons between them. Only now some beginnings are appearing in the respective literatures that suggest a common genealogy. There is still some reluctance to use each other's terminology. Perhaps *RQ*, the ALA Reference Service Division's official publication, has crossed the line a little more frequently and freely than has *American Documentation*, the official journal of ASIS. Yet there is a continuity between them that would strengthen both if Information Science would look backward and Reference would look forward more often. (I have illustrated this mutuality in the case of encyclopedia system design.)[18] Comparative Librarianship between Reference and Information Science proves that geographical boundary lines are no more important than disciplinary boundaries.

What comparisons can do for both information approaches is, first, compel continuous reexamination of the differences, real or alleged, that appear to exist. Second, it may encourage enough mutual regard to allow for reexamination without condescension of the principles and practices found on both sides of the line. Third, there is just the possibility that something has been overlooked in the one that can be combined with something neglected in the other, to introduce a new dimension into the information-gathering mission. Fourth, some fundamental assumptions about information presently shared by both camps may be challenged with a new look. For example, is the quantitative approach stimulated by computer retrieval the real heart of the information need—the gathering of separate facts? Or is it possible that what the so-called explosion awaits is an *implosion* of value retrieval? May it even be that the information crisis is no more acute than at any time in the history of civilization, because the increase in the number of facts has been more than matched by the hardware for retrieval that man's ingenuity has invented? The real crisis now, as ever before, is value retrieval, recovering significances. And on this problem, comparative study might provide some breakthroughs.

## Comparative Library Education

Because the professional literature appears to differentiate between Library Education and Education for Librarianship (although the ALA Library Education Division comprehends both), let us begin by defining each as a foreword to the first comparative judgment within the profession. In this essay, Library Education will be considered to be the *library education of the layman for library use*, from preschool to graduate school, as well as for the nonschool population. Education for librarianship will be extended to include postgraduate accredited professional education, not only the ALA master's, but the post-master's sixth year, the doctorate, and the undergraduate bachelor's that includes an ALA-NCATE type of course design. Furthermore, with growing recognition of the paraprofessional library technical assistant, it seems pertinent to consider the education of this middle group as well.

The first library education comparisons, therefore, should involve the levels of library education. Although the profession has been slow to articulate, if not actually reluctant to do so, recruitment and employment are forcing recognition of some kind of continuum. Offered here is what appears to be an emerging system of library education that encompasses not only preparation for library use by the layman, but education for professional service by the librarian.

What United States library education is suffering from now is a lack of comparative thinking among its levels, and particularly among its professional levels.

Dead ends for the bachelor undergraduate NCATE-like program, certificated by state departments of education for school librarianship, are still articulated awkwardly in too many ALA accredited master's programs, so that the student must repeat content or extend his calendar of preparation time, or both. This inadequate articulation between master and bachelor programs has received some attention in the past, especially in some states, and can therefore be said to be receiving comparatively more attention than coordinations between pairs of other levels. For example, the newest of all articulations caused by the paraprofessional education for library technical assistants, still opposed by some, faces a rocky road. Despite recognition in federal, state, and local systems of civil service of the need for aides and technicians, library education continues to neglect comparisons of levels of training in preparing for the different levels of duties.

Next to neglect of levels of training, comparative library education

## *Suggested Levels of Library Education*

| *Level* | *Objective* | *Preparation* |
| --- | --- | --- |
| Nonprofessional instruction | Library use in learning | Elementary, secondary schools, junior college, adults out of school |
| Nonprofessional research | Library use in research | Senior college, graduate school, adult specialists |
| Clerical | Library clerical duties | Secondary school, business education |
| Semiprofessional | Libraries paraprofessional duties | Junior college or lower undergraduate division |
| Professional 1 | Library professional duties: beginning | Senior college |
| Professional 2 | Library professional duties: advanced | Graduate school M. A. |
| Professional 3 | Library administration, instruction, research | Post-master, Ph.D. |

suffers most from neglect of basic subject comparisons. The subject, in recent years, has been complicated by the rise of peripheral professional subdivisions, such as Audiovisual Instruction, Information Science, Archivism, as well as several special librarianship categories, like medical, legal, and various pure and applied science librarianships. What should go into the curriculum that prepares the next generation to practice in our profession?

An examination of the increase in audiovisual techniques and a recognition that the audiovisual movement is but one of the two new waves in our library discipline will instruct us to revolutionize our basic courses in the area of Book Selection so that they become *generic* book selection or media selection courses. This is quite different from a course that concentrates on selection of hard-cover print, offers a strong unit on serials, and then pays its respect to audiovisual aids by gingerly indicating that such things as 16mm films exist, along with filmstrips, slides, and other audiovisual materials.

What is called for by the new dimension introduced into traditional Book Selection by AV is a three-pronged approach. Whereas Book Selection, as taught in library school and practiced in library service, has considered, basically, *subject*, and secondarily *level*, it must now consider *format* of equal significance. If there is any significance to the McLuhan furor it must be that the format of media (that is, the physical makeup) affects communication with different individuals in different ways.[19] Thus a film format may deliver its message more effectively to one individual, but a printed page may do this better with another person. Sometimes one subject is better presented through firsthand experience on the field trip, whereas another subject comes over better on film strip, slide, or transparency overlay. Consequently, it is important that library book selection mend its ways so as to consider a wider range of criteria for subject, level, and, above all, format.

Similarly, examination of Information Science as another library science wave of the twentieth century will instruct us to revolutionize our instruction in Reference. Although the information scientist is still too passive in his approach to information needs, he is more likely to offer assistance than the traditional Reference librarian, who waits for the question to be asked before answering it. From comparing the interest profile, all of us who work in the field of information feel encouraged to "initiate" the questions on issues that need answering. This comparison suggests a new dimension for those working with both Reference and Information Science. It is their job not only to find answers and materials, but to stimulate pertinent questions that might have been overlooked.

In addition to subject and level comparisons within the field, library education needs to compare itself with other kinds of education. When the neophyte librarian, fresh out of library school, dashes off his letter to the editor of the *Library Journal*, denouncing library school as the blot on the escutcheon of American education, he displays his inability to make accurate comparisons. Certainly all of this campus unrest is not entirely the fault of library school. Nor can the invectives against elementary and secondary education be caused by library education. Surely the protests against medical, legal, and other professional education prove that other students are not entirely pleased with the preparation they receive in their respective schools and colleges. What the student might better do, before writing his letter to the editor, is compare the education and protests in other professional areas with his own. He should study as well their solutions, and he should include some designs for a few prototypes he believes to be superior to be tried out on an experimental basis.

Of course, the symbol of all comparative librarianship is comparison with librarianship abroad. And this is no less so in the case of comparative library education. At least two entire issues of American professional journals have been devoted to aspects of Comparative Librarianship, one of these to comparative library education.[20] The *Journal of Library History* has two subtitles, one of which is "Comparative Librarianship."[21] As with the four major areas of librarianship discussed earlier, library education abroad differs from ours. One of the key differences between our library education and library education in the United Kingdom was pointed out in my essay in *Library Trends*.[22] Before we began our junior college paraprofessional library education, Japan preceded us. Our emerging recognition of varying levels of training for differing needs has long been anticipated in West Germany, in South Africa, in perhaps a half dozen other countries. Some of our professional debate about the place of the paraprofessional might be resolved by comparison with practice abroad.

### Some Other Comparisons

Part of our professional complex is to underestimate our discipline, our education, our research, and, above all, our professional literature and our professional philosophy. We do so, partially, because of our diffident, tiptoe, whispering vocational climate. But we do so even more because we lack comparisons. If we compare ourselves with some of the other disciplines, even the ones that have retained their prestige longest in the history of scholarship, we will be convinced that the art, if not the science, on which our vocation is based has an equal claim with philosophy to the definition "the sum of all knowledge." Another look, comparatively, at all education of the past and the present, general and special, will establish our library education as not only peer, but as containing some fundamental elements for all learning.

One of our two most self-disparaging professional stances is that the literature of librarianship is inferior. Inferior to what? That is never quite indicated. It is sufficient only to belittle the writing of librarians to become established as a sophisticate in our ranks. But assertions are based on the lack of comparative evaluations. All one has to do is browse, at random, through the journals of almost any of the other contemporary disciplines, or their applications, to rediscover how comparatively literate the librarian is in his writings. For example, how many of the articles abstracted in *Chemical Abstracts* reveal literary merit superior to writing found in library journals? This is not to rest smugly and say our publications cannot be improved. On the contrary, since the evaluation of writing is one of our top professional commitments, we must ever cultivate our own art of communication.

But we must also practice the tolerance of our profession with regard to answers to the question "What is art?" There are still a few of us who respond best to Tolstoy's answer in his famous little essay by that title. Others of us add the social element basic to the late Upton Sinclair's answer in *Mammonart*. But the sophisticated librarian these days who disparages the writing of librarians undoubtedly does so from the perspective of today's "liberated" exponents of literature. That is all right as long as these librarians' views are seasoned with the profession's tolerance and the comparative view of librarianship. It must always be remembered that such paperback celebrities as Faulkner, Capote, Nabokov, Albee, et al, may be rated as literary inferiors by some with fairly sensitive esthetic tastes. We will have to leave it to heaven to judge between those we appreciate. There is even a possibility that among the belittled writers who are also librarians one may sit at the right hand of the supreme literary critic up there.

The other of the two efforts of librarians that are frequently disparaged is their research. Since the early 1930s when, led by Chicago's new Graduate Library School, librarianship was converted to the scientific method, librarians have become increasingly apt disciples. The library literature will attest our commitment. It is doubtful if any discipline, outside of the natural and social sciences, can show a more favorable ratio of research to non-research publications. Indeed, it is now standard in library school to introduce research courses to train students how to do research. What should be disconcerting is that we, who base our practice on what is essentially a humanistic discipline, should so completely have accepted the folklore of the scientific method without ever indicating any doubts. It is unbecoming for us who investigate in the library art to repeat some scientists' smug observation: "What else is there?" At least some of us should dare to assume that the universe might have been put together by something other than man's scientific method, that perhaps when it comes to solving the ultimate riddle, research will be less helpful than revelation.


*Ultimately*

What librarianship needs is better comparative standards. The comparisons we now celebrate are overwhelmingly quantitative. In the four major areas of practice, the decisions we make are, at times, inordinately influenced by numbers. We count acquisitions—current and total—and measure the greatness of our collection, rather than qualitatively evaluating the ideas it is committed to disseminating. Our crusade for freedom has deteriorated into an endorsement of licentiousness. Our reports on preparations are predominantly counts of materials classified and cataloged rather than qualitative appraisals of access to ideas. When we account for dissemination efforts, the only standard is the per head circulation of bound books. A great public library records so many millions of questions answered each year. The questions may range from "What is the second law of thermodynamics?" to "Where is the ladies' rest room;" But each will count as one question in the total. Librarianship needs not only to make comparisons but qualitative ones, especially.

What is true of the four basic areas of library service is even more apparent in the divisions of librarianship that are qualitative in nature. Our investigations into the potentials of both our discipline and our practice have tended, steadily, toward research via the scientific method. We have almost turned our backs on our humanistic heritage by according second-class citizenship to all non-quantitative essays. We have inclined toward the belittling of our professional literature largely because it does not conform with the realism that dominates the literary scene today.

In terms of ultimate aims, librarianship must be called back to qualitative comparisons. We must more boldly think and act as if our occupation were a decisive one in the near-catastrophic decisions that confront mankind.

On the home front, we must seek to balance the overemphasis on realism and physical action advocated by our most potent media, the television networks, which are achieving a new dimension in totalitarianism by overpowering the national mind. Perhaps this can be accomplished best by contrasting our quiet voices with the blatant shouts of the tube. If we can arouse the American people to make comparisons, if we can somehow offer something more positive than the doomsday negations of our telecast news, perhaps we can start this nation back on the road to faith in itself and constructive achievement.

Abroad, we must present for exposure the Beautiful American. We made a start with USIS. We can do more by converting these United States libraries abroad into United Nations libraries in which all nations present their best qualities equally for comparison, including so-called Iron Curtain countries on an equal basis with so-called western countries. Because the key part of *comparative* is "equal footing."

Just as librarianship can improve itself by making comparisons, so can the profession lead the world out of its present negative outlook on all issues. The libraries of the world offer a common ground for documented dialogue on war and peace; on trade; on education; on a world culture that studies only how to advance all of mankind on the road to salvation.

NOTES

1. Louis Shores, "Why Comparative Librarianship?" *Wilson Library Bulletin* 41 (1966):200-206.
2. *Library Literature* (New York: H. W. Wilson Co.).
3. *Library Science Abstracts* (London: Library Association, 1968).
4. *Library Standards for Higher Educational Institutions* (Chicago: ALA-ACRL, 1942).
5. *Media Standards for Schools* (Chicago: AASL-DAVI, 1969).

6.  Jaroslav Drtina, "University Education for Librarianship in Czechoslovakia," *Journal of Education for Librarianship* 6 (1966): 258.
7.  Irina Bangrova and Nikandr Gavrilov, "A Soviet View of American Libraries," *Library Journal* 87 (1962):703-707.
8.  Tom Lehrer, "Smut," *That Was the Year That Was* (Reprise, 1965), Disc-mono.
9.  Louis Shores, *Around the Library World in 76 Days* (Hayward, Ca.: Peacock Press, 1966).
10. Louis R. Wilson, *Geography of Reading* (Chicago: University of Chicago Press, 1955).
11. R. W. Tyler and Douglas Waples, *What People Want to Read About* (Chicago: ALA and University of Chicago Press, 1931).
12. Louis Shores, "Our Quiet World," *Minnesota Libraries* (1969).
13. J. I. Wyer, *Reference Work* (Chicago: ALA, 1930).
14. S. C. Bradford, *Documentation* (London: Crosby Lockwood & Son, Ltd., 1948).
15. Ibid., p. 9.
16. C. N. Mooers, "The Educational Challenge of Information Science," *ADA Proceedings*, pt. 1 (1963):127.
17. See *American Documentation*, 1968, for example.
18. Louis Shores, "Encyclopedias and Information Systems Designs," *Progress in Library Science*, Robert L. Collison, ed. (London: Butterworths, 1967), pp. 116-133.
19. Marshall McLuhan, *Understanding Media* (New York: New American Library, Inc., 1966).
20. Louis Shores, "Comparative Library Education: Homework for a National Plan," *Journal of Education for Librarianship* 6 (1966):231-233.
21. *Journal of Library History, Philosophy and Comparative Librarianship* is the full title.
22. Louis Shores, "Qualifications of Personnel: Training and Certification," *Library Trends* 3 (1955):269-277.

# PART TWO

# Public Libraries and Media Centers

# 2/ The Public Libraries of Western Australia

FRANCIS A. SHARR

*The Library Board of Western Australia*

The postwar decade saw the birth of many new libraries in developing countries. It might almost be said that there is a postwar generation of libraries throughout the world, as there is of people. Just as each generation, facing its own challenges and opportunities, takes over the accumulated experience of its predecessors and adds its own contribution, so the libraries of this new generation are, or should be, doing the same. The Library Service of Western Australia is one such.

If Sir Isaac Newton could write "If I have seen further than most men it is by standing on the shoulders of giants," there is every reason why lesser mortals should acknowledge their debt to their predecessors. In 1953, when the service was planned in Western Australia, the giants were the public library services of England, Scandinavia, and the United States. This paper seeks to show how the lessons of their experience were applied to the very different situation in Western Australia and why in some respects new solutions were sought.

Libraries in the past have been characteristically urban phenomena. There cannot be many areas of the world less urban than Western Australia. It covers a million square miles, an area a third as large as the United States, with only one urban area exceeding twenty-five thousand population. In 1953 it earned its reasonably prosperous living from agriculture centered on small, widely spaced country towns. While this rustic pattern is being modified by the

enormous mineral developments now taking place, the essential
demographic pattern will not be greatly changed because modern
technology does not require large populations at the work site. For
example, Port Hedland was a sleepy little tropical port set in
mangrove swamps, with a population of twelve hundred, five years
ago. Five years hence, it will handle a larger tonnage than any other
port in the Southern Hemisphere, but will have a population of only
about ten thousand.

In the developed countries, from the time of the Industrial
Revolution, it was in the towns that the money was to be made.
There was therefore a steady creaming of talent from the country
which had its effect not only on demand for rural library services,
but also on attitudes toward libraries. Financial weakness leads to
conservatism and hence to opposition to agencies that introduce
disturbing new ideas. This is not the situation in Western Australia.
It is in the country that money is to be made, it is from the country
that the state earns its living, and it is on the intelligent application
of research that the prosperity of the country is based. Therefore,
there is need and demand for good quality library service in the
country, as good a quality as in the one major urban area, the
capital, Perth.

When L. R. McColvin made his survey of the Australian library
scene in 1946-1947, one of his firm recommendations was based on
the fact that experience had shown the necessity for public libraries
to be controlled by local authorities.[1] Admittedly McColvin had
lived through the thirties and forties in Europe and was acutely
aware of the dangers of totalitarian government to freedom of
thought. Although he may have regarded local authority as a
safeguard against that danger, his view represented accepted experience at that time and was adopted throughout Australia. What
McColvin did not mention, however, was that a local authority in
Australia is very different from a local authority in Britain. In
Western Australia, 80 percent of local authorities have a population
of less than six thousand and 60 percent less than twenty-five
hundred. In area, however, they are large. The median area outside

the metropolitan area is eleven hundred square miles, similar to that of the median English county. Clearly, they would be incapable of providing good quality library service from their own resources, or even with the added resources of a state subsidy, if their libraries remained entirely independent in the traditional British and American manner.

Most countries in the development stage exhibit at least five characteristics relevant to library development: shortage of skilled manpower; shortage of capital; shortage of indigenous publications; a preoccupation with practical problems, in contrast with speculative ones; and a lack of information resources. This does not imply that their people lack respect for the things of the mind, nor that they do not desire access to information. Indeed, in Western Australia the strength of demand for the informational aspects of library service, once there was a means of satisfying it, has been quite remarkable. These factors do, however, suggest the need not only for strict economy in the use both of funds and of professional staff (with consequent re-evaluation of some professional assumptions) but also that public appreciation, response, and support is more likely to be generated by an emphasis on the economic, technological, and educational contribution of library service to the community than on its recreational or general cultural aspects. This has proved to be the case in Western Australia, and the writer's experience in Nigeria indicated that it would be true there also.[2] It may be suggested that this is a factor in developing countries that is sometimes overlooked by advisers from established countries.

Public libraries in the older countries grew up and their traditions were established before the days of the current mass media. While the great urban libraries have always striven for depth and quality in their book stock, this has not everywhere been the aim in small and rural libraries. The Kenyon Report in Britain, for example, defined a major purpose of rural libraries: "to relieve the tedium of idle hours quite irrespective of intellectual profit or educational gain."[3]

In planning for the future almost from a tabula rasa in Western Australia, it seemed at the outset prudent to assess for what purposes books would be likely to continue to be used in the future, and in what fields, on the other hand, they might be supplanted by rival media. In this way the emphasis in the new service might be placed on those aspects most likely to be of enduring value and appeal. Books are undoubtedly—*pace* Marshall McLuhan—without rival for reference and factual purposes, for slow and careful study, for the conveyance of depth of concept and, within the limits of the written word, of depth of feeling. It follows that books will continue to be used for these purposes and that the people to whom books will continue to make the greatest appeal are those who value them for these purposes. Therefore, it seemed wise to concentrate policy and effort on the provision of books of quality and of information so that the service might both fulfill its most important social function and gather to itself the support of those who, convinced of the value of books, would be its staunchest friends.

The validity of this hypothesis has been amply demonstrated in the succeeding years not only by open public support, but by a steady increase in the use of serious works and information sources in both urban and rural libraries.

In 1951 the State Parliament passed an act to establish The Library Board of Western Australia, a statutory corporation charged not to provide library service itself, but to administer a program of state aid to local authorities for the purposes of developing public library service throughout the state. The aid was limited, in general, to a maximum of one dollar for each dollar expended by the local authority on its library. The Board was not empowered to establish libraries itself, nor, except in grave emergency, to take over and run existing libraries.

At that time there were a few existing libraries maintained in a very small way by local authorities—some of considerable age—but the greater part of the state had no library service. The Board therefore had the advantage of starting from a clean slate. On the other hand, it faced the difficulty that, as few people in the state had ever used a modern library, there was little demand for such a service. People do not demand things of which they have no knowledge.

The organization came into being with the appointment of the State Librarian in 1953. The basic problems to be solved initially were:

1. To devise a system which would enable local authorities (of the size indicated earlier) to provide effective library service throughout the state, in the country equally with the city;
2. To awaken demand for such a service;
3. To establish standards;
4. To persuade the government to provide the requisite funds.

The solutions then adopted and the methods of putting them into effect have not been essentially changed in the last sixteen years, during which time new libraries have been established by 120 out of the 146 local authorities in the state, and expenditure has increased from less than fifty thousand dollars to over a million dollars per annum.

Before 1900 there was no Australian government. The continent was divided into six independent states, which were isolated from the outside world and from each other both by distance and by their history. Each state established a "Public Library" in the capital city. These were not public libraries in the normal sense, but were in essence and in outlook miniature national libraries. They tended to model themselves on the British Museum.

About two years after the Library Board was established, the government decided that it should take over the Public Library of Western Australia, which, owing to financial starvation for many years, was not in a strong condition, though it had some excellent material dating from earlier days and a better overall stock than any other library in the state. The following decisions were made:

1. The library should fulfill the functions of a regional public reference library for the western third of Australia and not those of a national-type library.

2. The library should be reorganized in subject divisions to concentrate on the active provision of information service.

3. In addition to serving those who might come to it or

communicate with it directly, it should act as a strategic reserve of books and information to enrich the service of all local public libraries in the state, and should assist other types of libraries to the extent that they might wish.[4]

Many people fail to understand the Library Service of Western Australia because they assume that it must be like an organizational pattern with which they are familiar. It may be well, therefore, at this point to recapitulate some of the ways in which it is different.

It does not have one governing authority, unlike a large city library with branches, or an English county library. It comprises a Headquarters organization, governed by the Library Board; a State Reference Library likewise; and a large number of associated but independent public libraries controlled by local authorities.

The State Reference Library is unlike most American state libraries in that it is not particularly concerned with legislative functions, and it differs from many British and American public reference libraries by being operationally integrated into the total public library service, whereas they tend to operate separately from, and parallel to, the surrounding lending libraries.

The lending service differs from British county libraries not only because the libraries are independent libraries, not branches, but also because they may—and are encouraged to—call as of right on the resources of the major reference library of the region, which is geared to assist their users as much as its own. It differs from most American regional systems because the total book stock in all libraries, including the reference library, is in one ownership and is organized bibliographically as one unit, available to all participants.

There are many other differences, some of which will appear later, but these are fundamental.


*The System*

From the demographic and geographic factors indicated earlier, it was clear in the beginning that no pattern of organization existing elsewhere could be applied unaltered in Western Australia.

Experience in the older countries and in some other Australian states demonstrates that small independent libraries suffer three crippling difficulties.

1. The selection of a good, balanced, and comprehensive book stock is impeded by lack of experienced qualified staff, of bibliographical tools, of finance and also, perhaps, by the closeness of local pressures which influence the library's freedom in book selection and other matters.

2. Because of the relatively small number of readers, books tend to be read out before they are worn out. This leads to silting up of the shelves with partly worn books which have lost their appeal.

3. The needs of the user whose tastes or needs are out of the ordinary cannot be met except at extravagant cost. This is recognized by such readers, who are inhibited from asking for what they do not expect the library to supply. Two results follow. These potential library users, who are probably among those whose use of the library would be most beneficial to themselves and to the community, are not served. Secondly, because their needs are not made explicit, they tend to be ignored. This leads to the assumption that the demand on, and function of, the smaller public library is to provide little more than general recreational reading. Too often a form of Gresham's Law seems to operate in this situation.

Clearly it was necessary to find a means of overcoming these three difficulties if the service in Western Australia was to be effective over the whole state. At that time the most successful services in small towns and rural areas were those of Denmark, Sweden, and England. In Scandinavia small libraries retained their independence but received state subsidy in cash, together with some central assistance through the provision of advice and services, and were subject to state standards and inspection. In Britain, on the other hand, there was no system of subsidy. Rural libraries, by and large, were provided and controlled by large local authorities called counties, which did not provide the libraries of the larger towns. Small town libraries might either be controlled by the county or be entirely independent. There has always been a perhaps unfortunate assumption in Britain that the counties could assist local libraries only by taking them over and controlling them. English county libraries had, on the other hand, pioneered very efficient methods of operating a centralized mobile book stock serving a large number of separate libraries.

The West Australian system represents a fusion of these two approaches. From the Scandinavian it borrowed (as the Act required) the principle of subsidy, standards, and a measure of inspection; from the British the techniques of mobile stock organization. Both were adapted to the local scene. The principle of the reference library functioning additionally and actively as a strategic reserve of books and information to enrich the service of local libraries throughout the region (state) derived from disenchantment with the results of traditional reference library policy and from the principle that since all the people of the state were supporting the library through taxes, all should have the opportunity to benefit as equally as practicable.

The Library Board accepts responsibility for book supply, including processing, central cataloging, and organization, while the local authorities are responsible for premises and local staff. The Board does not issue a subsidy in cash. It buys and organizes books and then issues the books. These books are and remain the property of the Board; they are issued on loan. Each local authority, therefore, has an equity in a certain number of books but not in particular volumes. Local authorities are by no means precluded from acquiring additional books if they wish; a few do so (mainly reference work), but the majority are satisfied with the Board's supply.

It should be emphasized that the Board's responsibility is for book *supply*; it does not dictate book selection for the individual library.

Let us see how this system meets the three difficulties.

Book selection is the responsibility of the Chief Assistant Librarian, who is the next senior officer in the Headquarters organization under the State Librarian. His role is not to select books himself, but to coordinate, and if necessary amplify, the selections made by individual librarians to ensure that the state-wide service, as a whole, acquires the titles it needs in appropriate numbers. He is a very experienced librarian and has at his disposal what M. F. Tauber described as a formidable stock of bibliographical tools.

The problem of books being read out before they are worn out is met by exchanging a proportion of each library's stock at regular intervals, from weekly to bimonthly, depending on the size of the library. These exchanges serve three functions: to remove from libraries books which are worn out, obsolescent, or in need of repair; to maintain the stocks of the libraries in a condition fresh and attractive to readers; to enable a proportion of books of restricted appeal to be displayed at a library without remaining there. In a large library the third function is relatively unimportant because the very size of the choice available on the shelves takes care of it; the first two are important in all libraries. Therefore a graduated exchange ratio operates, ranging from 90 percent of total stock per annum in the smallest libraries (800 volumes) to 19 percent in the largest (100,000 volumes).

The needs of those whose interests are out of the ordinary, or who just want a non-fiction book which is not in their local library, are met by the Request and Information Service. The location of every non-fiction volume in the total stock is recorded at Headquarters. If a reader wants a particular book not locally available, he asks his local librarian for it, and the request is forwarded to Headquarters in Perth. In the last twelve years the number of such requests has increased by 50 percent every two years, and between 91 percent and 93 percent of the requests have been satisfied each year by interloan within the service, by purchase, or by external loan.

In addition to supplying books, the Request and Information Service is the means by which the information service of the State Reference Library is extended throughout the state. The users of all libraries are encouraged to make inquiries at their local library. If these cannot be answered locally, they are forwarded to Headquarters and passed to the appropriate subject library in the Reference

Library. It is responsible for producing as full an answer as possible by any appropriate means: arranging for a book to be lent, preparing photocopies of extracts, or even researching the answer itself and preparing an original statement. For this purpose it will not hesitate to obtain photocopies or microfilms from other Australian libraries, or from Europe or America if need be, to answer the question as fully as is practicable.

This active extension of the reference service could, if not firmly controlled, seriously impair the normal reference service to personal users. This is recognized and steps are taken to obviate the danger. Space, however, does not permit them to be detailed.

If users of individual libraries are to be given genuine access to the whole state-wide book stock, including that of the Reference Library, there must be a union catalog in each library. Such catalogs in card form are out of the question because of their bulk and the problems of filing. From the very beginning of the service, therefore, a printed catalog has been supplied to all libraries and kept up to date. Initially this was in loose-leaf form. Now it is Perfect-bound and issued annually. It currently consists of three volumes similar in format to telephone directories—and, like them, it is intended to be thrown away when superseded by the next issue.[5] Its cost of production is less than 1 percent of the cost of the service. As it adds more than 1 percent to the value of the service, it is justified.

When a new library is started the Library Board supplies the initial book stock, on a scale, at present, of one volume per head of population in the area defined as the service area of the library. It is hoped to raise this ratio, but at present it is financially impossible to do so without lowering the standard of books supplied. The stock is increased if the population grows, provided that the premises remain in line with minimum standards.

The definition of service areas is purely to permit rational administrative planning of sites, buildings, and book stock. It does not limit readers to particular libraries; indeed, every registered reader is entitled by law to use any public library in the state on presentation of his tickets.

The fixed ratio of books to population is perhaps an unusual feature of the service. It derives from three considerations. First, as the Board is issuing a state subsidy, in the form of books, the scale of issue must be related to objective factors open to scrutiny. A population basis is both objective and operationally realistic.

Second, it is common practice for public libraries, like personal libraries, to start with relatively few books and grow with time. There is, however, an essential difference between a personal and a public library. The first has to meet the needs and interests of only one person; the public library, on the other hands, has to please and assist many people with a spectrum of tastes and needs. Even at the recreational level, this requires a wider choice than the personal library. If the library is to meet informational and educational needs, the range must be wider still, and if a new library is to make a real impact on its community, it must present this choice initially.

Third, in the early days of British county libraries the aim was to cover the whole area with service as quickly as possible. This resulted in very small collections being issued widespread, in the box-of-books-in-the-village-school era. This policy did not result in effective library service, and it took a quarter of a century to undo the harm done. The Board in Western Australia was determined to avoid this mistake. It considered that one volume per head of population was the minimum (under mobile stock conditions) for effective service, with 800 volumes a minimum even if the population was below that figure. From this it follows that the speed at which new libraries can be established is determined by the availability of funds to supply this scale of book issuance while at the same time maintaining adequately the stocks of libraries already established.

The stock supplied to each library comprises 33 percent books for children, 40 percent adult non-fiction, and 27 percent adult fiction. Appropriate quick reference collections are supplied to all libraries. All these books are fully processed and ready for use; a catalog card is supplied for each work, to act as a stock record. From these unit cards the library may, at its discretion, copy-type entries for a local public catalog.

If there is an existing library, all its books must be vested in the

Library Board when the new stock is supplied. Normally they are all withdrawn immediately, or over a period. This is to insure that the new service has a new look and that all old, tatty, or obsolete material is removed. If a library has particular works that it specially wishes to keep, for association reasons for example, it may do so, but this is very seldom done. Australians are practical people and readily recognize that new books are better than old ones in a lending library, just as new cars are better than old ones on the road.

The methods of book selection will appear strange to many readers. In principle, selection is the responsibility of the local librarians. In the case of libraries with professional staff, it is a condition that they select all their own books. The unqualified librarians in smaller libraries are encouraged and assisted to make their own selections, but in default Headquarters' staff selects for them.

If small libraries are to be given an attractive stock of good quality, the exchange system is essential not only to remove books which are read out, but also because it is not economically sound to put expensive books or those of limited appeal in small libraries permanently. It is of the nature of the exchange system that books returned from one library in good condition move on to another. The only practicable method of selecting such books is from the shelves in Headquarters. Librarians must visit Headquarters, therefore, to make their selection of the used component in each exchange. Moving collections of books directly from one library to another is not regarded as satisfactory. The books for each library should be individually selected.

The librarians of small country libraries have neither the professional skill nor the bibliographical apparatus to select a wide range of new titles without seeing the books. There are no bookshops in small country towns. Therefore the only practicable method for them to select new books is from the shelves of Headquarters where a wide range is displayed.

It thus comes about that all selection for the smaller libraries is done from the shelves. Most librarians within 60 miles or so of Perth visit Headquarters every exchange, those between 60 and about 300 miles usually select every other exchange, while the more distant ones come to Headquarters whenever they have occasion to come to Perth, on holiday for example. Headquarters' staff selects the rest of their exchanges for them.

These visits serve also the valuable purpose of keeping local librarians in touch with the Headquarters' staff and afford opportunities to sort out problems and guide their work.

Libraries serving over ten thousand population normally have professional staff. They select their new books, in effect, by "ordering" from the Board, and they attend fortnightly book selection meetings chaired by the Chief Assistant Librarian. An advance order list is issued to each of these librarians fortnightly, but this does not limit their selection.

The Library Board currently (1968) spends US $470,000 per annum on books and related materials, or about 90 cents per head of the population now served. This is recognized to be inadequate, but it compares favorably with a total expenditure on books by the state and local authorities fifteen years ago of less than $10,000.

In brief, then, the state through the Library Board offers to local authorities books, central cataloging, and reference/information service; an interloan organization; central supply of stationery, furniture, and equipment; and general advisory service. To qualify for participation a local authority must provide, from its own funds, suitable premises, and local staffing.

The premises must at least conform to minimum standards of floor area fixed by the Board.[6] Headquarters offers consultancy service to library architects. The great majority of libraries are in new premises. The general standard of country libraries is high by international standards: local authorities take considerable pride in them.

In country districts of up to 3,500 population (town population of perhaps 500–1,000) an interesting design has evolved and become standard. The library is a separate wing of the local government office building. Access to it is past the main office counter which is always manned. Thus the library can be open daily throughout office hours even in very small places. Country people can use the library whenever they come into town, but the librarian is free to get on with other jobs in the office when her services are not required. This has proved a most efficient arrangement.

Above 3,500 population, a separate building is normal, and these buildings are not very different from libraries elsewhere. The Scandinavian gallery design has been adapted in the form of a mezzanine study area in a number of libraries and is becoming almost a characteristic pattern in the urban libraries.

In libraries up to 3,500 population the "librarian" is normally a girl in the local authority office. This method of staffing is, of course, connected with the building design mentioned above. Given the backing of a strong Headquarters organization and service, these girls can give good service, and some of them are very good indeed. They must be pleasant, accurate, and intelligent to hold a job in the office. Many become really keen on the library service, because it offers them variety of work and its own challenge.

Between 3,500 and 10,000 population, full-time staff is required. These librarians are mostly married women. They have no professional training, but most have a real interest—indeed dedication—in the work. With growing experience—and, again, backed by the Headquarters' services—they give a very satisfactory level of service.

No apology whatever is offered for staffing these smaller libraries with non-professionals. Apart from the impracticability of doing otherwise—in view of the shortage of librarians—it is not considered desirable to do otherwise. There would not be enough work demanding his qualifications to keep a young professional happy; his salary cost would be uneconomic in the smaller places; he would inevitably be a bird of passage on his way to higher things without commitment to the local community; lastly, he could not be given the range and depth of bibliographical experience which his professional development demands.

All local librarians are, on appointment, required to attend at Headquarters for a brief training course in the ways and ethics of the service. A *Handbook for Local Librarians*, which sets out recommended practice and advice, is issued to all libraries.[7] A newsletter, deliberately couched in an informal, chatty style, is issued quarterly to pass on new ideas and generally to give local librarians a sense of belonging. Most libraries are visited by the Chief Assistant Librarian or the State Librarian at least once a year to maintain contact, and most librarians visit Headquarters at intervals to select their new books. By all these means a corporate spirit and an understanding of the aims and working of the service is built up.

Nevertheless, it must be emphasized that local librarians are local employees. "The liberty of one ends where the liberty of another begins." Within their own libraries they are free to adopt what methods they wish, though most, in practice, follow the recommended procedures. It is only in their dealings with other libraries and with Headquarters that they have to conform to the general system in the interest of efficiency and for the avoidance of misunderstanding.

This overall pattern of staffing has much to commend it in rural areas and is probably applicable elsewhere. It is economical of skilled manpower and conforms with the principle of specialization of function by concentrating those tasks—selection, acquisition, cataloging, reference, and so forth—which require professional expertise and a sophisticated organization where they can benefit the maximum number of users, while distributing the essentially personal service of the individual library as widely as possible.

Except in one or two areas of extreme isolation (even by West Australian standards of distance) the Board does not supply books directly to individuals. Apart from the intention of the Act, the Board's view was originally that to supply those individuals who were aware of their need for books would blunt the edge of local demand for local libraries and so impede the provision of service to the far larger number who would realize the benefit of a library only when they saw and experienced it. This view has been abundantly proved right. Time and again it was the refusal of service to one individual that sparked the demand for a local library.

Despite the vast area of the state, regionalization of library service is not practicable. All the major channels of communication—airlines, roads, railways, postal services—radiate from Perth, the capital city. There are perhaps three country centers where regional headquarters could be established, but to embrace a viable number of libraries the regions would have to be so large in area that little personal contact would be possible. The cost of maintaining a regional book pool comparable with the Headquarters' pool in Perth would be high, and the money can be usefully spent on extending library services to places which have none. Several other Australian states have developed regional systems. The most successful may be in Tasmania, which also has a central book supply organization, but which is a small island fairly closely settled. In the other states, where regionalization has been adopted, it has been to mitigate the lack of a central state organization. In these states the government subsidy is paid in cash, not in books and service.

Centralized resources of music, drama, and foreign literature are available to all libraries. As a result of experiment, it was established that this was the most efficient method. In small libraries the numbers of any of these categories which can be normally stocked are insufficient to excite or satisfy local demand. It is better, therefore, to centralize the stock and issue it on request, either as individual titles, or acting sets of plays, or as loan collections to be exchanged at will. The music provision is the most highly developed. The Central Music Library offers specialized reference service and lending service of scores. Opened three years ago, it has a stock of about 4,000 volumes, 140 serial titles, 13,000 scores, and about 1,000 records for playing on the premises on high-quality equipment.[8] One local library also provides music-listening facilities. There is no record-lending service.

The Drama Library comprises acting sets of plays, and has its own catalog detailing number of scenes, number of characters, and so forth. The Foreign Literature Collection covers the main languages spoken by immigrants or students.

Control of standards is maintained effectively but unobtrusively by the Board's control of book provision policy.[9] As books are bought from the Board's funds, it has a right and a duty to determine overall book selection policy in conformity with the stated aims of the service, which briefly are: information, education, recreation—in that order of priority. It also controls the condition of the book stock, because binding and discarding are responsibilities of Headquarters. Standards both of quality and of condition may be claimed to be high. This strongly influences the service given in all libraries and serves to maintain essential standards.

The Board acknowledges responsibility to ensure that ultimately an efficient layout of libraries will cover the whole state. Any new library must therefore be so sited that it will fit into such an ultimate pattern, despite the vagaries of local government boundaries. The premises must conform to the minimum standards of the Board..

Beyond the measures already described, the Board does not exercise supervision of local staffs. It regards this as a local responsibility. Headquarters assists and advises but does not control, because the libraries are independent, not branches.

In the early days a good deal of missionary activity was necessary to initiate the establishment of libraries. Within a short time, however, this became unnecessary, as the success of the first libraries stimulated demand elsewhere. Rapidly, a waiting list of local authorities built up and, despite the progress that has been made, still persists. Unlike the situation in many parts of America, the decision to establish a library is made by the local authority and does not require an affirmative vote of electors. The electors may, however, demand a poll on any proposal to raise a loan. Only a few polls on library buildings have produced a negative vote, and in almost every case this has later been reversed.

There is no question that it has been the book selection policy, the exchange system, and the Request and Information Service that have generated the development and success of the service. They ensure that the stocks of all libraries are fresh and attractive to readers and that non-fiction not immediately available can be obtained on request. These are the two things that readers want above all, though they certainly also value attractive and efficient staff and premises.

The State Bibliographical Centre, a section of Headquarters, is operationally the hub of the whole system. It has four main functions: to conduct the bibliographical aspects of the Request and Information Service to public libraries; to encourage and facilitate library cooperation between libraries of all types in the state and, on request, between libraries in Western Australia and those elsewhere in the world; to maintain, for that purpose, union catalogs of books and serials held in all public, university, college, and special libraries in the state; and to provide bibliographical advice and service to the users of the State Reference Library. It was the first such Centre in Australia. Tasmania has since established a similar organization.

The library resources of Western Australia, though growing rapidly, are still not great. It is essential, therefore, that the best use be made of them. This needs organization and mobilization to make cooperation possible. Since the Board is an organ of the government itself, and since the responsibility of the public library service extends to the whole community while all other libraries serve only sections, the Board is the appropriate body to conduct the State Bibliographical Centre for the common good.

The acid test of any organization is whether it achieves the results intended. This question may be looked at from the state or the local point of view.

The attitude of the government and politicians is indicated by the increase of state appropriation from A$131,000 in 1955 (the year the reference library was taken over by the Board) to A$733,000 in 1968. The State Reference Library, once little used, is now quite overcrowded, and the government has promised a new building.

The response of local authorities may be judged from the fact that 120 libraries have been established since 1954 and still there is a waiting list for more.

The reaction of readers can perhaps be illustrated by two examples. The city of Fremantle had the oldest public library in the state, dating from 1851. The Council was proud of its library and supported it well. Its policy, however, was to provide a mainly recreational service in the mistaken belief that this was what the public wanted. In the first five years after the library became associated with the Board the number of registered readers rose from 2,400 to 10,907 (population 22,000); the number of books issued doubled, while the non-fiction issue increased four and a half times.

Moora, on the other hand, a wheat belt district of 1,500 square miles with a population of 3,300, including 850 in the town itself, had one of the best small country libraries in the state and 142 readers. Five years after entering the state service it had 1,042 readers; now it has 1,250.

Unquestionably, however, the most significant result achieved by the service is that the libraries in the country, as in the metropolitan area, are now alive with children and young people—the people who will build the future of the state. They are enjoying—and seizing—opportunities which the older generation never had. They will be better people in every way in consequence; better educated, better citizens, and better parents. The question is, can we improve our libraries fast enough to keep pace with their increasing demands?

The Library Service of Western Australia started from scratch. At that time no one had ever attempted to devise a coordinated library system to cover a million square miles. Ideas were borrowed from many sources, adapted and synthesized so that a new pattern of organization developed appropriate to the legal, demographic, and financial situation in Western Australia. In recent years the Board has been glad to welcome visitors and inquiries from many countries with still younger library services and so help, through them, to repay the debt it owed to the experience of those older countries which pioneered library services for the people.

NOTES

1. L. R. McColvin, *Public Libraries in Australia: Present Conditions and Future Possibilities* (Melbourne: Melbourne University Press, 1947).
2. F. A. Sharr, *The Library Needs of Northern Nigeria* (Kaduna, Nigeria: Ministry of Information, 1963).

3. *Report on Public Libraries in England and Wales*, Public Libraries Committee (London: Board of Education, Great Britain, 1937), p. 95.
4. F. A. Sharr, "The State Library of Western Australia," *Australian Library Journal* 6 (1957):161-163.
5. F. A. Sharr and others, "Production of a New Book Type Catalogue," *Library Resources and Technical Services* 10 (1966):143-154.
6. *Siting and Design of Public Library Buildings* (Perth: Library Board of Western Australia, 1962).
7. *Handbook for Local Librarians,* 4th ed. (Perth: Library Board of Western Australia, 1968).
8. S. McNamara, "A Music Library Service for Western Australia," *Australian Library Journal* 16 (1967):153-156.
9. *Book Provision and Book Selection: Policy and Practice* (Perth: Library Board of Western Australia, 1966).

# 3/ Public Library Services in the Inner City

MILTON S. BYAM

*St. John's University*

$A$s living places, cities have been both praised and excoriated.[1] A typical gibe at the city as a place to live is expressed in the statement that "New York is a great place to visit, but I'd hate to live there."

In spite of this remark and similar ones, the city has won. For the people have voted for the city with their feet—that is, by moving to them—since World War I. As a result, cities have grown tremendously, bursting their corporate boundaries to the point of encouraging the establishment of mini-cities around the core, inner, or central city. It is significant that, though most the larger cities lost population in the period between the 1950 and 1960 censuses, the metropolitan areas of which they are part grew appreciably in population.[2]

The central or inner cities also experienced remarkable shifts in population within their chartered boundaries. The shortages of living places after World War II, the extensive urban renewal projects designed to clean out slums, and the tremendous highway-building programs all served to remove people forcibly from their homes and send them house-hunting elsewhere. Some went to the suburban mini-cities just outside the central cities; others moved to suburban-type developments within the city boundaries. New York City's underdeveloped land—in Brooklyn's Mill Basin, in Queens, in Bayside, and in the entire borough of Richmond, for example—was suddenly discovered by builders, and new housing was made available to central city dwellers.

A more significant population shift was that of non-whites from rural areas to the cities.[3] The addition of these groups to city populations expanded their numbers and percentages in the population of the central cities. For the first time population shifts created large enclaves of non-whites in areas in which they had not existed before, areas which had prior to World War II existed only in the very largest cities, such as New York, Chicago, and Detroit. The size of the Negro population grew in some cases to almost a third of the population.[4] In this way cities were substituting a rural, unlettered population for their former residents.[5]

Public libraries are creatures of cities. Some of the world's best and largest libraries are to be found in cities that can support the shared services needed by their residents.[6] Such libraries were founded out of motives of benevolence and charity, and they promoted humanistic education.[7] It was the credo of the public librarian that reading would somehow make people better, and therefore he urged people to read.[8] With this vision of himself and his mission, the librarian did not hesitate to go anywhere and do anything to promote reading. Libraries promoted themselves as social service centers; their staff gave lectures, sponsored the formation of clubs by encouraging use of their meeting rooms.[9] Librarians developed special programs to aid immigrants in their quest for citizenship, gave book talks, and sought to interest children in books by extensive cooperation with the schools.[10] They reached out into the community by taking their books into prisons, hospitals, and firehouses.

Not all librarians participated, to be sure, but big city libraries were aware of the problems of their time and place and sought some resolution of them. As early as 1924, Joseph L. Wheeler suggested the need for a study of the community and outlined specific public relations responses for public librarians.[11] Over the years public libraries promoted and expanded their services by cajoling teachers into making visits to the libraries and by adding record, print-borrowing, and film services. In some ways, public libraries may have overreached themselves in their desire to make readers of everyone.

In the big cities they boasted highly centralized systems of branch libraries reaching into every community. By the 1950s book circulation in the public libraries was the highest in history, barring the depression. But libraries were strained by the impact of student demand created by those who had been the war babies.[12]

It would appear that the public librarian's dream had finally come true. They were indeed making readers out of everyone. Or were they? Or, like a rosy flush on the face of a sick man, did what looked on the surface like health really indicate illness? In other words, what was the underlying meaning of the heavy demand and the consequent strain?

Suddenly, the shifts in population were noticeable, with large Negro and Puerto Rican enclaves in the areas well supplied with branch libraries.

Suddenly, the constituency was expanded by people returning for service from the suburban communities to which their former patrons had escaped, and the shortage of professional librarians became a crisis.

Suddenly, with transistor radios in hand, every child could have the events of the world pressed against his ear during every waking moment of the day.

Suddenly, the computer came of age.

Suddenly, there was misbehavior in the streets that invaded the library itself, and the central city was forced to spend more and more on police, sanitation, education, and welfare services.

Suddenly, the excellent central city libraries were faced with a new world.

With a tightening city budget, a screaming new demand from peripheral areas, and decreasing library use in the older areas of the city, such libraries had the following choices. They could:

1. Abandon existing services for a new pattern of services to meet the needs of the disadvantaged;

2. Restructure the organizational and administrative pattern of the library so as to reduce costs;

3. Provide the traditional pattern of service to those who wanted

and needed it, while abandoning service in the areas in which disadvantaged populations lived, since they did not seem to want it;

4. Find new sources of funds to support traditional library services so that existing service could be maintained and so that expansion could be undertaken in disadvantaged communities.

It is to the credit of the library profession that it did not consider the abandonment of its services in disadvantaged communities. There were many reasons for this, including altruism. Further, many of the buildings in the poorer areas were solidly built Carnegie branches that were still useful. In addition, the anti-poverty campaign had made city administrations especially sensitive to increasing public services in these areas.

Still, librarians had to do something. They decided to look for more money.

In Pittsburgh, for example, county aid to central city public libraries allowed city libraries to permit outlying county residents to use the central library. New York, Maryland, Pennsylvania, and California, among others, passed laws providing aid to public libraries within their states.[13] The federal government, under broad-based education laws, supplied funds to public libraries by means of the Library Service and Construction Act. Aimed at specific ends, such as buildings or service to the handicapped, the laws did not in all cases provide the increase in central city library operating budgets required.[14] Since the money provided had not solved their problems, the libraries had to make further adjustments. Some, therefore, made changes in their modes of operation.

In the Brooklyn (New York) Public Library, the District Library Plan was launched.[15] This was a plan designed to reduce the need for scarce professional librarian skills by setting up a library satellite organization with professional librarians serving at one instead of five locations. The satellites were manned by nonprofessional library administrative staff. The Philadelphia Free Library launched its Regional Plan in north Philadelphia.[16] The Baltimore County Public Library and the Philadelphia Free Library trained college graduates who were not librarians to operate in libraries.[17] The state of New York attacked the problem of units of service that were too small through its aid program, which encouraged libraries to form systems in which they shared with each other professional librarians, material, and services.[18]

Still, these programs did little for the poor areas in cities. This was not caused by lack of recognition of the problem but rather by the failure of every type of program designed to stimulate the use of books in poorer areas. Down through the years the Brooklyn Public Library, for example, had tried many programs in the areas populated by poor people, seeking to awaken them to the joys of books and reading.[19] Some of the programs attempted include the following:

For the Negro, Puerto Rican, Hungarian, and others attending adult elementary classes, there were regular orientation programs designed to acquaint them with the library and its value.

For the youth in Bedford-Stuyvesant, a special lounge-type library with records and a relaxed setting was established.

"Know Your Fellow Americans" programs were planned and produced to introduce the Puerto Rican and the Hawaiian to his fellow citizens.

Consumer education programs were launched in a number of branches in deprived areas, in cooperation with Consumers' Union.

Band and orchestral concerts were given at branches throughout the system, including the deprived communities.

Tests were made to establish the effect of staff of similar ethnic background on community use. And staff double and triple the required size was tried to increase community involvement.

Tests were made of increased hours. And the effectiveness of increased numbers of copies of books as a factor in increased use was tested.

Books in Negro history were purchased in quantity; materials in the Spanish and Italian languages were made available.

Nothing happened.[20]

The branches in these areas continued to circulate about 70,000 volumes annually for populations of 25,000 to 50,000. Two-thirds of this circulation was accounted for by children, many of whom had visited the libraries in class groups.

However, the Brooklyn Public Library was not discouraged. It continued to try to reach disadvantaged populations and to convert them to library use by launching its community coordinator program in 1961. Under this program, a librarian was released from all normal chores and allowed to go into the Bedford-Stuyvesant community to stimulate library use.[21] Though there were no measurable results from this activity when the state made LSCA funds available, the Brooklyn Public Library expanded this program to three other areas. It also launched a pre-school storytelling program conducted by college graduates trained by the library.

Most notable of community coordinator activities was the "Three B" program of providing paperback materials in bars, beauty parlors, and barbershops, along with the auto-van that took books and library programs into slum neighborhood streets, often with a storyteller in tow. Both were attempts to stimulate library use by proximity of materials.

The Buffalo and Erie County Public Library expanded the resources of its North Jefferson Branch by setting up a traveling library-van with cartoons, music, and books.[22] The Rochester Public Library sought to train some of its staff in methods required of personnel in poorer areas.[23] The Queensborough Public Library established a storytelling program for pre-school children in poor neighborhoods and set up storytelling vans which could reach these tots in all weather and could move from community to community. The North-Manhattan Project of the New York Public Library sought to relate better to Harlem by intensifying its services there in the Countee Cullen Branch.[24] The Los Angeles Public Library established centralized and branch programs employing a bookmobile. With this plus spectacular programming it hoped to influence library use.[25]

Other libraries launched programs in the 1960s that did not depend on LSCA funds. The New Haven Public Library established a total community service branch library which provided games, toys, babysitting services, and recreation in one of its branch libraries.[26] Using anti-poverty funds from the Community Action Program, the

Enoch Pratt Free Library established a library in the slums of
Baltimore.[27] The Cleveland Public Library established what it called
"Reading Centers," which sought to solve one of the basic ghetto
problems: the inability of the poor to handle written materials with
skill.[28]

In all, libraries, particularly those in the larger cities, made many
attempts to overcome the lack of interest of the poor in libraries.[29]
Some of these were innovative, representing services never previously
offered by libraries, but generally they suffered from one basic
defect: they sought to make the poor users of normal library services
at a time when the poor did not need normal library services.

Television, transistor radios, and motion pictures had made the
poor as up-to-date about new concepts, thoughts, ideas, and
proposals as the most educated in our society, without putting them
through the embarrassment of reading children's books, admitting
their inability to read and write well, and acknowledging an inferior
status.

Today's television child is attuned to up-to-the minute "adult"
news—inflation, rioting, war, taxes, crime, bathing beauties—and is
bewildered when he enters the nineteenth century environment that
still characterizes the educational establishment where information is
scarce but ordered and structured by fragmented, classified patterns,
subjects and schedules.[30]

The rural Negro and Puerto Rican, fresh from the oral, face-to-face
tradition of the farm, found himself still in the same tradition in
front of the television screen. The library with its fixed location, its
rules, its role as an intermediary to the materials was, at best, a
secondary approach to what they needed to know.

Some librarians saw clearly their roles as transmission belts and
imparted information directly, no matter its form.[31] Other librarians insisted that books alone are the reason for libraries and viewed
suggestions to consider other forms of purveying information as
somehow wrong.[32]

At present in big cities, public libraries are under attack from the
city administrations. Two big city libraries have been without

directors for at least a year—Chicago and Cleveland. In private conversations, city administrators demand more innovative programs from their library administrators, while at the same time they reduce operating funds. Is it possible to add programs within the confines of a line-by-line budget? It is doubtful, particularly when the budgets themselves are also being reduced.[33]

One cannot say that the public librarian has not tried. The age-old dream of a literate and ever-improving society still remains his goal. He is faced, as is the rest of the world, with rapid technological and social change that has left all of society bewildered and confused. He cannot be criticized for the failure to find answers that others have not managed to find.

Still, the present is a time to take stock. Does the public library continue to have a role to play in educating the poor? Success has certainly not been demonstrated by overall increases in nationwide public library circulation statistics, which have shown an ominous decrease for the past two years.[34]

Obviously, one cannot seek out that large body of non-users with the same funds required to serve users without doing both jobs badly. Libraries must strengthen existing services to their users while somehow continuing to experiment with the means of attracting the non-user. But these experiments must not seek to attract the non-user to prosaic library services since even these services are not being used as well as they should be. According to one study, the public library did not service the poor, but rather an educated elite composed of students, housewives, and professional people.[35] It should be clear, therefore, that changes in approach are required. Indeed, libraries should be seeking to do what the books in hand seek to do—educate.

Libraries were born in a humanistic culture for the promotion of humanistic study. Like the schools and colleges of their times, they emphasized literature and languages. With the diminution of the humanities under the impact of a scientific and industrial society, libraries added scientific, technological, and industrial materials, but they still seek people with liberal arts backgrounds for their librarians.[36] Their personnel and their materials continue the humanistic tradition—a tradition characterized by one writer thus: "Whatever the virtue of this composite ideal, whatever nostalgias it may arouse, it has plainly not much to do with the world we live in now."[37]

In today's world, in which everything can be done by machine, the library should be experimenting with the direction infusion of information—not through disseminating print, teaching reading, or preparing book lists—but by providing the information required by each individual in the form in which he can best use it.

If a man cannot read easily, a filmstrip may be the best answer for him. Recipes may be passed on by tape or records. A single fact may be looked up by the librarian and given to the patron. The new eight millimeter sound single-concept cartridge film—borrowed for use at home or in the library—may teach a student more about gems and stones than any number of book pages. Talking books—now used by the blind and physically handicapped—may provide a better knowledge of foreign languages or Shakespeare's plays than the volumes on the shelves, and they may result in quieter use of the library by students.

Of course, this demands a different type of library from that now available to patrons in cities. It requires a move away from the membership concept, which so bemuses public librarians and insults the person who can scarcely write his own name, to a welcoming "use our services" approach. It calls for boards of trustees truly representative of the communities they serve, boards that reflect the very basic changes in the composition of our cities. It calls for librarians who help by digging up needed information, instead of waving airly at shelves of books in this or that number of the Dewey classification. They must also be knowledgeable about the newer materials so that they are aware that the best presentation of the information required may be in a chart, map, slide, filmstrip, film, or tape. They may even provide a copy of a page in a book.

Libraries of this type might well have film or tape cartridges right on their shelves next to the book. They might have a large amount of tape, recordings, eight millimeter and filmstrip projectors on the premises for use by the patron himself. Instead of treating periodicals, pamphlets, and other paper materials like awkward interlopers, their classifications would somehow reflect the presence of these materials and encourage their use. They would make their services relevant by providing answers immediately by means of telephone or television directly connected with the home or by means of teletype locations placed everywhere people might use them, and by moving information and facts around the way twentieth century people are used to having other things moved.

An added problem is that big city public library staffs are suffering from a great unease. This unease is caused by the decrease in library service resulting from reduced budgets, as well as from the failures of the administrators of the libraries themselves. These large library systems, spending millions of taxpayer dollars, are being administered by librarians who, like their systems, have grown to their present estate in the fashion devised for the pre-World War I era.

All by itself, the size of these systems creates a built-in inertia. But when one recalls that some of the larger libraries once maintained library schools of their own, for locally recruited young ladies for whom they had to provide a safe home-away-from-home, one realizes that a kind of paternalism was inevitable. This writer has been regaled by stories from older librarians about the almost dictatorial attention given their habits by branch librarians when the library training classes were still operating. According to the tales, these librarians approved their dress as well as their young men. Can an organization designed to carry out these functions avoid a kind of paternalistic administrative pattern which would chafe against the librarians of the sixties armed with master's degrees?

All of this cannot be put right simply by a kindly administrator or by an encouraging staff organization. It requires a kind of tough-minded reorganization of staff uses, assignments, rewards and penalties that treat the supervisory staff like the responsible people they are. In the present era, there is a good deal of talk about decentralization of large public libraries, as if any absolute principle all by itself could improve service, create innovation, and make a happy staff. Like the service provided, the staffs of the public libraries must be restructured and reorganized for the 1970s.

The age-old library ethic may well be changing under the impact of unionization of public libraries, which is going on at a furious pace. In a sense, unionization is just one more indication that the public library may have outlived its former role of proselytizer for education in the humanistic tradition. Like all other tax-supported services, the library is responsible for supplying a needed service—period. Those who need and want the service may protest the interruption of services caused by strikes. The librarians joining unions believe strongly such protest will result from possible strikes. If there are protests, they will probably come from those who *need* a book for school, for business, or for immediate information. The protests will not come from those the librarians would like to have made into readers.

Large city public libraries have to change their ideas about branch locations. There have been numerous studies made to show that branch libraries should be ten blocks, a half-mile, a mile, etc., from the people they are meant to service.[38] Yet every librarian serving in a branch library knows that as the distance from the branch increases past a quarter of a mile, fewer and fewer possible patrons from these further areas visit the library. A good example is the study of district library use in the Pennsylvania State study mentioned earlier.[39]

Library building design was established for an era when kerosene, wood, and coal were used for heat, and candles, oil, and gas were used for light. Such considerations had to affect the pattern of service provided by them. For example, it was logical to provide reading rooms in this context. But today, even the poorest homes are provided with water, centralized heat, and electricity.

Society still requires some place in which to collect and store information and to make it available, if only to prevent wasteful duplication of effort and the advancement of impressions and feelings as facts. Viewed in this context, buildings, persons trained in the liberal arts, and library collections themselves may well take other forms than those presently in use. Big city public libraries could easily provide for the physical circulation of books and reader advisory services presently being given from a third of its present outlets or fewer.[40] It could then indulge in a burst of other services including bookmobiles, storytelling vans, motion picture showings, and mailed books, records, and film services. In this way, funds could be found for experiments with television, teletype, and other means of electronic communication of information directly to the homes of the public.

The big cities have the resources. They have a stake in the existence of a large population needing their services. They should stop trying to entice non-users into existing facilities that do not seem to meet their needs. They should seek ways to provide what is needed, where it is needed, if truth and scientific knowledge are to continue to have validity. It is fearful to consider a situation in which all of the poor acquire their knowledge orally. The spoken becomes fact, or distorted, becomes the rallying cry for demagogues. Only the public library has demonstrated an interest in and ability to educate all of society. Only it can maintain the promotion of factual exchange. The question is, does it have the will?

Its past would say that it does.

### NOTES

1. Jane Jacobs, *Death and Life of Great American Cities* (New York: Random House, 1967). Note the praise accorded village life by the Booth Tarkingtons and William Allen Whites and the movies of the 1930s based on this and other similar themes, such as Frank Capra's *Mr. Deeds Goes to Town*, (1936).

2.

| Standard Metropolitan Statistical Area | 1960 | | 1950 | |
|---|---|---|---|---|
| | Metro Area | Central City | Metro Area | Central City |
| Boston | 3,177,000 | 697,197 | 2,410,572 | 801,444 |
| Chicago | 6,591,000 | 3,550,404 | 5,177,868 | 3,620,962 |
| Cleveland | 1,971,000 | 876,050 | 1,532,574 | 914,808 |
| Detroit | 3,972,000 | 1,670,144 | 3,016,197 | 1,849,568 |
| Los Angeles | 7,776,000 | 2,823,183 | 4,151,687 | 2,221,125 |
| New York | 11,260,000 | 7,781,984 | 9,555,943 | 7,891,957 |
| Philadelphia | 4,617,000 | 2,002,512 | 3,671,048 | 2,071,605 |
| St. Louis | 2,203,000 | 750,026 | 1,775,334 | 856,796 |
| San Francisco | 2,935,000 | 1,107,864 | 2,135,934 | 1,159,932 |

Source: U. S. Bureau of the Census

3. Almost 40 percent of the population was rural in 1950. In 1960, 20 percent was rural.

4.

*Non-White Population in Selected Northern Cities, 1960*

| City | Population | Non-White | % |
|---|---|---|---|
| Baltimore, Md. | 939,024 | 328,416 | 35.0 |
| Camden, N. J. | 117,159 | 26,892 | 23.8 |
| Chicago, Ill. | 3,550,404 | 837,656 | 23.6 |
| Cleveland, O. | 876,050 | 253,108 | 28.9 |
| Detroit, Mich. | 1,670,144 | 487,174 | 29.2 |
| Gary, Ind. | 178,320 | 69,340 | 38.9 |
| Newark, N. J. | 405,220 | 139,331 | 34.4 |
| Oakland, Calif. | 367,548 | 97,025 | 26.4 |
| Philadelphia, Pa. | 2,002,512 | 535,033 | 26.7 |

Source: U. S. Bureau of the Census

5. Philip M. Hauser, and Martin Taitel, "Population Trends: Prologue to Library Development," *Library Trends* 10 (July 1961):32.

6.

*Public Libraries in Selected American Cities*

| City | Volumes | Circulation | Income (1967) |
|---|---|---|---|
| Boston | 2,415,141 | 2,735,946 | $ 4,824,222 |
| Chicago | 3,556,340 | 9,303,609 | 9,036,137 |
| Cleveland | 3,330,861 | 5,765,909 | 6,116,342 |
| Detroit | 2,142,436 | 4,178,613 | 6,559,899 |
| Los Angeles | 3,371,420 | 13,175,616 | 9,564,361 |
| New York Public Library | 3,231,696) | | 12,379,862) |
| | 7,894,022) | 12,308,318 | 19,746,072) |
| Queensborough Public Library | 2,281,861 | 8,375,142 | 8,795,350 |
| Boston Public Library | 2,691,279 | 9,060,290 | 9,660,841 |
| Philadelphia | 2,531,741 | 5,984,814 | 7,221,984 |
| St. Louis | 1,244,425 | 3,047,590 | 3,084,610 |
| San Francisco | 1,111,239 | 3,255,643 | 3,728,418 |

7.  Milton S. Byam, "History of Branch Libraries," *Library Trends* 14 (April 1966): 368-373.

8.  Robert D. Leigh, *The Public Library in the United States* (New York: Columbia University Press, 1950), pp. 12-14.

9.  Arthur Bostwick, "The Public Library, the Public School and the Social Center Movement," *A Librarian's Open Shelf* (New York: Books for Libraries, 1920), pp. 145-155.

10. William S. Learned, *The American Public Library and the Diffusion of Knowledge* (New York: Harcourt, Brace & Co., 1924), pp. 35-56.

11. Joseph L. Wheeler, *The Library and the Community* (Chicago: American Library Association, 1924).

12. Annual Index Values for a sample of 41 American Public Libraries, 1956-1967.

(1960=100)

|                          | 1956 | '57 | '58 | '59 | '60 | '61 | '62 | '63 | '64 | '65 | '66 | '67 |
|--------------------------|------|-----|-----|-----|-----|-----|-----|-----|-----|-----|-----|-----|
| Circulation Index Value  | 81   | 85  | 92  | 95  | 100 | 106 | 107 | 110 | 116 | 117 | 114 | 112 |
| Expenditure Index Value  | 72   | 80  | 86  | 93  | 100 | 105 | 112 | 123 | 134 | 145 | 151 | 163 |

Source: A.L.A. Bulletin May 1968 p. 492

See also American Library Association, *Student Use of Libraries* (Chicago: American Library Association, 1924).

13. H. C. Campbell, *Metropolitan Public Library Planning Throughout the World* (Oxford: Pergamon Press, 1967), p. 154; *Emerging Library Systems* (Albany: State Education Department, 1967); Kenneth F. Duchac, "Public Library Development in Maryland," *Library Journal* 92 (15 March 1967): 1113-1116; Lowell A. Martin, *Library Service in Pennsylvania, Present and Proposed* (Harrisburg: Pennsylvania State Library, 1958); "Master Plan for Public Libraries in California Adopted by the California Library Association at Coronado, October 26, 1962," *California Librarian* 24(January 1963):17-28.

14. In some cases, the effect was negative since the library spent a good deal of its budget and staff time preparing proposals which were not approved.

15. Milton S. Byam, "Brooklyn's District Library Scheme," *Wilson Library Bulletin* 35(January 1961):365-367.

16. Henry M. Kapenstein, "Northeast Regional Library," *Catholic Library World* 36(March 1965):431-34.

17. Duchac, "Public Library in Maryland."
18. *Emerging Library Systems.*
19. Eleanor T. Smith, "Public Library Service to the Economically and Culturally Deprived," *The Library Reaches Out*, Kate Coplan, ed. (New York: Oceana Publications, Inc., 1965), pp. 213-239
20. Priscilla Dunhill, "Dust Gathers on the Library," *The Reporter* 38(13 June 1968):34-36.
21. *Neighborhood Library Centers and Services* (New York: National Book Committee, 1966).
22. *Bookmark* (Albany: New York State Library, January 1966), p. 136.
23. Harold S. Hacker, "Urban Failures and Cities," *Library Journal* 90 (1 May 1965):2077-2079.
24. *A Study of Four Library Programs for Disadvantaged Persons* (Albany: New York State University, 1967).
25. "Report of Library Services and Construction Act: Project 3842," mimeographed (Los Angeles: Los Angeles Public Library, 1 January–30 June 1966).
26. Meredith Bloss, "Take a Giant Step," *Library Journal* 91 (15 January 1966):323-326.
27. Evelyn Levy, "Library Services in the Inner City," *Wilson Library Bulletin* 41 (January 1967):470-477.
28. T. E. Barensfeld, "Limited Adult Reader," *Library Journal* 92 (15 September 1967):3004-3007.
29. Neighborhood Library Centers.
30. Marshall McLuhan, and Quentin Fiore, *The Medium is the Massage* (New York: Bantam Books, Inc., 1967), p. 18.
31. Marjorie P. Holt, "Help for the Disadvantaged," *RQ* 6 (Fall 1966):40-43.
32. Roger H. McDonough, "An Inaugural Address" *American Library Association Bulletin* 62(July-August 1968):873-878.
33. The *New York Times* of 12 January 1968, reported that the City of Newark was considering closing its public library and museum. This was later (March 12) rescinded for nine months. Public library budgets have, in fact, increased but the increases have been absorbed to a large extent by mandated cost of salaries, pensions, social security and other fringe benefits. See the study by William F. Hellmuth, "Trends in Urban Fiscal Policies," *The Public Library and the City*, Ralph Conaut, ed. (Cambridge: MIT Press, 1965).
34. See Annual Index above, note 12.

35. Bernard Berelson, *Library's Public* (New York: Columbia University Press, 1949), pp.123-135.
36. J. H. Plumb, ed. *Crisis in the Humanities* (Baltimore, Md: Penguin Books, Inc., 1964), pp. 7-10; *Bulletin*, School of Library Science, Columbia University (1968-1969), p. 9.
37. Graham Hough, "Crisis in Literary Education," *Crisis in the Humanities*, p. 97.
38. Leonard Grundt, *Efficient Patterns for Adequate Library Service in a Large City* (Urbana: University of Illinois, 1968), pp. 3-4.
39. Thomas W. Shaughnessy, "A Study of Distance and Time as Factors Influencing the Use of District Center Libraries," Appendix to Lowell Martin, *Progress and Problems of Pennsylvania Libraries* (Harrisburg, Pa.: Pennsylvania State Library, 1967).
40. At its peak, the Brooklyn Public Library circulated 10 million volumes from fifty-five separate building locations. The Ingersoll Library (the Central Building) was responsible for a million of these. Ten large buildings could therefore have absorbed this circulation.

# 4/School Libraries and Librarianship

CAROLYN I. WHITENACK

*Purdue University*

Education in the decade of the 1960s could be characterized as a decade of dissatisfaction, of ferment, and of reexamination of the system of education that we have established. A very important part of that system is the school library program. It, too, has undergone a crucial study by those most expert in its field, resulting in a restatement of philosophy, purposes, and services in the recently issued national *Standards for School Media Programs.*[1]

These *Standards* were prepared jointly by the two professional associations directly associated with teaching and learning resources—a Joint Committee of the American Association of School Librarians and the Department of Audiovisual Instruction of the National Education Association in cooperation with an Advisory Board consisting of representatives from twenty-eight professional and civic associations. The discussion following is concerned primarily with interpreting the modern school library program in the individual school as expressed in these *Standards*.

Terminology and patterns of administration differ among schools. There are school libraries, instructional materials centers, learning resources centers, instructional media centers, library media centers, and audiovisual centers. Again the terms as defined in the *Standards* will be used because they tend to exemplify the vital, enthusiastic, quality program required for today's education. Definitions of terms are cited early for clarity:

Media—Printed and audiovisual forms of communication and their accompanying technology.

Media program—All the instructional and other services furnished to students and teachers by a media center and its staff.

Media center—A learning center in a school where a full range of print and audiovisual media, necessary equipment, and services from media specialists are accessible to students and teachers.

Media staff—The personnel who carry on the activities of a media center and its program.

Media specialist—An individual who has broad professional preparation in educational media. If he is responsible for instructional decisions, he meets requirements for teaching. Within this field there may be several types of specialization, such as (a) level of instruction, (b) areas of curriculum, (c) type of media, and (d) type of service. In addition, other media specialists, who are not responsible for instructional decisions, are members of the professional media staff and need not have teacher certification, e.g., certain types of personnel in television and other media preparation areas.

* Media technician—A media staff member who has training below the media specialist level, but who has special competencies in one or more of the following fields: graphics production and display, information and materials processing, photographic production, and equipment operation and simple maintenance.

Media aide—A media staff member with clerical or secretarial competencies.

System media center—A center at the school system level to provide supporting and supplemented services to school media centers in individual schools of the system.

Unified media program—A program in which instructional and other services related to both print and audiovisual media are administered in a single unified program under one director.

Teaching station—Any part of the school (usually but not always a classroom) where formal instruction takes place. Media centers are not included within this definition, although it is recognized that instruction is part of the media program.[2]

## Concepts

The first concept which I should like to emphasize is that of the *learner as the center* of the school media program. As stated in the *Standards*, "The process of education is essentially creative. It employs the intellectual, physical, and social skills of pupils in a learning process which begins with a clear enunciation of desirable human values as expressed in attitudes and actions of students . . . ."[3]

"The education experiences which will be most helpful must be identified, and the most effective tools and materials located. The pupil will not only need to learn skills of reading, but those of observation, listening, and social interaction. He will need to develop a spirit of inquiry, self-motivation, self-discipline, and self-evaluation . . . ."[4] Learning is very private and individual. The best learning occurs when the student is mentally active—selecting, responding, making discriminations and value judgments, and taking action upon important ideas, experiences, and resources as they relate to him personally in such a way that learning takes place and that further learning is continued on his own initiative. Each child is unique in his needs and abilities. The climate for learning throughout the school, but most certainly in the school media center, must provoke an inquiring mind, must cater to the intellectual and curious, and must develop a process of independent thinking. This program opens doors to the world of culture, literature, science, discovery, and free inquiry.

Reading is the key to success in independent study. Not reading per se, but reading critically—in the same way that one takes meaning from the printed page, from the television screen, from the radio program, from the film, the filmstrip, the resource of whatever format, and brings that knowledge to bear upon the decision-making process. The recent Commissioner of Education, Dr. James Allen, has identified reading as one of the most crucial problems of today's school, and has set as a primary goal for the seventies, "every student a reader." How can they read without reading materials in media centers?

Reading is also the essential ingredient to continuing one's education throughout life. Greater use of independent study in all subject areas will tend to help all students improve their reading skills during all the years of elementary and secondary education, and it will also reinforce reading skills necessary in higher education and throughout adult life.

Students learn best from their own activity. Better ways of grouping students—ungraded classes, ability grouping, advanced placement, accelerated groups, and enrichment classes—all make it possible for students to be organized in different ways to use learning resources to meet their diverse needs. Teachers, parents, peers, and institutions are the sources of many ideas, experiences, and materials. Traditionally, books and libraries have been the primary means of recording and communicating ideas. Today we have new approaches to reading, and well-designed and illustrated books as well as many quality paperbacks enhance the learning environment. Also in recent years there have been many audiovisual developments such as programmed learning, tapes, educational television programs, new kinds of projected materials, teaching machines, and other special teaching devices. Each type of material has a contribution to make to the educational process. The distinctive qualities of each resource should be recognized and all appropriate resources should be used in the learning situation.

The problem of continuing to extend and diversify educational opportunities, especially as these relate to the freedom of each student to learn in his own way, maximizes the need for an abundance of resources in a variety of formats and at many levels of instruction. The second concept, *a unified program of printed and audiovisual materials and resources or a multi-media approach to learning*, has received prominent attention in recent years. "Students, in the pursuit of their studies, use a cross-media or multi-media or single medium approach, and receive appropriate guidance from the school librarians (i.e., media specialists) in the selection of these materials and in their effective use. This principle means more than showing a student how to use a filmstrip viewer, or machinery for teaching tapes, or an 8mm sound film projector, or the micro-reader, or the apparatus for listening to recordings, or the dial equipment for banks of resources now making their appearance, or the apparatus for making transparencies, or machines and devices for programmed instruction. The program of teaching the use of library resources (i.e., media) includes guidance in teaching students viewing and listening skills."[5]

In a problem oriented curriculum, students are encouraged to use a diversity of experiences and react in many different ways. Working together, the teacher and the media specialist collect information, observe, and encourage students to use a reservoir of media in organizing their information and formulating conclusions. The media specialist surveys all media available. A good teacher varies the materials used—textbooks, library books, audiovisual media, lecture, discussions, tests, and the like. Some materials may need to be created. Often a book will be used, sometimes a film, filmstrip, or tape recording, or a combination of these will be chosen. Students differ in styles of learning: some respond better to visual materials, others to auditory media, whereas still others chose verbal resources. The important concept is that the best resource or resources of high quality be chosen for the particular learning situation and for the particular student or groups of students. As students have more time and reason for using media, and as media of instruction become more important, media specialists become co-directors of learning with teachers, helping to decide why, how, when, and where to use media.

Third, *the school media program is a program of learning and media services throughout the school.* The rationale of this program will be affected by the educational philosophy of the school, the organization of the curriculum, the administrative policies and practices of the school, the teachers' knowledge of and attitude toward learning resources, the availability of full-time media professionals to assist in the selection and use of media, the conditions under which these media will be used, and the availability of these materials at the time needed. Rigid programs of lockstep education, with media resources stored in the back of study halls, operated by students and part-time staff, and poorly supported by tax funds, do not meet the demands of today's student. In quality schools students study and learn in media centers, in laboratories, classrooms, electronic learning centers, in study carrels, in small group seminars, and wherever students and teachers are. In schools that provide flexibility of scheduling and that emphasize the learner, the move is away from the textbook-centered classroom and teacher-centered teaching. Rather, resources will be located in all stations used by students and teachers.

Therefore, a good media service program serves the objectives of the total educational program of the school by:

1. Providing media professionals with sufficent supportive staff to consult, organize, and manage media resources, services, and facilities, in media centers, in subcenters, in classrooms or wherever learning takes place.

2. Locating, gathering, organizing, coordinating, promoting, and distributing a rich variety of quality learning resources for use by teachers and students as individuals and in groups to improve learning, and by including involvement of teachers and students in the selection process.

3. Making available facilities, services, and equipment necessary for the selection, organization, management, and use of printed and audiovisual resources, including availability at all hours of the school day, before and after school, and extended hours.

4. Offering leadership and by counseling and guiding teachers and students in motivation, utilization, and experimentation in terms of the best media or combination of media for the particular learning situation.

5. Supplying a quality media environment with efficient work spaces for students, faculty, and media staff for reading, listening, and viewing activities.

6. Providing reference resources and specialized reference staff in reference areas to meet the informational needs of the faculty and staff.

7. Furnishing facilities for and assistance in the production of self-created instructional materials, displays, and demonstrations to meet the special needs of students and teachers.

8. Exploring the uses of modern technology, including exploratory use of computers, in attacking the control and synthesis of knowledge to encourage more learning in less time.

9. Encouraging supervisory and other supplemental services from districts or larger units, including investigating the desirability and cost of central services required in processing the varied learning media for all the schools of a cooperating area.

10. Offering information on new educational and curricular developments and participating in networks of knowledge for the benefit of students and teachers.

Such a program must have staff; collections of materials, equipment, and devices; facilities; and funds. Each part is dependent upon the other. Basic to the program is the support of school board members, school administrators, curriculum specialists, classroom teachers, and community leaders. The concern for quality education must be shared by all citizens.

The next general concept is that of the *professional media staff* in sufficient numbers, some generalists and others with specialization, supported by technicians and aides *as indispensable to a good media program*. The *Standards* call for at least one professional, supported by a technician and an aide or clerk, for each 250 students for a school with an enrollment of 2,000 students or less. As enrollments go higher, adjustment will be needed. The greatest need in today's schools is adequate media staff who are adequately trained. Personnel educated for diverse aspects of the program will insure the necessary organization and use of media. Training for professional media specialists will encompass a variety of skills and experiences. Some of the more important of these are:

1. A thorough knowledge of the psychology of learning, understanding of the needs, purposes, and behavior of the users of media centers, and the ability to act as co-directors of learning with teachers.

2.  Certification as teachers as well as special certification in media fields, with the ability to develop instructional objectives in behavioral terms, analyze, try out, and modify units of study, and assist teachers and learners in this modification.
3.  Knowledge of the historic role of the library and the present and future of its functions and materials, as well as a knowledge of the growth of communications theory, including storage and retrieval of information.
4.  Awareness of the new technology of education and the ability to promote unified treatment of ideas, whether they come through computers, filmstrips, books, or other media, or a combination of these.
5.  Experience with the full range of instructional resources, including the perception, display, and presentation of all types of media.
6.  Acquaintance with the broad scope of instructional research as it relates to the uses of media, and continued awareness of the implications for education of such research.
7.  Deftness in the management of media and people, including management control and professional direction of para-professionals.

   In years past, the disciplines of library science and audiovisual education have provided foundation and background for media specialists, but professional education for school media specialists needs to be redesigned and restructured. The scope and sequence of graduate professional education for the school media generalist and specialist is urgent. A most promising new venture is the School Library Manpower Project of the American Association of School Librarians, funded by the Knapp Foundation of North Carolina. The first phase of task analysis of jobs performed in media centers was completed in 1969, and the analysis was reported by the Research Division of the National Education Association.[6]
   The subject matter of this new discipline—school media services—will draw on psychology, sociology, administration, curriculum, business management, communications theory, computer sciences,

educational research, and other fields. Institutes, workshops, and conferences have done much to upgrade the profession; much remains to be done. Cooperative programs between librarianship and audiovisual departments need to be developed in schools of higher education that presently have separate departments. School media specialists should be freed from traditional requirements and permitted to elect at least a third of their program in the other department.

Supportive staff also will be an important aspect of media programs. Not only will highly trained librarians, audiovisual coordinators, and media specialists be necessary, but also technicians, clerks, and other para-professionals will be needed. Media center directors will need special competencies in personnel management, leadership, communication, interpersonal relationships, and administrative ability.

Media specialization will also provide staff who may wish to work with specific media, at different levels of learning, or with subject areas: reference media preparation, television, programmed learning, computer utilization, media processing, and specific disciplines. The media staff should complement each other in specialization and competencies.

A hypothetical school of a thousand students could stratify its staff in the following way.

### Head of Media Program

Director
1—aide
1—clerk

| *Professional* | *Supportive* |
| --- | --- |
| 1—primarily reference and media guidance | [ 1—aide<br>[ 1—clerk |
| 1—primarily audiovisual and graphics preparation | [ 1—technician<br>[ 1—clerk |
| 1—primarily television | [ 1—engineer<br>[ 1—clerk |

*Developing an up-to-date quality collection of media* is the next concept. Great quantities of materials of all kinds are needed— books, films, filmstrips, recordings, tapes, pamphlets, magazines, newspapers, and realia. Media must be available to support and enrich every area of the curriculum and for the wide range of ability and maturity levels. The gamut of interests of boys and girls must be provided for. Students and teachers are actively involved in selection and evaluation. The collection must be sufficiently large and well stocked to be used efficiently for research, for reference, for recreation, for enrichment, and for guidance. (Consult the *Standards* for quantity.)

The materials should be of the highest quality in content and presentation. In addition to providing information, media should develop appreciation for our own heritage and for the cultures of other peoples and should enable the student to grow in maturity, judgment, and tolerance. It is essential that the collection be one which broadens rather than limits the horizons of students.

Some types of materials and devices for teaching will not be available from commercial sources, so students, teachers, and media staff will need to create them. These include displays and exhibits, bulletin boards, mounted pictures, posters and charts, transparencies, slides, filmstrips, and 8mm films.

The school should have a written selection policy formulated by students, faculty, and media specialists and endorsed by the administration, school board, and community. This policy should indicate the general objectives and procedures of selection, and affirm such freedoms as described in the *Library Bill of Rights, The School Library Bill of Rights,* and *The Students' Right to Read.*[7]

Media equipment and devices essential to proper utilization of materials should be available in sufficient quantity and quality to insure easy management by groups and individuals. Portable equipment should be available for home loan of materials. (Consult the *Standards* for quantity.)

Circulation and loan regulations should encourage students in the widest possible use of all materials. Organization of resources should facilitate use. Some schools are arranging printed and audiovisual materials in a multimedia sequence side by side on open shelves by subject classification. Technical processing of materials in larger units such as regional or state centers is highly desirable. Card catalogs and/or printed book catalogs invite exploration of media and are essential as inventories of resources.

Maintenance of the collection and services is dependent on financial support—not less than 6 percent of the national average per pupil operational cost should be spent per student per year as stated in the *Standards*.[8] The 1968-1969 estimated national average was $680.00. Flexibility of purchase procedures throughout the school year is desirable.

*Facilities with a quality environment that is functional in design, centrally located, and efficient in work and use areas invite student and faculty utilization.* Attractive arrangements of space and furniture, good lighting, acoustical and temperature control, and noise-reducing floor covering are recommended. Adequate space for listening and viewing as well as reading are necessary services of the media center. Laboratory production areas for making transparencies, 35mm slides, recordings, and other created media are essential. Electronic storage and retrieval equipment and dial access information systems require space for users as well as electronic equipment. Optional spaces are areas for television and radio production and storage of computers. Enough electrical outlets and communications relays for electronic equipment are essential.

Suggested space utilization based on the recommendations of the *Standards* appears on the following pages.[9]

*Effective media services at the school level are dependent on supplementary services at the district, regional, state, and national levels.* Supervisory and advisory services, central processing, cataloging and collections of materials too expensive to own in the individual school, e.g. films, are among the functions offered by larger organizational units. Regional and multi-state planning to provide networks of knowledge with computer capability are projected for the future. Inservice education, professional advancement, and extensive professional collections are additional assets. Media selection and evaluation with examination collections are new developments.

Practically all state departments of education have directors of media services, sometimes divided into school library and audiovisual services. It is important to local development that state programs be unified, if possible, or coordinated in such a way that administrative organization does not become a barrier to function of media. The most comprehensive statements of policy are available in two handbooks from the Council of Chief State School Officers.[10] The state media service staff also interprets the program to other state supervisory staff and serves as a liaison with federal programs.

Leadership at the national level has established and put into operation a program of federal planning and funding for media resources to state and local systems. Title II of ESEA 1965 is often referred to as an example of wise administration of federal funds. Title III of ESEA of 1965 and Title III of NDEA of 1968 have assisted with proper media equipment.

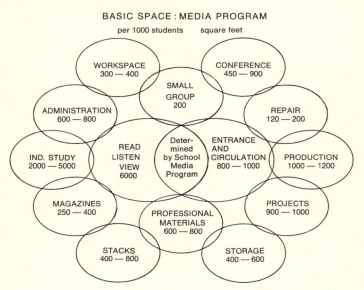

BASIC SPACE : MEDIA PROGRAM

per 1000 students        square feet

WORKSPACE 300 — 400

CONFERENCE 450 — 900

SMALL GROUP 200

ADMINISTRATION 600 — 800

REPAIR 120 — 200

IND. STUDY 2000 — 5000

READ LISTEN VIEW 6000

Determined by School Media Program

ENTRANCE AND CIRCULATION 800 — 1000

PRODUCTION 1000 — 1200

MAGAZINES 250 — 400

PROJECTS 900 — 1000

PROFESSIONAL MATERIALS 600 — 800

STACKS 400 — 800

STORAGE 400 — 600

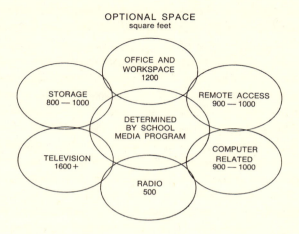

OPTIONAL SPACE
square feet

OFFICE AND WORKSPACE 1200

STORAGE 800 — 1000

REMOTE ACCESS 900 — 1000

DETERMINED BY SCHOOL MEDIA PROGRAM

TELEVISION 1600 +

COMPUTER RELATED 900 — 1000

RADIO 500

A planned strategy of programs, meetings, publicity, and implementation of these new *Standards*, involving administrators, curriculum specialists, teachers, the community, commercial interest, and school boards at all levels of action by the supervisors and leaders of present media programs will give opportunities for gaining local, state, and national support for media specialists and media services. A national implementation project similar to the Knapp School Libraries Demonstration Project is urgently needed.[11]

## Consummations

Education and media are ever changing. The school's educational program and its media program are always evolving; nothing is truly consummated. As one goal is shifted, another appears. The following are generally accepted consummations:

1. There is a mounting body of testimony in the professional literature that attests to the principle that effective media programs require staff, resources, and services readily available to the user. Educators have long given obeisance to the importance of the individual. The user will be served even if he must bypass conventional modes of securing information.

2. Standards of accrediting agencies accept the concept that a quality school can be judged by the quality of its school media program. All state departments of education have qualitative and quantitative standards for the use of media resources. One important criterion of a quality school is its school media—library and audiovisual—program. The North Central Association of Colleges and Secondary Schools has revised its policies and principles and standards for approval of secondary and junior high schools, which now include a prominent section on media service. The Southern Association of Colleges and Schools has developed qualitative standards for elementary schools including the schools' media services. *The Evaluative Criteria*, a cooperative national study used by many schools throughout the six major regional associations, has a section "Educational Media Services—Library and Audio-Visual," which has been revised in view of the recent *Standards*.

3. Education is a state function. The responsibility of school boards of education for support of all educational endeavors, including the school media program, is practiced throughout the land. State departments of education make periodic reviews of the schools' education program, including the school's media services. Most departments have some requirements for financial support at the local and state level. There is developing a firm philosophy of joint responsibility of local, state, and federal funds for education that include the support of the media program.

4. The joint development of *Standards for School Media Programs* by the two leading professional associations directly involved in media services, in cooperation with other national associations concerned with quality education, improves the opportunities for acceptance and implementation. The excitement and attention given the *Standards* and the acceptance of the new terminology have been rewarding to the members of the two national associations that developed this innovation. Many schools have achieved excellence in their media programs, and many others desire a new stimulus to improve their instructional programs.

5. A basic program of certification is practiced in every state. Although it is true that these requirements need evaluation and

change, it is also true that a pattern of the professionalization of the school media staff has been established. The separate patterns for school librarians and audiovisual coordinators must be corrected at once.

*Prospects*

1. Implementation of the *Standards* will improve the quality of teaching and learning in the nation's elementary and secondary schools. Presently many of the nation's elementary schools exist without media services. A disparity exists between the national *Standards* and what is provided in most secondary and junior high schools. As parents, enlightened citizens, and community leaders are told the story "like it is" today, programs of reading, viewing, and listening are bound to improve. The need for rapid implementation, experimentation, and innovation will have to be encouraged. Adequate qualified staff to direct and manage programs of resources in ample spaces should improve.

2. The school librarian, the audiovisual specialist, and/or the media specialist have the opportunity of becoming instructional leaders by serving as catalysts in the curriculum and directing independent learning. Their reference and bibliographic skills as well as their knowledge of the diverse collection of quality materials makes them essential to the learning task and active in instruction. Their numbers will increase. We have enough people; we need to recruit from these people many new professionals and supportive technicians and aides. A massive effort must be made. With the development of community colleges and new professional education programs with "career ladders" for media service personnel, the manpower problem will become less critical.

3. New programs of professional education of school media personnel will develop. A school media professional is neither a librarian nor an audiovisual specialist. He is a new educational professional with the best of these two professions retained and with new skills in psychology, leadership, management, and communications.

4. All state and regional standards and certification patterns need to be revised. Many inadequacies exist; some standards and certification requirements are too rigid. Experimentation should be encouraged.

5. The need for better media statistics at local, state, and federal levels calls for consensus in record keeping. The recently organized National Center for Educational Statistics may be helpful. Presently no one knows expenditures, resources, and manpower needed.

6. Empirical, analytical, experimental, and descriptive research is limited or almost nonexistent concerning today's school media program. Increased numbers of doctoral candidates have provided a few studies, but lack of funds is a major handicap.

7. Adequate reviewing and bibliographic control of all forms of media are services urgently needed now, but they must remain a prospect for the future. A very bright new star in this dark cloud is the reviewing of non-print media in the *Booklist* under the editorship of Paul Brawley.

8. Adequate media resources for inner-city schools and the thinly populated rural areas is a prospect for the future. It is unbelievable that this nation will continue to permit its poor to be deprived of food for the body and resources for the mind.

9. Provision for centralized technical processes, including cataloging at the source and district or larger unit media services, are available in only a few systems. Centers which are established in the future should be planned to take advantage of the new technologies of education and information.

10. Networks of knowledge to meet the informational and research needs of youth hold promise. School media professionals are experimenting with dial-controlled random access, audio-video retrieval systems. Most of these materials are not available commercially, and units are expensive and not always reliable. Yet the potential is there.

The knowledge of the ages readily available to the user in school, in his home, or wherever he desires, is a worthy vision and goal, and also a possible one. Presently, in every elementary and secondary school, a well-stocked media center directed by skilled media specialists with supplementary services from system centers would markedly improve the learning opportunities of each student.

## NOTES

1. *Standards for School Media Programs*. ALA and NEA, 1969.
2. Ibid., p. xvi.
3. Ibid., p. 1.
4. Ibid.
5. Frances Henne, *Learning to Learn in School Libraries*, p. 15.
6. The special report, *School Library Personnel: Task Analysis Survey*, should be requested from Robert Case, Director, School Library Manpower Project, American Library Association, 50 East Huron Street, Chicago, Illinois 60611.
7. *The Library Bill of Rights* was adopted by the Council of the Council of the American Library Association in 1948 and revised in 1967; *The School Library Bill of Rights* was approved by the American Association of School Librarians and endorsed by the Council of the American Library Association in 1955; and *The Students' Right to Read* was issued by the National Council of Teachers of English in 1962.
8. *Standards for School Media Programs*, p. 35.
9. Ibid., pp. 40-43.
10. Council of Chief State School Officers, *Responsibilities of State Departments of Education for School Library Services* (Washington, D. C.: The Council, 1961); Council of Chief State School Officers, *State Department of Education Leadership in Developing the Use of New Educational Media* (Washington, D. C.: The Council, 1964).
11. Peggy Sullivan, ed. *Realization: The Final Report of the Knapp School Libraries Project.* ALA, 1968.

## BIBLIOGRAPHY

American Association of School Librarians and ALA Council, 1955.
Saunders, Helen E. *The Modern School Library*. Metuchen, N. J.: Scarecrow Press, 1968. *School Library Bill of Rights.*

ALA American Association of School Librarians and NEA, Department of Audio-Visual Instruction. *Standards for School Media Programs.* ALA, 1969.

American Library Association. *ALA Bulletin,* January 1969.

——. *Standards for School Library Programs,* ALA, 1960.

Brown, James W., Ruth H. Aubrey and Elizabeth S. Noel, comps. *Multi-media and the Changing School Library,* California State Department of Education, 1969.

Brown, James W., Richard B. Lewis and Fred F. Harcleroad. *AV Instruction: Media and Methods.* New York: McGraw-Hill, 1969.

Brown, James W. and Norberg, Kenneth. *Administering Educational Media.* New York: McGraw-Hill, 1965.

*Bulletin of the National Association of Secondary School Principals,* January, 1966.

Council of Chief State School Officers. *Responsibilities of State Departments of Education for School Library Services.* Washington, D. C.: The Council, 1961.

Council of Chief State School Officers. *State Department of Education Leadership in Developing the Use of New Educational Media.* Washington, D. C.: The Council, 1964.

Council of American Library Association. *Library Bill of Rights,* 1948, rev. 1967.

Dale, Edgar. *Audiovisual Methods of Teaching.* New York: Dryden Press, 1969.

Darling, Richard L. and others. "IMC-Library Services." *Instructor* 77 (November 1967): 83-94.

Delaney, Jack J. *The New School Librarian.* Hamden, Conn.: Shoe String Press, 1968.

*Educational Leadership,* Vol. 21, January 1964.

Ellsworth, Ralph E. *The School Library,* Educational Facilities Laboratories, 1963.

Gaver, Mary. *Effectiveness of Centralized Library Service in Elementary Schools.* 2d ed., New Brunswick, N. J.: Rutgers University Press, 1963.

——. *Evaluating Library Resources for Elementary School Libraries.* New Brunswick: ssh press, 1962.

——. *Every Child Needs a School Library.* Chicago: ALA, 1962.

——. *Patterns of Development in Elementary School Libraries Today.* 2d ed. Chicago: Encyclopedia Britannica, 1965.

——. *Patterns of Development in the Elementary School Library Today, A Five Year Report on Emerging Media Centers.* 3d ed.

Chicago: Encyclopedia Britannica, 1969.

Graham, Mae, ed. "The Changing Nature of the School Library," *Library Trends* 17 (April 1969).

Henne, Frances. *Learning to Learn in School Libraries.* Reprint *School Libraries.* May, 1966.

Jones, Milbrey L. "Secondary Library Services: A Search for Essentials." *Teachers College Record* 68 (December 1966): 200-210.

Knirk, Frederick G. and John W. Childs. *Instructional Technology.* New York: Holt, Rinehart & Winston, 1968.

Lohrer, Alice, ed. *The School Library Materials Center: Its Resources and their Utilization.* Champaign, Ill.: Allerton Park Institute, 1964.

Lowrie, Jean E. *Elementary School Libraries.* Metuchen, N. J.: Scarecrow Press, 1961.

Meierhenry, Wesley C. *Media and Educational Innovation.* Lincoln: University of Nebraska Press, 1966.

Michigan Department of Education. *The Instructional Materials Center.* Bulletin No. 369, 1965.

*Multi Media Approach to Learning:* Report of a Special Conference sponsored by Knapp School Libraries Project, Provo, Utah, 1967.

National Council of Teachers of English. *The Student's Right to Read.* Champaign, Ill.: The Council, 1962.

National Education Association, Department of Audio-Visual Instruction. *Highlights of Schools Using Educational Media.* Washington, D. C.: NEA, 1967.

National Education Association. Department of Rural Education. *School Library Programs in Rural Areas.* Washington, D. C.: NEA, 1966.

National Study of Secondary School Evaluation. *Evaluative Criteria.* The Study, 1969.

Nelson Association Inc., *School Libraries in the United States.* A Report prepared for the National Advisory Commission on Libraries, November, 1967. Available from ERIC, University of Minnesota Graduate Library School.

Rufsvold, Margaret I. and Carolyn Guss. *Guides to Newer Educational Media,* 2d ed. ALA, 1967 (Revision in process).

Srygley, Sara Krentzman, ed. "School Library Services and Administration at the School District Level," *Library Trends* 16 (April 1968).

Sullivan Peggy, ed. *Realization: The Final Report of the Knapp*

*School Libraries Project.* Chicago: ALA, 1968.
U. S., Department of Health, Education and Welfare. *Library Facilities for Elementary and Secondary Schools.* Office of Education. Special Publication No. 10, 1965.
_____. *The School Library as a Materials Center.* Office of Education, 1962.
_____. *Descriptive Case Studies of Nine Elementary School Media Centers in Three Inner Cities.* Title II, 1969.
_____. *Emphasis on Excellence in School Media Programs.* Title II, 1969.
Wofford, Azile May. *The School Library at Work; Acquisition, Organization, Use and Maintenance of Materials in the School Library.* New York: H. W. Wilson, 1959.


*Periodicals*

*ALA Bulletin.* American Library Association, 50 E. Huron Street, Chicago, Illinois 60611. (with ALA Membership)
*Audio-Visual Communications Review.* Department of Audiovisual Instruction, 50 E. Huron Street, Chicago, Illinois 60611. (with DAVI Membership)
*Audiovisual Instruction.* Department of Audiovisual Instruction, NEA, 1201 16 Street, N. W., Washington, D. C. 20036. (with DAVI Membership)
*Education Leadership.* The Association for Supervision and Curriculum Development, NEA (with ASCD Membership)
*Educational Screen and Audio-Visual Guide.* Educational Screen, Inc., 2000 Lincoln Park West Building, Chicago, Illinois 60614.
*Education Technology.* Educational Technology Publication, 456 Sylvan Avenue, Englewood Cliffs, New Jersey 07632.
*Library Journal.* R. R. Bowker Co., 1180 Avenue of the Americas, New York, New York 10036.
*Library Trends.* University of Illinois Graduate School of Library Science, Urbana, Illinois 61801.
*School Libraries.* American Association of School Librarians, 50 East Huron Street, Chicago, Illinois 60611. Quarterly. (with AASL Membership)
*Top of the News.* American Library Association, 50 E. Huron St., Chicago, Illinois 60611. (with ALA Membership)
*Wilson Library Bulletin.* H. W. Wilson Co., 950 University Avenue, Bronx, New York 10452.

# PART THREE

# Academic Libraries

# 5/ *Canadian University Libraries*

JOHN P. WILKINSON

*University of Toronto*

Pattern: a fully recognized form . . . and established mode of
behavior . . . beliefs, and values held in common
by the member of a group.

Service: to meet the needs of . . . to provide information or
other assistance to . . .

*(Webster's Third New International Dictionary)*

Some years ago Neal Harlow, now of Rutgers, in addressing the
Canadian Library Association, stated that "problem one in the
education of librarians is that no general theory of professional
behavior has been widely accepted . . . no theoretical base, no
prototype upon which to pattern education and practice. We have
been content to do what comes naturally.[1] To which Walter Stone,
at the University of Pittsburgh, has added, "No other professional
service group has paid so little attention as have librarians to the
need for continuing self-study and research and to the importance of
recruiting and training specialists for competency in the application
of research methods."[2]

To explore the implications of such statements with respect to
patterns of service in Canadian university libraries, the present writer
has just completed a series of flying visits to major university
libraries across Canada.[3] These visits were intended not to provide
yet another description of the components of service, but to
investigate the climate of opinion against which our service patterns

are currently projected. We have been subjected to a deluge of descriptive surveys and "normative" standards; but we do not seem to have examined adequately one of the most basic questions of all—the relationship between "need" and "response."

The present paper presents what may be termed a pre-study of the above relationship. Time did not permit investigations in depth of either need or response; but the current rationale (or lack of it) underlying the connection between the two variables is examined for Canadian university libraries, since an understanding of that rationale would seem essential before meaningful research into any part of the pattern can be undertaken. Before librarianship embarks upon major and costly investigations of user or non-user needs; before we undertake expensive analyses of manual or automated responses; and before we utilize model simulation, systems design, or any other sophisticated criteria of critical path requirements, we must understand the mental sets underlying patterns of service currently evidenced in our libraries.

Before discussing the present study, however, ad hoc agreement upon certain terms and concepts is desirable. "Need" is a basic physiological or psychological attribute, and is perhaps more likely to be unconscious or even latent than to be fully self-recognized and kinetic. Need, therefore, must be distinguished from "demand," for the latter is very probably but a partial and possibly inaccurate reflection of the former. Moreover, while basic needs—such as the need for information—are relatively stable, demands based upon those needs are subject to a wide range of environmental influences and are inherently unstable. Responses based upon manifestations of expressed demands are, therefore, based upon a shifting and uncertain foundation.

"Response" is understood here to encompass the total range of physical and intellectual answers to a relevant need. Thus reference service is as much a response as are the resources it utilizes, and the building is as much a response as the book. Mental attitudes are as respondent as are machines, and an ethos is as responsive as any equipment. Moreover, the *relationship* between response and need— the application of the total response variable to the conscious and unconscious, present and potential need variable—may be designated as "service." It is with this relationship rather than with the variables per se that research should, of course, be most creatively concerned. Thus, for example, "use studies," insofar as they are based upon recorded circulation rather than the much more elusive satisfaction of need, have limited value in library research because they relate to one aspect of response—the *in situ* resources—rather than to the relationship between response and need.[4]

The importance of investigation of the type for which the present study may be regarded as a prototype seems to this writer to be very great. A generally held rationale of service based upon a systematic understanding of the needs which that service is intended to meet is necessary to the survival both of the individual librarian and of librarianship as a profession. Ad hoc responses to apparent demands will not ensure social approval at a time when society itself is involved in a period of widespread, though probably superficial, change. It is no coincidence that the occupation of chief librarian has been ranked, in terms of probable mortality rates, just below that of wartime tail gunners and submariners (and peacetime university presidents!), for, without a researched rationale upon which to depend, the librarian is largely at the mercy of shifting and conflicting demands—demands that may themselves be baseless. Similarly, in macrocosm, librarianship as a social validity must, like any other viable social organism, demonstrate a theoretical base predicated upon an understanding of the broad social needs that spawned it; for the future of any organism which responds unwittingly to pressures that may be at best ephemeral and at worst misleading must be uncertain.

In an attempt, therefore, to determine the climate of opinion in Canadian university libraries with respect to the rationale underlying patterns of service, a series of questions was directed in essentially open-ended interviews to the various chief librarians, senior librarians, and members of university faculties whom the present writer sought out.[5] The questions were designed to determine not what but *why* patterns existed, and they were answered with great frankness by all concerned. In part, the frankness resulted from assurances that no individual institution, let alone individual, would be identified in this paper. But to a far greater extent the candid and generous assistance appears to have arisen from a feeling on the part of librarians and teaching faculty alike that the rationale of service in academic libraries represents an urgent, even vital problem. To all those whose confidences and close cooperation made this study possible, I take this opportunity to express my gratitude.

## *The Definition of "Service"*

Question one in the interview represented an attempt to obtain a definition of "service." The definition of service was generally consistent across the country and was useful primarily as the basis for further questions. Service, respondents agreed, was the dynamic response to existing and potential needs for the present and the foreseeable future. It was frequently stressed, however, that the existence of a service may in itself generate a need; and that needs will vary from department to department. Such qualifications suggest a possible confusion between "need" and "demand," for a service that serves no prerequisite need (as distinct from a service that recognizes a latent need and hatches it into a kinetic demand) is, it can be argued, invalid. Similarly, as Dean Swanson of Chicago has pointed out, one of the basic problems in determining needs, as distinct from demands, is that respondents will normally suggest those services they want in terms of the services they have come to expect.[6] Indeed, the university librarians themselves appear at times to fall into this trap, in that service was defined by some in terms of material responses alone. Certainly, the majority of those interviewed restricted their concepts of service to what Samuel Rothstein has termed "moderate" service as distinct from "liberal" service, with an attendant emphasis upon a bibliographic approach.[7] However, as has been said, the basic definition across Canada of academic library service revealed a consistent recognition of the interdependency of need and response that provided ingress into the remainder of the study.

## Community Parameters

Question two tried to discover the present limitations placed upon the parameters of the community served by Canadian university libraries, and the answers to this question were again generally consistent. However, in this area a minor variant, possibly related to the relative isolation of the region in which a library is located, became apparent. In general, the Canadian university library limits its active service to its own academic community. (However, most libraries will not turn away serious users, except sometimes pre-university students, who wish to use non-stack resources in the library.) Respondents gave a threefold rationale for limiting service to members of the library's own community: (a) the resources of our university libraries are inadequate to meet the needs even of their own communities, let alone to service a broader community; (b) the funding of Canadian university libraries is intended to support campus service; (c) to service members of other library communities would be to, undercut the services (and therefore the funding claims) of such other libraries as exist in a region. For this last reason, many university libraries will offer services only by referral from a relevant library outside the university system.

That this "parameter" rationale is, however, flexible to the point of opportunism becomes evident when we examine the *actual* modifications in various libraries; and, indeed, as has been noted, there exists a body of opinion of sufficient divergence and strength to warrant its inclusion as a variant pattern. In almost every library visited there was the feeling that the university library does have an obligation (if for no other reason than that of good public relations) not to turn away potential users. Thus many libraries will extend their *in situ* use rulings to permit borrowing when the user has received specific, *limited* permission from a senior member of the library's staff to borrow. Moreover, libraries with medical or law adjuncts invariably extend their service in those areas to the professional community beyond the university community *as such*;

and the same type of professional extension appears to apply to the scientific and business communities. With respect to the variant pattern, a significant minority (about one quarter) of the libraries visited saw a formal commitment to the non-academic community for services falling within the resources of the university library. There were two lines of reasoning for this variant pattern. In some cases the reasoning was simply that the region had at some time contributed capital to the development of the library and had thereby acquired limited rights. In at least three cases, however, the opinion was expressed that, because the financial support for the university came from regional taxes, the ongoing service responsibilities of the university library must also be to the total population of the region. This second opinion represents the reverse of the argument that the funding of Canadian universities is intended to support only campus service.

The pattern of service in terms of its community parameters is based, it would seem, upon a conscious rationale, but the answers to question two suggested at times to this writer—and the suggestion was reinforced by answers to later questions—that Canadian university librarians frequently develop a philosophy of expediency. It is recognized, of course, that questions of practicability may often force a detour in the critical path to an objective; but, if the detour is permitted to become a goal in itself, librarianship is deprived of any consistent theoretical base. Thus several librarians, having stated the economic and political reasons for limiting active service to their immediate community, added their wish that the situation could be otherwise. Although the wish could be made privately, however, it was emphasized that no public expression of such a philosophy would be expedient because "existing resources would not be able to handle the demand," and because "ways now exist for getting around the formal regulations if both reader and library so desire."

The dilemma inherent in this attitude seems to the present writer reminiscent of the old riddle of the primacy of the chicken or the egg. University library resources in Canada are inadequate to support services to a wider community; therefore, we cannot publicize or even plan for wider services; therefore we cannot develop arguments for funding to support such plans; therefore university library resources in Canada are inadequate. The only way to break out of the circle (assuming that university libraries are justified in remaining largely self-sufficient) may be to regard the "research level collection" as a regional resource. If this were done, the emphasis of service would presumably be based not upon the category of the borrower, but upon the relevancy of his need to the scope of the university's collection.

Indeed, it may be that a failure to distinguish between the category or status of the borrower and the relevancy of his need is the underlying issue in the current conflict between some total service advocates and many university librarians. If university libraries could permit non-university readers to use materials unique to the academic collections on a formal, publicized basis, they would meet the objectives of total service without infringing upon the collection responsibilities of other types of libraries, and probably without greatly increasing their own user load. Unfortunately, the university librarian has not regarded it as expedient to publicize services beyond the confines of his campus, has not felt it philosophically necessary to challenge the dictates of expediency, and has not succeeded in making his position clear even to his own colleagues in other types of libraries. To say that any "approved" need will, in fact, be met by unpublicized means is not to turn the thrust of the above thesis, for, as one chief librarian suggested, the university library's basis of support rests upon publicized services, not passive responses, and the academic community alone may already be too restrictive a source of support for the research library. Moreover, one of the ironies in this area is that, even though most university libraries *are* serving selected individuals or even groups from the non-academic community, they offer the service in such a way that they derive little public or professional credit for their efforts.

*Investigation of Need*

The third and fourth questions posed to respondents in this study concerned the degree to which the rationale of service in Canadian university libraries is based upon systematic investigation. The answers to the first question regarding definitions of service established the generally accepted relationship between need (now limited, by replies to the second question, to needs within the academic community) and response, and led to a defining of service as the manifestation of this relationship. It seemed logical, therefore, to assume that no valid rationale of service could be developed unless university libraries had investigated the needs they exist to meet. As Basil Stuart-Stubbs has written, "librarians do not create libraries. Libraries are created for the users of libraries . . . ."[8] Question three, then, asked simply, "How has your library proceeded to investigate the need to which it responds?"

The answers to this question indicated that very few Canadian university libraries have thus far conducted any systematic or sophisticated investigation into the needs to which they hope they are responding. Although several libraries have recently appointed staff personnel for research and development, such personnel are just beginning to rise above the apparently inevitable paper work to initiate investigation into areas such as that of "need." Indeed, the overall impression left by the responses received is that Canadian university librarians might have been a lot happier if the study had been directed to them a decade from now. On the other hand, university libraries in this country have been offering services for over a century, and it does not seem too soon to ask on what bases such services have so far been developed.

Insofar as needs have thus far been investigated, the rationale appears to be that the closest we can come to ascertaining needs is to invite demands. Thus many libraries have distributed questionnaires to their faculty—sometimes twice yearly, sometimes once in five years—and some libraries have questioned their students or made systematic use of the answers received from questionnaires preliminary to Robert Downs' 1967 report on Canadian academic libraries.[9] Moreover, most libraries reported having faculty book representatives in the various teaching departments, frequently linked to the library through subject specialists on the library's staff.

The library's representatives are normally specialists in relatively broad areas such as fine arts, music, modern languages, and history, and the link may be made under the aegis of a reference department, a subject division, or a bibliographic or selection department. But, whatever terms are used, the links, where they exist, are intended to facilitate collection development and to ensure that bibliographic demands can be met "instantly."

So far as it goes, this rationale does not contradict the definition of service given in answer to question one, but some of the implications this writer found being drawn from the rationale seem to distort the initial concept of service as a relating of responses to needs. As almost every respondent stated, the entire emphasis of Canadian university libraries has thus far of necessity been placed upon the acquisition of resources rather than upon the servicing of them. Even the organization of the material for use has been, largely, uncritically derivative. In its most extreme form this stress has taken the form of dealer selection or blanket ordering which, as one chief librarian pointed out, either places the primary responsibility for selection outside the library or reduces the librarian to a collector rather than a selector. As one respondent phrased it, "if we have everything in an area, we don't have to investigate the need," and as another answer stated, "Now money is no problem and everything asked for is bought."

Admittedly dealer selection ordering is predicated upon prior selection of "areas of excellence" by the library, and upon the right to make "negative selections" for return after shipments are received. Nevertheless, the implications of this type of rationale may easily become distorted to suggest that, given sufficient resources, the demand can always be met, and that the underlying needs and appropriate responses do not have to be understood. A parallel argument might be that a company which markets a sufficiently wide range of products can dispense with marketing surveys, since every consumer need will be met somewhere within the company's range of "service." This argument may well hold true if economic factors are ignored. Indeed, one librarian did suggest that the whole concept of market analysis is quite unnecessary.

To this writer, however, any skewed stress upon one aspect (resources) of one component (responses) of the need-service-resources sequence is dangerous to the long-term development of the total sequence; although it is true, as one respondent noted, that the library probably should not attempt to meet all relevant needs, for librarians should be familiar with the larger information system of which libraries are but a part. It is also true that at times it is not needs but expressed demands that must preoccupy the library as a politically conscious organism. On the other hand, if service is the relating of responses (including resources) to needs, then no part of that service can be satisfied by emphasis upon the resources alone, for the relating of responses to needs involves far more than the presence of material on a shelf. The relationship involves, for example, the underlying need for material, which may turn out to be informational or non-container oriented. It involves, as Stuart-Stubbs points out, the degree of accessibility needed, which may not correspond to the accessibility demanded.[10] It involves the level of responsiveness needed from the service agent, which may dictate different or higher qualifications than those currently found among library personnel. Finally, the relationship involves a more aggressive role for the librarian in reassessing the emphasis which should be placed upon the several components of the need-service-response syndrome, not after the resources have been acquired but while they are being developed. Definitive collections will not necessarily ensure that all needs are met, and may not even be relevant to the meeting of many needs. Library selectors whose response is essentially to known or anticipated demands may well be responding to invalid manifestations (however loudly they are expressed) of needs they only partially comprehend. A thoroughly researched rationale should precede, not succeed, development of service in Canadian university libraries.


## Basis of Service

The fourth question asked in the interviews—"Upon what base (researched, standardized, or pragmatic) do present services at your library rest?"—was intended to re-enforce and possibly to expand upon the answers received to question three. It was explained to respondents that "researched" meant "based upon research of whatever degree of sophistication conducted in your library or elsewhere"; that "standardized" meant "depending upon standards, such as the CACUL *Guide to Canadian University Library Standards*"[11]; and that "pragmatic" meant "partaking of a practical, *ad hoc* approach, as opposed to the other bases suggested." The answers to this question indicated that the overwhelming majority of Canadian university libraries base their services upon a purely pragmatic approach.

This general answer is not surprising in view of the essentially empirical concept of resource development revealed by the answers to the preceding question. Question four did, however, occasion further and sometimes unexpected observations from respondents. With respect to standards as a base, it was pointed out that library standards are themselves pedantic and pragmatic, developing descriptive norms rather than researched rationalizations. Most of the larger libraries suggested that they had outgrown existing standards. And, though several librarians indicated that they did sometimes use points from the standards to support decisions already reached, the consensus seemed to be that standards have so far failed to provide Canadian university librarians with any overall rationale.

With respect to research as a base in question four, the point was made that, despite the addition of research personnel to several library staffs, a significant pattern of researched service may be possible only if regional research centers are established to work upon broader areas to develop more general implications than are possible for individual libraries. Such regional centers may generate sufficient prestige to obtain funds for research, whereas individual libraries have difficulty persuading their respective university presidents that there is indeed a research content to librarianship. Finally, and perhaps related to the previous point, it was suggested that it is "unfair and spurious" to blame university libraries for not encouraging research into librarianship when the universities themselves are so blatantly unable to research into their own needs and objectives.

Without denying these points of view, however, it should be noted that regional research centers will still need organized and cooperative "laboratories." Moreover, there is little evidence that librarians have tried to present well-developed and carefully cogent research proposals to university presidents. Finally, though universities themselves may appear at times disorganized, academic libraries are presumably not discouraged by their parent bodies from developing operational research. In other words, if a responsibility does exist for research in librarianship, libraries themselves must assume the greater share of such responsibility.

With respect to pragmatism as a base, it was pointed out that such pragmatism often rests upon a personal philosophy of liberal service and that there is a constant interchange of information, particularly among chief librarians. "Libraries do things on an *ad hoc* basis, but they let others copy them." Moreover, as one library that had a strong base of data for potential research explained wearily, libraries may be pragmatists simply because they have neither the quantity nor selection of staff to develop on any other base. Canadian university librarians, then, appear at times to be unwilling pragmatists, but pragmatists nonetheless. Personal philosophies can probably be regarded as no more than untested hypotheses. It may be, therefore, that we can distinguish a pattern of pragmatic service in Canada; but even this may be a contradiction in terms for, as one respondent to this question commented, "The trouble with pragmatism is that you don't know whether your response is valid or even whether you understand the challenge."

*Need and Response*

Questions five and six dealt with the identification of the data necessary to evaluations of need and of response. Any study concerned with patterns of service will probably be essentially philosophical, because patterns themselves represent modes of behaviour, beliefs, and values. But underlying the question of patterns in Canada are urgent political and economic issues. It is conceivable, for example, that within the next five years a government might confront a Canadian university library, through its parent institution, with an ultimatum that ordered funding to be based henceforth upon the needs that the library had to meet. Question five asked, therefore, "What data would you consider basic to an evaluation of need?"

Discussions here soon revealed, however, that an underlying issue had to be met before question five could be answered. There were, it appeared, needs and needs in the minds of librarians, and some needs were less relevant to the university library than were others. Even given unlimited resources, for example, should university libraries offer "special library" responses? Here again, university librarians appeared to respond pragmatically in terms of their specific clientele. Thus the medical and law librarians, and to a lesser extent the science librarians, tended to favor an open-ended approach to an evaluation of need, with a "liberal" response if warranted, whereas the humanities and social science librarians tended to adopt a didactic approach centered upon the material itself. As one librarian remarked, "the expectation of service is less present among the humanists and social scientists and their needs can be met without extensive evaluation." Clearly, to a librarian of such persuasion, the data basic to an evaluation of relevant social science and humanities needs would be very limited.

Despite an underlying bias for or against certain types of user needs, however, the answers of most of the respondents to question five showed that they did agree that the data related to need were presently unknown and could become clear only through closer contact with faculty and students. Indeed, many responses seemed to suggest service concepts in this regard so subservient as to be virtually passive and probably unconducive to sophisticated analyses of need. It is of interest that so many of the suggestions for the gathering of data centered on the presence of librarians in "user committees" and so few on the type of research recorded by Voigt and Line.[12] Moreover, two major caveats regarding faculty contacts tended to further weaken the academic librarian's present approach to the evaluation of need. First, it was pointed out that, to really understand faculty needs, librarians must speak the faculty language, share the faculty life and ethos, and blend into the faculty scene far more than they do now. Secondly, it was stressed that professors often "dream in color"; that individual demands run the whole gamut of human eccentricity; and that, at any rate, expressed needs are too often only a reflection of an individual's desire for bibliographic status. In other words, librarians would seem to agree that opinion surveys are unlikely to uncover valid evidence of basic needs. Yet such surveys underlie most library approaches to the needs problem.

Moreover, if subjective opinion surveys have limited value in this instance, arguments as to whether librarians, or library assistants, or professional specialists are best able to elicit faculty opinions—arguments that marked the course of this question—seem tangential to the main issue. Instead, librarians' interests should be directed, as one of their number remarked, to ensuring that librarians take educational methods courses in order to understand the processes and goals of education and that they "know how to design questionnaires, undertake sampling studies, and perform statistical analyses." Computers should be available to handle variables and relationships, thus freeing librarians from their preoccupation with macro-units (the containers) and enabling them to emphasize micro-units (the contents). Librarians, several respondents agreed, should be prepared to concentrate upon such areas of interest while planning to eventually turn many of their processing functions over to commercial outlets, which may in time also fabricate prepackaged and precoded units of knowledge. Indeed, it may be, as one respondent suggested, that "twenty years from now librarians will deal either in information or in waste paper;" but, in the meantime, we appear remarkably uncertain of the data base underlying any evaluation of need, and certain only that, as one chief librarian remarked, "As long as we can keep them happy on both sides of the firing line, we're alive!"

Question six asked what data librarians considered basic to an evaluation of response. Not surprisingly, since so few respondents had been able to begin identifying the data basic to an evaluation of need, even fewer could essay opinions on what data would be necessary to response evaluation. Indeed, to some the question itself seemed largely academic, as evidenced from their replies: "The lack of complaints show we respond well without investigating the needs." "Compliments are frequent so our responses must be frequently apt." "We know we're popular!" and "I would confess to a rather large discouragement with vocational research, for so much of the research that has been done has been irrelevant or unproductive; or else it has been borrowed uncritically from other disciplines; or else it has seemed motivated by little more than a desire for 'respectability'."

Question six, then, elicited the vaguest response of all the questions asked. Canadian university librarians seemed less interested in evaluating their service responses than they had been, for example, in investigating needs. An unrecognized need may become a threatening demand, but an unrecognized response remains just that. Again, the approach of librarians to this, as to the other questions in the study, was essentially pragmatic and, within its limits, consistent. With respect to an evaluation of response, the rationale seemed to be that responses must be quick, not researched, that "Trouble must be met before it can explode, and the need is primarily for sensitivity and good communication," and that "the emphasis is upon 'crisis management' not 'crisis prevention'." Thus, in effect, the Canadian librarians were saying that their time must be devoted to surviving each new threat, so that regretfully they have no hours left for preventive research. However, one respondent—a business manager, not a professional librarian—offered a different interpretation for the lack of interest in evaluating library responses. To this respondent, the reason for the lack of interest lay in the lack of cost consciousness among librarians, and he expressed dismay at the paucity of budget planning and fiscal feedback he had found in university libraries. It appeared, therefore, to this respondent (still thinking as a business man) that librarians far too often lack any semblance of "profit plans"—the "profit" being service—and so feel no necessity to balance their responses against the needs to be met.

## Servicing Independent Study Programs

One way of attempting to understand a pattern of service is to ask how the service responds to a particular type of need. Does the response change as the need changes, and how, and why? Question seven in the study asked: "How specifically does your library cater to the needs generated by independent study programs?"

Of the independent study programs, Robert Downs has written, "Pedagogically superior to either the textbook or reserve book . . . independent work and study on the part of the student . . . requires that the student have some training in how to make efficient use of books and libraries . . . and be made responsible for using the library's total resources, finding materials relating to his assignments in whatever sources that may be available."[13] Recent proposals for campus organization and development have assumed that more emphasis on independent study is inevitable and desirable. Therefore, library interest and involvement in the new programs was predictably high although the interest of Canadian university librarians appeared to be more with the housekeeping implications than with the pedagogical nuances of the programs.

In several libraries it was believed that independent study was not being developed to any extent on the campus because there was no evidence of the impact of such study on the use of the library, but the relationship between independent study and library use may be considerably more complex than such a belief or Dr. Downs' statement would suggest. In courses in which the student is not book oriented, as for example in some of the science courses, independent study based upon a problem-solving approach may lead, as one medical respondent reported, to less rather than greater dependency on the resources of the library. Moreover, and of more general significance, preliminary findings from research in progress at a major Canadian university library suggest that there may be little quantitative difference between the use made of a library by students in a traditional course and in an independent study program.[14]

A better index of the growth of the independent study approach on a campus may be the diminution of the reserve shelf, although, as Henry Wriston, former president of Brown University, has pointed out, the contents of that shelf may supply an index of diminishing expectations on the part of individual professors rather than a reflection of the impact of an entire program. However, although the size of reserve collections in Canadian university libraries is decreasing, the immediate reason is not the impact of independent study programs, but the increasing initiative shown by librarians in checking the unjustified growth of reserve collections. Influenced in part by studies on reserve use, such as those by Lois Carrier, university librarians are whittling away steadily at faculty-inspired segregated short-term loan collections.[15] On the other hand, many respondents report increasing use of reserves among senior undergraduates, and at least one Canadian university library has just established a graduate reserve room in addition to its undergraduate reserve area. With respect to any rationale of library service toward independent study programs, it can be said only that the libraries have not yet felt the need to respond to such programs, either in terms of reference service or in terms of collection organization, and that, in this area, the library's appreciation of use may be more realistic than that of many classroom teachers.

## The Rationale behind Specific Aspects of Service

Questions eight, nine, and ten in the interviews were intended to investigate the rationale behind specific aspects of service. The three aspects chosen were ones distinguished by Robert Downs in his 1967 report on the resources of Canadian academic libraries, namely, orientation programs, library schedules, and length of loans.[16] In each case the emphasis of the present study was on the "why" not the "what" of the decisions reached, and with respect to the orientation programs, there were three parts to the question asked. Do you have a program, how did you determine its content, and how do you evaluate the program?

Almost every university library has an orientation program. Downs described the possible variations on the theme, but the variations do appear to share a common rationale—the assumption that students need to be taught formally how to use a university library. Only two libraries reported that they were depending upon individual service rather than group instruction to teach use of the library. The content of group instruction was normally chosen by the librarians to give to the students what the librarians thought the students ought to know.[17] The basis for the librarians' choice varied all the way from an arbitrary selection of elements "designed to make things easier for the librarians" (a worthy goal compatible with also making things easier for the students) to systematic opinion surveys of all first year students. In only one case, however, did a library carry its desire to give the students what they wanted to know to the perhaps logical conclusion of having the students themselves prepare a script and presentation, with the library acting as the information backstop. Significantly, this single experiment in the ultimate grass roots approach was criticized by other libraries as expecting students to know that which they would not know they needed to know.

Provisions for measuring the effectiveness of ongoing programs were frequently gross and unreliable, so that the somewhat paternalistic rationale behind the inception of many orientation programs tended to be re-enforced by the evaluation procedures or lack of procedures. The commonest measure was to ask students known to the librarians what they thought of the program, though some libraries did distribute evaluation questionnaires. The library mentioned above, which had used second-year students to prepare the script, used first-year students to evaluate the presentation by revising it for the subsequent year. Only three libraries made systematic use of objective feedback by determining whether the number of directional and functional questions received at the information or reference desk decreased after the directional and functional orientation program had been completed. In each case a decrease was recorded. Only two libraries used any formal analysis of consumption data in developing their program, though many libraries sought the "educated opinions" of reference staff. One of the reasons for the low use of objective feedback techniques was that, despite the plethora of statistics kept by university libraries, very few of the libraries visited kept statistics designed to meet predetermined, problem-oriented objectives. Thus, with respect to the orientation programs, although the objectives of the programs were reasonably clear, the presentation and evaluation techniques frequently did not appear to have been developed with the program objectives in mind.

The rationale underlying library schedules was that users have a right to insist upon reasonable hours of service. Such reasoning was undoubtedly expedient, but stemmed also from a genuine conviction on the part of most librarians that a supportive service must comply with demands even more than with needs. This distinction between needs and demands was made clear by a senior librarian who noted, "If we worked on a rationale of need we would have shorter hours because to keep the library open for twenty people who don't *have* to study here from midnight to one in the morning isn't economically justifiable; but right now we're responding to a demand not justified by either need or use."

To some extent, however, the decision to meet demands (usually from students) was modified uncritically by the results of head-counts from the period contiguous to the extension period requested, and respondents noted the willingness of students to be persuaded by the evidence of such counts. Moreover, head-counts have also been extrapolated to adjust as well as to extend hours, and counts have been conducted in trial periods as well as in adjacent hours. Also, in a few cases, hours were extended in advance of expressed demand because of external factors such as early arriving commuters or the later hours in neighboring libraries. But, in every case, however, the new hours created their own demand, so that, as one respondent put it, "If there is one thing certain about scheduling, it is that you never reduce your hours!"

What is missing behind such a rationale of service, however, is investigation into need as distinct from demand. What does a user need, minute by minute, in an academic library? Is the need for materials or is it for study space? Can needs be met better at certain times than at others? Are there really right and wrong ways of satisfying needs? One study was supposed to have shown that longer and longer library hours were subsidizing longer and longer student dinner periods, presumably because there is an optimum length of time in which any given student can or will study. Is this possibly apocryphal conclusion justified? Should library users learn to discipline themselves to library hours as they do to banking hours, so that libraries could give maximum service during shorter hours? Or is the cost of maintaining access so inexpensive and adequate that cost is not a factor in scheduling? And is such investigation justified, or are responses to be based, as one librarian phrased it, on "surveys and sit-ins," because sophisticated research "just isn't politically worth the time"?

Whether or not sophisticated research can be justified regarding library schedules, such investigation into the rationale justifying the length of loans in university libraries would certainly seem to be politically expedient. The answers to question ten—"What rationale underlies the length of loans in your library?"—made it clear that this question, together with the closely related topic of fines, is one of the most explosive issues being probed by the new student power groups. The dominant pattern of library service with respect to loans still appears to be the traditional two weeks to students, with shorter loans on special formats and materials in demand, and with longer loans for faculty and some graduate borrowers. However, the traditional pattern is being increasingly challenged, and the rationale behind current experimentation in loan periods is of particular importance for us in that it tends to throw the entire topic of patterns of service in Canadian university libraries into focus.

True to their philosophy of expediency and subsidiary service, librarians have not generally initiated changes in policy respecting loan periods and fines, except for minor administratively convenient modifications such as placing the date due on a Monday. The majority who still held with the basic two-week loan for students did so "because it is traditional," "because it matches our feelings regarding demand and use—the old touch system," "because it seems to be the 'right' span for the students' needs and memories," and "because it is a round figure and the one used by other libraries." Such a rationale, firmly founded upon pragmatic justifications within a framework of expertise and accepted practice, nevertheless shows how inherently unstable pure pragmatism is, for now the traditions have been dismembered, and the "experts" have been challenged out of countenance by other experts no better supported with facts than they. Thus, once the egalitarian movement had destroyed the concept of a special status for faculty, and once the faculty had been cowed into surrendering any or all of its traditional rights, the responses of the libraries swung as widely toward uniform loan periods and "common equivalent sanctions" as they had once toward prerogatives for faculty and administration. A significant minority of the libraries visited had adopted or were about to adopt one-week loans instead of two-week loans; or fines for students and faculty (to be enforced, particularly when on-line loan systems were introduced, by suspension of library privileges for delinquents); or no fines for anyone; or an across-the-board combination of an indefinite loan period with the machinery for recall. Such measures were just as unwittingly responsive to the pressures of a new regime as the measures they replaced had been responsive to traditional demands, and very few libraries could offer any rationale of loan periods beyond that of uncontrolled empiricism.

## Interlibrary Cooperation

Question eleven explored the views of chief librarians, on interlibrary cooperation and "areas of excellence." The point of this question was to investigate the extent to which the rationale of service had been strong enough to transcend those feelings of parochialism which naturally characterize any consciously independent organism. The answers received revealed that, formally at least, the barriers to cooperation had been surmounted, and that four major forums for interlibrary discussion existed: the librarian's Committee of the Association of Atlantic Universities for eastern Canada; the committee on Library Co-operation of the Conference of Rectors and Principals, the Ontario Council of University Librarians (OCUL) for central Canada, and the Council of the Western Canadian University Librarians (COWCUL) for western Canada. With one exception, these forums were too new to have had much impact upon patterns of service. But the exception, OCUL, had been so successful with its "Inter University Transit System" that the System was presented as the highlight of "collective autonomy" in the *Second Annual Review* of the Committee of Presidents of Universities of Ontario.[18]

It would appear, indeed, that although three of the four interlibrary councils had been formed as subcommittees of presidential committees (the western COWCUL being an independent creation), their members have surged ahead of their university administrations in developing plans for practical cooperation. There are, however, two major limitations to such cooperation. The first lies beyond the powers of the librarians to control. It involves the need for the universities to agree upon areas of teaching excellence before agreements can be reached upon areas of collection excellence. The second limitation is more subtle and more related to the librarians themselves. It involves, again, the essential pragmatism of academic librarianship, which discourages initiative in pressing for unproven or potentially high risk ventures. Therefore, although university librarians have been conspicuous leaders in cooperative plans designed to improve housekeeping aspects of their operations, they have been less successful in developing any rationale of service based on cooperative acquisition, processing, and storage. The result is that although discussions in these areas have been initiated, particularly in the Far West and in Ontario, the true potential for university leadership inherent in such organizations as OCUL and COWCUL has yet to be realized.

The purpose of this study has been to investigate the climate of opinion—the beliefs and values—of university librarians throughout Canada as to their reasoned responses to the needs of their communities; to examine, in other words, the pattern of service in Canadian university libraries. The existence of such a pattern, an established mode of behavior, has become clear as the study progressed. It is a pattern unaffected by regional interests and disparities, such as the isolation of the prairies or the economic deprivation of Quebec. It is a pattern of pragmatism: a belief that the meaning of service can be summed up in its practical consequences, and that no further understanding of the relationship between need and response is necessary than that which can be provided by a description of the consequences of that relationship. It is a pragmatism that has grown naturally out of the preoccupation of university librarians with quantitative demands. There has always been the demand for more books, presumably because the larger the collection the greater the likelihood of any given title being present. There has been the demand for more librarians to process the books, on the assumption, it may be supposed, that a book on a shelf is meeting a need and that a librarian is the best person to put it there. There has been, particularly of late, the demand for more space to house the increased number of books and librarians, supposedly because access to the growing collection has to be immediate and the processing even faster than that.

With so pragmatic a pattern dominant in Canada, there has been little opportunity for a climate of opinion to develop favoring research and the more sophisticated services resulting from research. The users have not demanded changes in the type of response but only in the degree of service, and the libraries have not responded with any but the most practical and ad hoc expedients. It would be unrealistic to suggest that this pattern will change overnight, or that the climate of opinion is showing a universal shift. But there is a growing realization that "the library of the future will have to seek out government funding as never before," as one respondent said, "and the government of the future will demand researched data as never before." Gradually, therefore, the university libraries of Canada are appointing researchers to their staffs. Gradually, the climate of opinion is shifting to favor time for research as a legitimate charge against the library's budget. The search for recent graduates is now concentrating upon the qualities of subject expertise, creativity, initiative, and management potential. When qualified librarians are found they will themselves further change the climate of opinion and influence later patterns of service.

Thus the definition of service arising from the study contains the potential for dynamic, liberalized, information-centered responses if needs for such services exist. In the meantime, current demands are regarded as a manifestation of a limited, container-oriented need, and Canadian academic library responses are similarly limited. The potential parameters of the university library's community may far transcend the academic community. For the present, however, librarians are content to concentrate upon the local, known demands. Canadian university librarians recognized the importance of conducting systematic investigations into both need and response, but have not felt it practical as yet to seek the financial and intellectual support of the universities for such investigations. Though they deplored the lack of data about users' needs, librarians could see as a practical consequence of their concern no more sophisticated solution than closer faculty contact, while the practical consequences of a lack of response data caused even less concern. Again, the rationale behind specific aspects of service rested upon a feeling that demands must be met whether justified by need or not, but the recognition that research could and should modify such simplistic pragmatism was present and now waits only on the provision of money and personnel. Thus, finally, the interlibrary forums have shown remarkable success in dealing with the practical aspects of housekeeping operations, but have shown perhaps disturbing caution in venturing into high risk areas requiring careful and sophisticated feasbility research.

Both a pattern of pragmatism and a climate of research readiness are revealed in the foregoing study. If the climate can now be encouraged by governments, by library schools, and by university libraries themselves, the too narrowly pragmatic approach to service now current in university libraries will change. Within the next decade the established beliefs and values held in common by Canadian university librarians should be based upon a new and far-reaching theory of professional behaviour.

NOTES

1. Neal Harlow, "The Educational Problem" *Canadian Library* 22 (September 1965): 87.
2. C. Walter Stone, "A Design for Tomorrow," *Proceedings of the National Conference on the Implications of the New Media for the Teaching of Library Science* (Urbana: University of Illinois Graduate School of Library Science, 1963), p. 31.
3. The opportunity is here taken to express the thanks of the author to the Humanities and Social Sciences Committee of the University of Toronto for their generous grant in aid for this research; to the Director of the School of Library Science of the University of Toronto; and to the librarians visited for their unstinting cooperation and essential assistance.
4. Robert B. Downs, *Resources of Canadian Academic and Research Libraries* (Ottawa: Association of Universities and Colleges of Canada, 1967), p. 81.
5. See Appendix.
6. Don R. Swanson, Address to the 20th Annual Conference of the Canadian Library Association. Toronto, June 1965.
7. Samuel Rothstein, *The Development of Reference Services through Academic Tradition, Public Library Practice and Special Librarianship*, ACRL Monographs, no. 14. (Chicago: Association of College and Reference Libraries, 1955), pp. 76-77.
8. Basil Stuart-Stubbs, "The Downs Report in Perspective," *Financial Implications of the Downs Report on Canadian Academic and Research Libraries*, ed. Robert H. Blackburn

(Toronto: Association of Universities and Colleges of Canada, 1969), p. 17.

9. Downs, *Resources of Canadian Libraries*, p. 127.
10. Stuart-Stubbs, "Downs Report," p. 18.
11. Canadian Association of College and University Libraries, *Guide to Canadian University Library Standards, Report of the University Library Standards Committee of CACUL, 1961-1964* (Toronto: CALCUL, June 1965).
12. Melvin J. Voigt, *Scientists' Approaches to Information* (Chicago: American Library Association, 1961); Maurice B. Line, "University Libraries and the Information Needs of the Researcher: A Provider's View," *Aslib Proceedings* 18 (July 1966):178-184.
13. Downs, *Resources of Canadian Libraries*, p. 83.
14. For further information on this study, the reader is advised to contact Miss G. F. Dobbin, Systems Librarian, The University of British Columbia, Vancouver, Canada.
15. Lois J. Carrier, "Are University Reserve Collections Justified?" *APLA Bulletin* 30 (September 1966): 85-88, 99-103. _____,"Undergraduate Use of Reserve Material in Six Selected Subjects," (MLS Thesis, University of Toronto, 1968).
16. Downs, *Resources of Canadian Libraries*, pp. 81-92.
17. Ibid., p. 84.
18. The Committee of Presidents of Universities of Ontario. Ontario Council of University Librarians, *Inter-university Transit System Anniversary Report, 1967-1968*. Toronto: CPUO, 1968; The Committee of Presidents of Universities of Ontario, *Collective Autonomy: Second Annual Review, 1967/68*. Toronto: University of Toronto Press, 1968.

APPENDIX/*List of Universities and Chief Librarians Visited*

Alberta, University of, Edmonton, Alberta; B. B. Peel.
British Columbia, University of, Vancouver, B. C.; Basil Stuart-Stubbs.

Calgary, University of, Calgary, Alberta; T. M. Walker.
Carleton University, Ottawa, Ontario; H. G. Gifford.
Dalhousie College and University, Halifax, N. S.; L. G. Vagianos.
Guelph, University of, Guelph, Ontario; L. G. MacRae.
Laurentian University of Sudbury, Ontario; Rev. P. E. Filion, S. J.
Laval, Université, Quebec, P. Q.; Abbé Joseph-Marie Blanchet.
Manitoba, University of, Winnipeg, Manitoba; D. T. Wilder.
McGill University, Montreal, P. Q.; Keith Crouch.
McMaster University, Hamilton, Ontario; W. B. Ready.
Memorial University of Newfoundland, St. John's, Newfoundland;
    D. L. Ryan.
Montréal, Université de, Montreal, P. Q.; Daniel Reicher.
New Brunswick, University of, Fredericton, N. B.; G. E. Gunn.
Queen's University, Kingston, Ontario; D. A. Redmond.
Saskatchewan, University of, Saskatoon, Saskatchewan; D. C.
    Appelt.
Simon Fraser University, Burnaby, B. C.; D. A. Baird.
Sir George Williams University, Montreal, P. Q.; Helen Howard.
Toronto, University of, Toronto, Ontario; R. H. Blackburn.
Victoria, University of, Victoria, B. C; D. W. Halliwell.
Waterloo, University of, Waterloo, Ontario; D. E. Lewis.
Western Ontario, University of, London, Ontario; J. J. Talman.
Windsor, University of, Windsor, Ontario; W. F. Dollar.
York University, Toronto, Ontario; T. F. O'Connell.

# 6/ Organization and Services of University Libraries in West Africa

A. J. E. DEAN

*University of Ibadan*

The English-speaking countries of West Africa, the Gambia, Sierra Leone, Liberia, Ghana, and Nigeria cover an area of nearly half a million square miles in the equatorial belt and present a picture of infinite variety—an Atlantic littoral of beaches, lagoons, tidal creeks, swamps, a forested hinterland and, in the case of Ghana and Nigeria, interior plains merging with the savannah fringes of the Sahara. Altogether about 67 million people speaking a great variety of languages, but with English as a common tongue, inhabit the region. Nigeria is by far the largest country of the five, with a population of 56 million, and the Gambia the smallest, with a population of 300 thousand. All, with the exception of the Gambia, have considerable economic potential, but at the moment the gross national product per capita in each territory is far below the world average.

The Gambia, Sierra Leone, Ghana, and Nigeria were all formerly British colonies and attained full independence, after a period of internal self-government, between the years 1957 and 1965. Liberia, on the other hand, came into existence as an enclave under American influence, being declared an independent Republic in 1847 and recognized as autonomous by the United States in 1862.

Although institutions of higher learning are not new to West Africa, both Fourah Bay College and Liberia College having been founded in the nineteenth century, higher education, together with the comprehensive university and college library systems implied by

TABLE 1/Senior Staff and Student Enrollment in
Universities and Colleges of English-Speaking West Africa, 1967-1968

| Universities and Colleges | Foundation Date | Senior Staff (Academic Administrative, Library) | Students (Undergraduate, Postgraduate) | Remarks |
|---|---|---|---|---|
| Ghana, pop. 7,945,000 | | | | |
| University of Ghana, Legon | 1948 | 587 | 2,522 | Attained university status, 1961 |
| University of Science & Technology, Kumasi | 1951 | 355 | 1,374 | Attained university status, 1961 |
| University College of Cape Coast | 1962 | 285 | 1,120 | University status from foundation |
| Liberia, pop. 1,016,000 | | | | |
| University of Liberia | 1862 | 111 | 825 | Attained university status, 1951 |
| Nigeria, pop. 55,653,821 | | | | |
| University of Ibadan | 1948 | 551 | 2,749 | Attained university status, 1962 |
| University of Nigeria, Nsukka[a] | 1960 | 362 | 2,587 | University status from foundation |
| University of Ife | 1961 | 333 | 1,256 | University status from foundation |
| Ahmadu Bello University[b] | 1962 | 598 | 1,390 | University status from foundation |
| University of Lagos[c] | 1962 | 389 | 1,877 | University status from foundation |
| Sierra Leone, pop. 2,183,000 | | | | |
| Fourah Bay College, University of Sierra Leone | 1827 | 161 | 600 | Both institutions incorporated into the University of Sierra Leone by the |
| Njala University College, University of Sierra Leone | 1964 | 106 | 306 | University of Sierra Leone Act, 1967 |

[a] University of Nigeria, closed as a result of national emergency. 1965-1966 figures given.

[b] Includes Central Campus plus Abdullahi Bayero College, Kano; Institute for Agricultural Research, Samaru; and Institute of Administration, Zaria.

[c] Includes Central Campus plus College of Medicine and College of Education.

the term, has come into its own only during the past twenty years. In this brief survey an attempt will be made to appraise the library activities of all degree-giving universities and colleges in English-speaking West Africa with a minimum enrollment of three hundred students. A statistical picture of these foundations, which number eleven altogether, is given in Table 1. The Gambia is not included because it has neither the population nor the economic strength to sustain an indigenous college at the moment. The enrollment limitation excludes only one or two very small institutions, the omission of which will not affect the validity of any conclusions drawn. Most of the figures given in Tables 1-4 are based upon information provided by the librarians of the institutions concerned in response to a questionnaire circulated in November 1968.

In all, there are well over 3,500 teachers, librarians, and senior administrators and nearly 17,000 students in the universities and colleges of the region. The overall ratio of students to population is 1:4,000 and of students to literate population is 1:740, a literacy rate of 18.5 percent being assumed. Poor though these ratios are, they are a very considerable improvement upon the situation prevailing even ten years ago. It is worth noting for the purpose of comparison that the student/population ratio in Britain is 1:265 and in Canada 1:97. West Africa has made rapid progress, but there is still much ground to be covered.

It is relevant to consider the major factors that have contributed most decisively to the progress of higher education and library development in English-speaking West Africa. Possibly the most dynamic force has been the enthusiasm for learning generated by African nationalist leaders throughout the region. A further stimulus, in the area of British influence, was the encouragement and help given by successive British governments both before and after independence. Mention should also be made of the impact on educational and library planning on the international agencies, metropolitan cultural agencies, and the foundations, particularly in recent years.

African nationalist leaders even in the earliest days were conscious of the fact that a literate and informed public was a sine qua non of economic and political progress. They were thus keenly aware of the importance of libraries of every description in educational programs. This awareness is reflected in the views of Kwame Nkrumah expressed at the official opening of the Accra Central Library in 1956. He said:

> when my studies took me to the United States of America and to England, I realised how vital to the student and, indeed, to every ambitious man and woman, was a good library. For a small subscription I could be the proud possessor—for a short while at least—of the best books on almost any subject that interested me. In my struggling days in London I can without doubt say that my happiest hours were spent browsing among the books in the British Museum. A good national library and a good national museum and a good cultural center are the custodians of a nation's culture and wisdom.[1]

It was this kind of attitude demonstrated by the leaders of the new nations in English-speaking West Africa that made possible the foundation of impressive universities and extensive library systems. I say impressive advisedly, because West African university development in the last few years has moved at a pace unparalleled by any other emergent region of the world. These universities, each centered on a growing library, are the concrete expression of the determination of African leaders to bring West Africa as rapidly and as efficiently as possible into the technological age.

It is doubtful if higher education in Sierra Leone, Ghana, and Nigeria could ever have reached its present stage of development without the active encouragement of Britain. The recommendations of the two Parliamentary Commissions, chaired respectively by Cyril Asquith and Walter Elliot, which reported in 1945, laid the foundation of the postwar wave of university development in the colonies.[2] They placed particular emphasis upon the importance of the library as the central academic institution of the university, and the Asquith *Report* stated quite categorically: "We cannot emphasize too strongly the paramount importance of . . . the building up of a university library [in the colonial universities] to rank with university libraries elsewhere."[3] It was, as a matter of fact, immediately as a consequence of those two Commissions (although not without some initial difficulties) that university colleges were established at Legon, Ghana, and Ibadan, Nigeria, in 1948. It should also be noted that initially both these institutions awarded the degree of the University of London in the same way that Fourah Bay College was awarding the degree of the University of Durham. It was strongly felt that new colonial colleges should evolve under the tutelage of a senior university until they had gained sufficient academic experience to award their own degrees. Indeed, this special relationship with the University of London lasted in the case of Legon until 1961 and in the case of Ibadan until 1962, that is, until these bodies achieved full university stature. All the institutions listed in Table 1 now award indigenous qualifications, but close and informal ties still exist with the universities of the metropolitan world.

There was a further development of major importance in respect to colonial education arising out of the Asquith *Report*, and this was the establishment of the Inter-University Council for Higher Education in the Colonies under the Secretaryship of Walter Adams. This body was charged with the task of cooperating with existing colonial universities and with fostering the development of other institutions of higher learning in the colonial territories in their advance to university status. One of the first acts of the Council was to appoint a Library Adviser to assist in planning library systems in the colonial colleges. Successive advisers to the Council have given generous and ungrudging service to the college and later university libraries of the countries of the emergent Commonwealth, assisting in the recruitment and appointment of staff, searching for scarce books and scarcer serials, arranging microfilming and photocopying services, scanning plans of library buildings, and so forth. The Inter-University Council has served and continues to serve with distinction the universities and academic libraries of Sierra Leone, Ghana, and Nigeria. It will be clearly seen, therefore, that before and after independence Britain was determined that these three West Africa territories should have an opportunity of developing programs of higher education comparable with the best in the metropolitan world and, moreover, programs which clearly identify the university library as the focal point of university activity.

It is also appropriate to mention the increasing influence in recent years on the university libraries of West Africa of external agencies, international bodies, cultural organizations of various metropolitan governments, and also the major foundations, Rockefeller, Ford, and Carnegie. The Carnegie Corporation, in particular, has, to a great extent, been responsible for the introduction of certain aspects of American library practice into the region.

Foreign influences have clearly been of considerable importance in shaping the pattern of university and college library development in West Africa. Sierra Leone, Ghana, and Nigeria have been greatly influenced by the former colonial power, Britain, and to a lesser extent by the United States. In Liberian library development, American influence has been paramount, and had we included in our survey the universities of French-speaking West Africa, we would have noted the pervasive impact of French library traditions. However, it should be stressed that all these institutions under consideration are now achieving their own specific identity and, while maintaining close relations with Europe and America, are tending to adapt rather than to adopt the library patterns of the metropolitan world.

## Organizational Patterns

In the following analysis of university and college library systems, comments will be grouped under several broad headings—government; finance; departmental structure; content and organization of collections and buildings.

### GOVERNMENT

In Sierra Leone, Ghana, and Nigeria a pattern of government

familiar to civic universities of Britain is perceptible; a University Council determines policy and has as its chief executive a vice-chancellor. Council is advised upon all academic matters by the Senate or the Academic Board (these terms are often interchangeable) consisting entirely of university teachers, the university librarian, and so forth, and excluding the administrative officers of the university. The Senate is normally a vigorous and inquiring body, the views of which are accorded the highest respect by the Council. In ten out of eleven institutions investigated the librarian enjoys professorial status and privileges, and in one only is he equated with a lower academic grade. In almost all cases the librarian is responsible directly to the vice-chancellor and is advised on library policy by a library subcommittee of the Senate. This organizational structure is typified by the University of Ibadan Library. (See Chart) In only two institutions—the University of Ghana and Fourah Bay College—is the librarian directly responsible to the library subcommittee for the administration of library policy rather than to the vice-chancellor. Where this kind of situation prevails, there is a danger that directives from a lay committee may take precedence over the librarian's professional viewpoint—a situation that is less likely to occur when the librarian is directly responsible to the chief executive of the university. However, too much should not be made of this, since the impact of the librarian upon the goverment of the university library is as much a matter of his own personality as of his constitutional position.

An examination of annual reports indicates that library committees generally represent a cross section of academic interests, although this pattern is not necessarily laid down in regulations and, indeed, may be dependent upon the good sense of Senate to effect when selecting representatives. The librarian is normally a voting member of his committee and either he or his deputy acts as secretary. The chair at meetings is usually taken by the vice-chancellor or his nominee, although in one case, the University of Lagos, the librarian acts as chairman.

The university librarian is normally a member of the Senate and

ORGANIZATIONAL STRUCTURE OF UNIVERSITY OF IBADAN LIBRARY

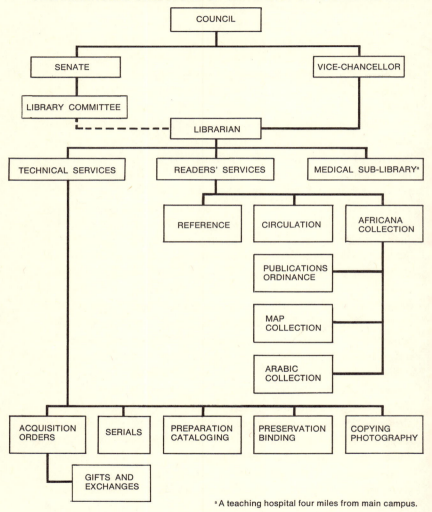

ᵃ A teaching hospital four miles from main campus.

sometimes of the Faculty Boards as well. He is also, by reason of his membership in the Senate, entitled to be elected to other committees in the university and can advance quite a long way up the governing hierarchy.

The American tradition of university government, which is not too dissimilar from the British, prevails at the University of Liberia, and a Board of Trustees presides over the institution. The composition of this Board and its activities are broadly similar to the Council of the British university. The chief executive of the Board is the president and the librarian is directly responsible to him. There is an Advisory Council consisting of faculty representatives, the librarian, and officers of the administration, all of whom assist the Board of Trustees in developing university policy, while a Faculty Library Committee advises the librarian on library matters.

In the American system of university government, fewer matters are referred to committees than in the British pattern. The executive powers of the university president tend to be greater than those of the vice-chancellor. The kind of committee structure, which characterizes universities following the British tradition, would soon break down if applied to such large and complex institutions as American universities. The librarian in the American context tends to be regarded first and last as an administrator, whereas in the British he is regarded somewhat ambiguously, first as an academic and second as an administrator. Consequently, under the British system, university librarians are able to climb the same ladder in the hierarchy as other academics. Indeed, quite recently the librarian in one university in West Africa was elected deputy vice-chancellor for a period of four years.

An important trend in the library government of institutions of higher learning in West Africa is the growing prestige of the librarian in the councils of the university, a prestige that is higher than in many metropolitan countries. As was remarked in a previous paper, "the appalling scarcity of books [in Africa] gives the librarian as the custodian of the materials of learning a standing and favoured position which he lacks in more prosperous lands!"[4] Nonetheless, it does not seem to me that professorial status is a sufficient recognition of the librarian's importance in the academic community, particularly in the larger universities, such as Ghana and Ibadan, where responsibilities are of such an order that the librarian might reasonably be accorded decanal status. With this enhanced standing he would have access to *all* committees in which university policy is decided and which consequently have such a vital bearing upon library development.

### FINANCE

The annual recurrent expenditure of the universities and colleges surveyed amounts to one and three-quarter million dollars. The majority of these funds are obtained from government, the balance being donated by various metropolitan agencies. (Fees paid by students themselves represent a very small proportion of the university budget and, in any case, a high proportion of these are derived from scholarships awarded by government). It is not possible to assess capital expenditure on library development over the years, but the proportion covered by grants from external agencies is greater than in the case of recurrent expenditure.

In West Africa, generally, university library estimates—both recurrent and developmental—are prepared by the librarian, scrutinized by the library committee, and passed to the finance committee for consideration in the light of competing demands from other departments in the university. The success of the librarian in obtaining an adequate share of the funds allocated to the university is normally a function of his standing in that institution. Estimates tend to be prepared on an ad hoc basis in the form of a line budget, and little attention has been paid to the development of standard formulae for the rationalization of expenditure. An attempt is made to prepare quinquennium estimates as well as annual estimates in most of the institutions under consideration, but recurrent financial crises and other unanticipated changes in the demands made upon the university make these estimates a most unreliable guide.

Table 2 gives expenditure statistics relating to the institutions

TABLE 2/Annual Recurrent Library Expenditure, 1967-1968

| University and College Libraries | Total library budget | Percentage spent on books & serials | Percentage spent on salaries & wages | Percentage spent under other headings | Percentage of total university or college budget spent on library |
|---|---|---|---|---|---|
| **Ghana** | | | | | |
| University of Ghana, Legon | $190,701 | 53.5 | 43 | 3.5 | 4.06 |
| University of Science & Technology, Kumasi | 102,627 | 51.5 | 33 | 15.5 | 2.73[a] |
| University College of Cape Coast | 105,840 | 51 | 38 | 11 | 5.00 |
| **Liberia** | | | | | |
| University of Liberia | 58,422 | 29 | 69 | 2 | 7.00 |
| **Nigeria** | | | | | |
| University of Ibadan | 323,239 | 36 | 58 | 6 | 3.66 |
| University of Nigeria, Nsukka[b] | - | - | - | - | - |
| University of Ife | 245,674 | 56.5 | 38 | 5.5 | 5.29 |
| Ahmadu Bello University | 283,705 | 29 | 62 | 9 | 4.25 |
| University of Lagos | 374,986 | 44 | 47.5 | 8.5 | 4.40 |
| **Sierra Leone** | | | | | |
| Fourah Bay College, University of Sierra Leone | 78,324 | 37 | 49 | 14 | 5.06 |
| Njala University College, University of Sierra Leone[c] | - | - | - | - | - |
| Average | $195,946 | 43 | 48.5 | 8.5 | 4.61 |

[a] Librarian states that university budget was inflated through unusually heavy expenditure under certain headings; consequently the percentage of the budget spent on the library appears unusually small.

[b] Not in session; no figures available.

[c] Library depends heavily on United States Agency for International Development in the form of capital grants and no true picture of recurrent expenditure can yet be given.

surveyed, and it will be seen that an average of 43 percent of the recurrent budget was spent on books and periodicals, 48.5 percent on salaries, and 8.5 percent under other headings during the session 1967-1968. Excluding other headings, the proportion of book expenditure to salary expenditure is in a ratio of 47:53. This corresponds, more by chance than judgment, very closely to the British SCONUL recommended ratio of 50:50 or 45:55[5] This seems to me a very reasonable standard, and those libraries deviating wildly from it might well examine the implications with advantage. However, it should be remembered that quite frequently local factors make the application of these rough guidelines impracticable, and there is necessarily *constant* relationship between the cost of acquisitions and the cost of people to service them. In Table 2 it will be seen that expenditure on staff salaries and wages seems disproportionately high in the University of Liberia Library and in Ahmadu Bello University Library. In the first case, a seemingly excessive expenditure on salaries is caused by the necessity of employing a high proportion of expatriates, and in the second case, results from the fragmented nature of the campus. Where, as in Ahmadu Bello, the constituent institutions in a university are spread over a wide area, heavier manpower costs are inevitable. Thus, any standards accepted must inevitably be reviewed and modified in the light of local needs.

Reference to Table 2 shows that an average of 4.61 percent of university and college annual recurrent expenditure is spent on libraries. This figure is inadequate, a fact which will become quite obvious when stock, staff, and services are examined at a later stage. The University Grants Committee (U. K.) recommendation in respect to library provision for a university of medium size is 6 percent[6] of overall expenditure. If this proposal is appropriate for Britain, then a lower figure could hardly be suggested for West Africa, where libraries—because of their comparative isolation and inability to participate in schemes of subject specialization—must each provide a much wider subject coverage than the academic libraries of the metropolitan world. It is quite clear that universities in the developing countries should aim to spend rather more, proportionately, on their libraries than is spent in more prosperous areas. Although it is somewhat hazardous to suggest a standard, it seems reasonable to propose that West African universities and colleges should spend 6.5 percent of their overall budget on library services. This may seem a considerable increase when compared with present expenditure, but any lower recommendation would underestimate the significance of library services to learning.

## DEPARTMENTAL STRUCTURE

The departmental structure of the University of Ibadan (see Chart) is reasonably typical of the more mature library in the region and conforms very much to the existing pattern in many British and American libraries of the same type and size. The usual pattern is the familiar breakdown of librarian's office at the top of the hierarchy with two departments in the level below—technical services and readers' services, each under the direction of a senior officer. In the smaller institutions, though, the heads of sections may well report directly to the librarian without any intermediate coordinator.

### LIBRARIAN'S OFFICE

In theory, the librarian, in collaboration with departmental heads, plans and directs library policy from his office, but this position is the exception rather than the rule even in the larger libraries. For the most part he divides his time between his office and filling in for other people in departments lower down the hierarchy. It is not too unusual to find the librarian checking the cataloging or classification or even taking a turn at the reference desk. This situation, which theorists will probably rightly regard as administratively disastrous, arises out of the fact that professional personnel were for so many years in short supply in West Africa, (and for that matter in some areas still are) particularly at the higher levels.

### TECHNICAL SERVICES

There is some variation in the makeup of technical services divisions in West Africa, but for the most part they contain orders and acquisitions, serials, cataloging, binding, and photocopying units, although in the case of the University of Ghana, for example, binding, photocopying, and printing are the responsibility of the superintendent of special services, who reports directly to the librarian.

As far as orders and acquisitions are concerned, the most contentious issue is that of book selection. Most of the universities and colleges in this survey are small and, therefore, because of the shortage of subject specialists, tend to be dependent upon the academic staff for the selection of materials, the head of acquisitions taking responsibility for bibliographical and reference sections of the library and for filling in gaps generally. Unfortunately, even as university libraries have grown in size this method of acquisition has persisted, and academic staff generally have more control over the selection of books than is desirable if a reasonably balanced stock is to be achieved. Too often the stock of a university library reflects the subject interest of the most forceful among the heads of academic departments rather than providing a representative collection covering the whole spectrum of knowledge.

When we come to cataloging and classification, we find many variations in practice. Although the classified catalog tends to predominate because of the impact of British practice, the dictionary catalog is gaining ground in the newer libraries. When we come to examine the form of the classified catalog in West Africa, numerous difficulties come to light. The classified section is often merely a shelf list and often lacks any subject approach except for that provided by the index of the classification schedule itself. As a general comment, it is fair to say that catalog provision in a number of libraries is poor, and in the worst cases access by serendipity is the rule. Difficulties in producing a coherent and consistent cataloging and classification policy have been due, to some extent, to the lack of continuity amongst personnel in cataloging departments often caused by the practice of employing expatriate librarians upon short-term appointments. There has also been a notable lack of appreciation at higher levels in library hierarchies of the confusion that an inadequate cataloging policy can create as the demands of a university become increasingly sophisticated.

In the libraries surveyed, eight apply the ALA and three the AA rules; seven use the Library of Congress classification scheme, three use Dewey, and one uses Bliss. The economies associated with the use of the Library of Congress classification for university libraries are so apparent that at least one library, the Kashim Ibrahim Library of Ahmadu Bello University, is reclassifying the whole library by this scheme and dispensing with Bliss. It should be noted also that several of the special libraries, comprehended within the university library systems considered, use different schemes from those applied in the main library.

As far as types of catalogs are concerned, the card catalog is generally favoured, but Kumasi, for example, uses a sheaf catalog. A stripdex catalog was adopted some years ago at the Kashim Ibrahim Library, but is now being replaced by cards.

Unit card cataloging tends to be the practice in several of the larger libraries. However, it is distressing to report that in quite sizable libraries catalogers still plod away remorselessly producing typewritten cards with all their attendant disadvantages.

As far as the reproduction of cards is concerned, the University of Ghana Library, for example, utilizes a Minigraph duplicator and the University of Lagos replicates cards by an offset process and is hoping soon to introduce a Flexowriter.

In the field of special services, binding and photocopying, provision in West Africa is good. There are several first-class binderies attached to the universities and colleges, and photocopying units are normally well supplied with equipment—microfilm cameras, reflex copiers, and electrostatic copiers of one sort or another. One gap has been the failure to arrange for hiring the Xerox 914, but difficulties in this respect appear at last to have been overcome, and it is expected to see them in general service before too long. It should be noted that one library, at least, has access to an extremely good printing service and that is Ibadan, where a very efficient press has been in operation for several years.

*READERS' SERVICES*

Readers' services divisions, for the most part, comprise reference, special collections, and circulation departments. With one or two exceptions, readers' services in West African libraries are undistinguished, a defect common to the British university library systems until quite recently. In a recent article on the Makerere University College Library, Glen Sitzman comments on the distress often felt in academic circles in respect to a library "which maintains a vast storehouse of information yet never felt the need of developing the reference and information service."[7] In fact, reference service in libraries throughout tropical Africa leaves much to be desired. Students receive guidance of a sort, it is true. Freshmen in most institutions, for example, are given some initial orientation. The librarian normally meets incoming students and gives them a brief introduction to library use, but for the most part, they are too overcome by their new surroundings to absorb very much. Sometimes there is a follow-up and more specific instruction in library use is given to small groups assembled upon the basis of subjects studied. However, it is not uncommon for students to enter and leave the university with a completely imperfect idea of the purpose of the university library in an academic community. In general, there tends to be rather more emphasis on aid to faculty and postgraduate students than to the undergraduates who need it most. Quite good guides of one sort or another are issued to students in many institutions, but it is doubtful if very much attention is ever paid to them.

The idea of employing subject or form specialists in reference work rather than just generalists is slowly gaining ground, and specialists are slowly beginning to coordinate book selection in their particular fields. At the moment, though, most of the specialists on the staff of university and college libraries are appointed to develop special collections rather than each specific section of the classified sequence, but that at least is a step in the right direction.

Among the other responsibilities of the readers' services division is the circulation department. In West Africa one finds quite a wide variety of charging systems ranging from Brown to Bookamatic. In the smaller libraries with few professional staff, the main guidance to readers is as often as not provided by the circulation desk assistants. Deplorable though this situation may be, it is probably better than no assistance at all.

THE CONTENT AND ORGANIZATION OF THE COLLECTION

Statistics relating to the size and growth rate of library collections of the institutions surveyed are given in Table 3. Altogether they contain a total of over a million volumes. Only five collections exceed a hundred thousand volumes and only three libraries acquire more than ten thousand books a year, a figure which certainly does not permit a representative coverage of the world's annual output of

*TABLE 3/Library Stock and Acquisitions, 1967-1968*

| University and College Libraries | Total Book Stock | Acquisitions | Periodical Subscrip- tions |
|---|---|---|---|
| Ghana | | | |
| University of Ghana, Legon | 218,000 | 6,382 | 4,200 |
| University of Science & Technology, Kumasi | 52,846 | 4,483 | 1,480 |
| University College of Cape Coast | 50,000 | 8,000 | 1,246 |
| Liberia | | | |
| University of Liberia | 45,000 | 4,000 | 300 |
| Nigeria | | | |
| University of Ibadan | 230,000 | 9,058 | 4,000 |
| University of Nigeria, Nsukka[a] | 102,642 | 11,321 | 2,777 |
| University of Ife | 65,000 | 7,500 | 1,604 |
| Ahmadu Bello University | 157,205 | 13,195 | 3,280 |
| University of Lagos | 113,316 | 18,280 | 2,980 |
| Sierra Leone | | | |
| Fourah Bay College, University of Sierra Leone | 67,662 | 2,093 | 1,155 |
| Njala University College, University of Sierra Leone | 21,000 | 2,150 | 600 |

[a]1966-1967 figures.

scholarly literature at the level required by students and faculty. The situation in respect to periodical subscriptions is rather more promising, and six institutions subscribe to over fifteen hundred titles.

Although the University College of Sierra Leone, Fourah Bay, is the oldest establishment considered, its library development has been slow until quite recently through scarcity of funds. The largest and most comprehensive collections are possessed by the Universities of Ibadan and Ghana. These libraries are particularly rich in back runs of serials, bibliographical and reference tools of every description and, of course, Africana. In fact, every library collects Africana with considerable enthusiasm.

Most libraries maintain special collections—internal and external—on a basis of subject matter, form of material or reader interest. While the university librarian has, of course, complete responsibility for all internal collections, there is no concensus regarding responsibility for the organization of those collections maintained outside the central library. There tend to be two schools of thought on the subject. One school holds that university library service should be centralized, that external collections should be avoided and, if they do come into existence in spite of official discouragement, no responsibility should be accepted for them. The other school argues that a decentralized library service is desirable, that faculty service points under the supervision of the main library are essential, and that full control must be maintained over all collections except those which, through their special nature, are under autonomous professional direction. Although there is something to be said for a policy of centralized services in the early days of a university's existence, if it is not modified as the institution matures, teaching departments tend to build their own collections without consultation with the main library and often without professional guidance. This kind of development naturally leads to considerable confusion. It is clear, therefore, that as a university grows in complexity and becomes dispersed over a wider area, a policy of controlled decentralization should be accepted, with the main library providing service at various points on the campus. Although this inevitably results in some duplication, the additional expenditure is justified by improved facilities. What is particularly vital, and what it should not be necessary to state, is that whatever policy is followed a union catalog of all library materials held on the campus should be maintained in the central library, irrespective of whether they come under the control of the university librarian or not.

In the early days of the academic libraries of West Africa, the professional cadre consisted entirely of expatriates. These have to a great extent been replaced by West African graduates with either an overseas or a local professional qualification. However, in five of the institutions surveyed, the senior librarian is still an expatriate. There is still difficulty in finding indigenous staff for higher posts, but this situation will soon be changed as local graduates gain experience and gradually move up the library hierarchies throughout the region.

In Table 4 the staff position in the various university and college libraries examined is shown. Altogether these institutions have a total staff of 690; 127 professionals and 563 in other grades. The overall ratio of professional to non-professional staff is 1:4.4, the ratio for Nigeria is 1:42, and for Ghana 1:53. This difference between ratios for Nigeria and Ghana results in part from the existence of a long established program of professional library education at university level in Nigeria. It is doubtful if comparision with metropolitan standards in respect of professional to non-professional staff ratio is of much significance at the moment. More non-professionals are employed proportionately in West Africa than, for example, in Europe or America, because their productivity is lower. This situation could be improved by the introduction of more training courses for all intermediate and junior grades. Inspection of Table 4 also shows that professional staff are generally spread rather thinly, a fact borne out by certain inadequacies in respect to services. It is obvious that there are clearly not enough professionals in proportion to non-professional staff in many of the libraries examined for adequate direction and supervision.

As far as qualifications are concerned, most senior library staff are graduates with American, British, or indigenous qualifications, and all hold faculty rank. Increasing attention is being paid in recruitment to the class of first degree obtained, since it is agreed that senior staff cannot expect to be equated with teaching staff for the purposes of pay and privileges if their basic qualifications are in general weaker than those of the faculty. Insufficient attention, however, is still paid to the actual subjects studied for the first degree by candidates for library posts. Generalists are still being sought rather than specialists, and little attempt is made to ensure that the spectrum of subjects taught in the university is represented

*TABLE 4/Personnel, 1967-1968*

| University and College Libraries | Number of professional staff | Number of other staff | Total staff | Ratio of professional to non-professional staff |
|---|---|---|---|---|
| Ghana | | | | |
| University of Ghana, Legon | 11 | 66 | 77 | 1 : 6 |
| University of Science & Technology, Kumasi | 7 | 23 | 30 | 1 : 3 |
| University College of Cape Coast | 8 | 50 | 58 | 1 : 6 |
| Liberia | | | | |
| University of Liberia | 6 | 15 | 21 | 1 : 2.5 |
| Nigeria | | | | |
| University of Ibadan | 24 | 78 | 102 | 1 : 3 |
| University of Nigeria, Nsukka[a] | 23 | 88 | 111 | 1 : 4 |
| University of Ife | 13 | 34 | 47 | 1 : 2.5 |
| Ahmadu Bello University[b] | 10 | 77 | 87 | 1 : 8 |
| University of Lagos | 20 | 100 | 120 | 1 : 5 |
| Sierra Leone | | | | |
| Fourah Bay College, University of Sierra Leone | 5 | 31 | 36 | 1 : 6 |
| Njala University College, University of Sierra Leone | 3 | 9 | 12 | 1 : 3 |
| Overall Ratio | | | | 1 : 4.4 |

[a] 1966-1967 figures.

[b] 5 graduate assistants in training not included.

by corresponding academic background on the part of the library staff.

In conclusion, it must be emphasized that most of the libraries examined could exercise much more imagination than they do in the field of personnel management. There are few procedural manuals, rarely sufficient staff meetings, few adequate programs of in-service training (Ahmadu Bello University is a notable exception), nor is the professional development of senior staff sufficiently encouraged.

BUILDINGS

The buildings of the university and college libraries considered vary enormously, but most have been built during the past fifteen years. Among the older buildings which are not air-conditioned, the most notable is the Ibadan University Library designed by Maxwell Fry and Jane Drew and opened in 1954. It is one of the most beautiful and ingeniously designed buildings to be seen in tropical Africa, in very marked contrast to the library of the University of Ghana opened in 1958.

In the past four years a number of new university libraries have been completed in West Africa, all of them, with one exception, fully air-conditioned. New buildings have been erected for the University of Lagos, the University of Ife, Fourah Bay College, Njala University College, and an extension has been made to the University of Ibadan Library. The University of Ife building is only partially air-conditioned, but provision has been made for full air-conditioning at a later date.

There is a growing appreciation in West Africa of the principles underlying modern trends in planning the library building—that form must follow function; that a building must be both externally and internally flexible in order to accommodate changes in patterns of library service; and that the building must be compact and not too fragmented for easy supervision. The newer library buildings to some extent reflect the acceptance of these principles. For example, the new University of Lagos building, which was opened at Yaba in 1965, is fully air-conditioned, modular in structure, square, four stories high, with an extremely flexible interior and provision for future expansion. At the moment it has a basic floor area of 63,000 square feet and will accommodate 250,000 books and 800 readers.

In West Africa, generally, universities tend to be thinking in terms of providing accommodation for between a quarter and a half million books, seats for about a quarter of their readers and, very sensibly, phasing their library building programs over a period of years.

*Evaluation*

The development of university and college libraries in English-speaking West Africa, as in other parts of emergent Africa, has been handicapped to some extent by external factors—isolation brought about by inadequate communication; a trying climate in a few cases; economic and political difficulties which have had a not unexpected impact upon financial provision; an absence of a library tradition in homes and schools; a lack of solid national and public library infrastructure upon which academic libraries in parts of Europe and America depend so much for fringe benefits; and a lack of expertise in the servicing and operation of the various sophisticated items of equipment which are considered essential to the modern library.

Related to these factors are the major defects which we see in the university library systems in West Africa: (a) insufficient funds, (b) insufficient trained manpower, (c) a neglect of overall long-term planning in the design of systems, (d) the prevalence of outdated ideas.

The analysis of expenditure given in Table 2 shows that libraries are often allocated too little of the university budget for adequate service and that the distribution of funds between materials and people to service them often lacks balance. However, it should not be thought that in all cases a sufficiency of funds will necessarily solve all problems. For example, even the most generous salaries may not ensure that a senior library post is appropriately filled, if no African candidates are available with suitable qualifications and if no expatriate candidates are willing to risk their security by taking a post without tenure. Nor, indeed, can a sudden increase in a library's prosperity solve problems of isolation and poor communications, situations that can only be ameliorated concurrently with economic and educational advance.

The shortage of professonally trained manpower, particularly at the higher levels, accounts for certain of the deficiencies which have been noted in the library practices in West Africa. However, this particular problem is well on the way to solution, thanks to the various programs of indigenous library education initiated since 1960.

From the remarks made in the preceding sections it will be seen that in many university and college libraries in West Africa objectives have almost always been determined upon an ad hoc basis, little attempt having been made to anticipate academic development in the design of organizational patterns and services. In developing countries, rather more than elsewhere, the determination of university objectives upon which library planning can be based has presented considerable difficulties because of recurrent crises, frequent changes in educational policy, and an irregular flow of funds.

A further defect mentioned has been the impact of outdated ideas upon library service. Until quite recently many of the university and college library systems of West Africa were to some extent isolated from the mainstream of world library development. The leaders of the profession in the region were extremely active, but found difficulty in keeping abreast of current practice. The reasons for this are not far to seek. First, most university and college librarians in West Africa had a heavier schedule than elsewhere through the constant need to improvise, and there was little time left for professional readings. Second, professional communication between the various institutions within West Africa and between West Africa and other parts of the world tended to be somewhat ponderous. Third, in the early days there could be none of the ferment of discussion and argument that characterized metropolitan library circles since professionals in West Africa were few and far between.

In the foregoing survey, the eleven major university and college libraries have been examined in some detail, and certain conclusions have been drawn concerning their structure and services. It should, however, be made quite clear that, although for the most part they share a common environment, they each and every one are at a different stage of development. Some libraries are quite old and some quite new, some rich and some poor. This makes generalization difficult. Had it been possible to examine a larger population, it would have been feasible to categorize by stage of development, identify those institutions within each category giving optimum service, and make rather more detailed proposals for the development of each category of library upon the basis of the data analyzed.

As far as the future is concerned, it is clear that the primary objectives must be to increase library budgets, to survey existing libraries with a view to ascertaining how far the needs of readers are being satisfied, and to establish a code of standards as guidelines for effective development. In proposing standards it will be necessary to sift information in respect to all the major university library systems of Africa, without restricting the exercise to a small region. It is quite clear that an investigation of West African university library systems alone will not produce sufficient data upon which to base sound recommendations in respect to practice.

Many of the university and college libraries of West Africa frequently possess enviable accommodations, elegant furnishings, and even impressive basic book stocks, but beneath the facade deficiencies are too frequently found. University authorities are for the most part aware of these imperfections and are clearly eager that the development of their library services keeps pace with the growing sophistication of their teaching and research programs. It is necessary to observe, however, that whatever the defects of the academic library systems of West Africa, achievements over the past twenty years have been remarkable and, if a note of criticism has been sounded, it should not be forgotten that university library services in many economically favored metropolitan countries are infinitely worse.

## NOTES

1. Evelyn J. A. Evans, *A Tropical Library Service: The Story of Ghana's Libraries* (London: Deutsch, 1964), p. 49.
2. J. Asquith, chairman, *Report*, Commission on Higher Education in the Colonies, Colonial Office of Great Britain (London: H.M.S.O., 1945); W. Elliot, chairman, *Report*, Commission on Higher Education in West Africa, Colonial Office of Great Britain (London: H.M.S.O., 1945).
3. Asquith, *Report*, p. 18.
4. A. J. E. Dean, "The Balme Library, University of Ghana: History, Structure, and Development, 1948-1965," *Nigerian Libraries* 3, no. 2 (August 1967), p. 83.
5. T. Parry, chairman, *Report of the Committee on Libraries*, University Grants Committee, Great Britain (London: H.M.S.O., 1967), p. 277.
6. Ibid., p. 156.
7. Glenn L. Sitzman, "Uganda's University Library," *College and Research Libraries* 29, no. 3 (May 1968), p. 203.

# 7 / Automation in the Academic Library in the United States

CLAYTON A. SHEPHERD

*Indiana University*

The library traditionally has been an important link between the author and the reader in the process of information transfer, a chain which is initiated by the author and carried through from the publisher to the library acquisition of the material, its organization and cataloging, and finally, its circulation to its users. Each of the operations within the library complex need not be seen as discrete and independent activities, but rather as subsystems which are parts of the total service organization. These operations are often such that they lend themselves readily to automated processing, especially if the library is seen as an organism with closely interrelated functions.

The electronic computer and ancillary machinery, such as punch-card equipment, can be applied easily to many essential library operations. Although originally designed to perform mathematical computations, the computer has proven itself time after time in various applications oriented toward nonscientific areas, such as accounting, stock inventory control, personnel records, maintenance, etc. The computer has an advantage in such applications because it is ideally suited to process large amounts of material at high speeds and to perform its functions accurately. Thus, it is no accident that libraries turned to the computer to meet increasing demands of time and labor soon after its emergence as a business tool.

The university library, therefore, has been active in library automation. Certainly the high volume of users the university library serves is an important reason, although there are many types of libraries serving large numbers. Further, the university library is likely to handle a broad spectrum of subject material (although this is true of other libraries too), and it often, in addition, builds extensive collections in depth in particular subject areas. More important, the university library is found in an environment of research and innovation. If there is a school for library science on campus, the library can turn to it for assistance in automation, and the library, in turn, can act as a fertile test bed for library school research. Further, many universities provide access to a computer on campus as a research tool, thus allowing a double opportunity for experimentation and the development of novel approaches to library operation. It is not surprising that in the university library environment some of the most significant strides are made in automation practices and procedures.

## What is "Automation"?

In the mid-1950s it was determined that the electronic computer could be employed in specialized industrial operations that previously had been monitored and controlled, in some cases by entire staffs of highly skilled workers. Although this is only one type of operation to which the computer has been applied, it has been a highly significant one—especially since it has taken over repetitive tasks and has freed industrial personnel to concentrate on planning and development problems. The term "automation" has been traditionally applied in these situations; it calls to mind a device, monitored by a single individual, which controls an entire band of machines. Various process-control devices fall into this category.

Yet we must raise the question as to whether the term "automation" in its exact sense can be applied to library procedures. The application of computing equipment has certainly freed the time and aided the effort of library personnel, with the result that they have greater opportunity to concentrate on the various intellectual tasks so necessary to library operation. However, the degree to which operations are automated—strictly "hands-off"—is open to question. The usual pattern of computer application in various library activities can be likened more easily to those found in accounting procedures and stock inventory control, which essentially are record-keeping functions rather than controlling functions. Thus, if we are to use the term "automation," we should use it guardedly so that we labor under no misapprehensions about the automatic nature of these processes. Perhaps "mechanization" would have been a better term, especially since the word implies a wide range of equipment and technique—the situation that holds in library contexts. But the term "automation" seems to be here to stay as far as library applications are concerned.

## Automated Operations in the Contemporary University Library

A survey carried out in mid-1966 indicated that there were at that time 638 libraries using data processing equipment, and three-fourths of those were academic or special libraries. They represented 90 percent of the 942 libraries with firm plans for automation.[1] It would be impractical to catalog all the existing cases within the American university library complex that have undergone automation of one or more of their operations. In the first place, the literature is incomplete, and second, the picture is constantly changing. Therefore, only a few of the most recent examples in each area will be discussed, especially those with unique or noteworthy characteristics.

ACQUISITIONS

In both the acquisitions and serials ordering procedures in a typical university library, many operations are analogous to those in business and industry having to do with stock ordering, inventory control, and related accounting procedures. Not all automation programs in this area depend upon sophisticated computing equipment. The University of Maryland, for example, carries out its acquisitions operations on an IBM 407 accounting machine. An order deck is processed, including the generation of the purchase order. Records for the cataloging department are produced, and an auxiliary listing for bill payment and management control is generated.[2] A combination of manual and machine operations to accomplish certain acquisitions procedures was reported by Ralph Shaw at the University of Hawaii Library.[3] In a system that has been in operation for more than a year and a half, better and faster control is now achieved than had been by the manual accounting system previously used, yet it costs about one-thirteenth as much. An example of economies that can be gained from automating several functions at once is illustrated by the system at Texas College of Arts and Industries. The library is able to use the computer at no cost for its acquisitions operations, since the cost is written off by the circulation and serials departments. In automating their acquisitions procedures, this university took the lead from the Pennsylvania State University system in incorporating the use of the change card, which furnishes cancellation data if an item is unavailable from a dealer, and which deletes all information pertaining to that order from the computer. If, however, an item is received, cost data are generated and input to the computer for accounting purposes; the change card then accompanies the item received to the cataloging procedures. The second change card receives the code number and, after keypunching, is used by the computer in providing a card acquisitions list.[4]

The University of Michigan Library was also concerned about costs in automating its acquisitions program. Feasibility studies had indicated that the system would be more costly at the time it was installed than the manual method. However, it was recognized that input volume could increase considerably without a concurrent increase in clerical staff. Rather modest equipment is being used there, as at other installations—in this case, an IBM 1460 computer.[5]

SERIALS CONTROL

In the survey previously mentioned, Jackson indicated that "the most usual current use of EAM [electronic accounting machine, i.e., punch card] equipment is for serials control." Serials control also seems to be the most prevalent area of application (in the university libraries) using more sophisticated equipment, Eugene Jackson reports.[6] Indeed, because of the multiplicity of input items and the variation and irregularity of publishing period among serials, this area traditionally has caused the librarian a great deal of concern and has been considered fair game for automation. The haphazardness of the issuing policies of various publications has been pointed out by Roper. A serial may be identified by volume and year; by volume, issue, and year; by issue and year, and so on. In a 1965 issue of *American Documentation*, David Bishop and others posited a theory of publication that revolved around the related concepts of frequency and interval.[7] Publication patterns are often conceived of in terms of frequency, but serials of different frequencies may, in fact, have the same publication pattern. Conversely, serials with different publication patterns may have the same frequency. Irregular frequency has often caused problems in serials controls systems. The authors emphasize the concept of predictability, which they say is implicit in the idea of pattern. Thus, the computer is able to produce a check-in card that will predict certain characteristics of the next issue expected by the library. These check-in cards form the nucleus of the serials record system at the UCLA Biomedical Library. Fred Roper describes this feature of the system as follows:

For each *title* the library currently subscribes to, the computer generates one card for the *next expected issue*. It is here that the UCLA system departs most obviously from the other systems in use. Rather than predicting the issues that should arrive during a specific time period, the computer recognizes that there *will* be a next issue and accordingly generates a check-in card for that issue, regardless of when it will arrive in the library. The check-in card will contain in most instances enough information to identify completely the particular issue expected, i.e., the elements of the internal number system needed to identify the publication.[8]

With such a system, the library apparently avoids a number of headaches arising out of the complex patterns of serials publication.

The interest in serials control and in making serials publications available to the user is exemplified by a project headed by Donald Hammer at Purdue University and funded by the Indiana State

Library in Indianapolis. The project is in the process of compiling a list of serials holdings at several academic and public libraries in the state of Indiana; this compiled list will be reproduced and distributed to all participating libraries. The overwhelming advantage in such a program is that it will provide an important communications link among the various libraries and will expedite the interchange of serials holdings not present in all libraries. Unfortunately, once again data input seems to constitute the difficulty, especially at Indiana University where there are over fifteen thousand titles in the serials collection and limited manpower with which to record serials holdings information for input to the computer. Nevertheless, the availability of such a list should more than outweigh the effort required in its preparation.

CATALOGING

The book catalog, of course, has long been recognized as an important adjunct to the card catalog, especially in locations in which the card catalog is not readily available. Many university libraries are generating book catalogs by computer; their style and use are somewhat similar, by and large, and will not be described here.

Richard Johnson, however, has reported on an interesting variation: At Stanford University, where the main entry concept has been abandoned, the system instead arranges works alphabetically by title under each subject heading and not by author. Experience indicates that this arrangement is quite satisfactory, especially for a selective collection.[9]

The most significant development in catalog automation over the past few years has been the implementation of the MARC Project by the Library of Congress.[10] The MARC Pilot Project grew out of a series of conferences, the first having been held in 1965, to investigate the feasibility of converting catalog data to machine-readable form. Sixteen libraries were selected to participate in the project; of these sixteen, eleven were universities with varying kinds of computing equipment. Since that time, magnetic tapes bearing information contained on LC cards, together with computer programs which enabled their reproduction in LC card format, have been distributed. After certain modifications of the MARC format, the MARC II system was developed; at present tapes of this format are being distributed in a standardized form and are being used to advantage in the automation of cataloging procedures in various university libraries. One of the major advantages is that the basic bibliographic entry is already being provided.

These tapes are proving to be extremely useful, not only as a basis upon which to build an automated cataloging system, but as a source of information for selective dissemination of information programs as well. The practicality of the latter use has been demonstrated at Indiana University by a research project in which interest profiles of several faculty members from various departments were compared with the MARC tapes. Bibliographic information selected therefrom was distributed. This material was valuable to faculty members in keeping abreast of new publications in their fields of interest.[11]

Although Project INTREX will be discussed in greater detail later, it should be pointed out first that an important feature developed in conjunction with this project is the augmented library catalog. Alan R. Benenfeld, in a discussion of Project INTREX, indicated that the catalog is deliberately experimental:

There are no ties to existing or past catalog structures which might otherwise constrain achievement of our experimental objectives. There is freedom to change both order and format of data elements to meet varying experimental conditions.

Second, the author indicates that the system is time-shared; that is, it is accessible to a number of users at remote locations who can have direct access to the catalog. Third, he indicates that it is "augmented," that is, that it goes beyond traditional catalogs and indexes in terms of the depth of information in the catalog. He suggests that "a large number of bibliographic data elements associated with diverse bibliographic forms have been identified and synthesized into a hospitable single catalog structure."[12] These features are especially significant in terms of Project INTREX's stated goal of providing a central resource for an information transfer network to extend throughout the academic community. Since access to information is the touchstone of any library, especially one participating with others on a network basis and one in which a commonality of terminology is mandatory, such effort as is seen in Project INTREX will stimulate network development. The augmented library catalog as an object of research is being used to discover answers to questions of the commonality or differences in the needs of users in the university community, as well as to establish criteria for optimum search and display.

REFERENCE

One of the primary goals of the library is the retrieval of information. However, when the term "information retrieval" is encountered, it immediately calls to mind elaborate systems of indexing and filing organization and the complex Boolean combination of terms required to extract specific, detailed information from the file. Although such complex operations seem to be far removed from the traditional reference service provided by librarians, the two functions can be seen as different not in kind but merely in degree. Whereas the conventional definition of library automation excludes "information retrieval" operations, this area should not be ignored by library administrators, nor, more specifically, by reference librarians themselves, nor should it be ignored by the designers of automated reference systems.

Yet the need for information retrieval, per se, in the conventional library, has been seriously questioned. Andrew Osborn has put it this way:

From the beginning with Vannevar Bush's paper of 1945 in *The Atlantic Monthly*, a two-pronged attack has been launched: on the one hand, libraries are branded as inept, inefficient; on the other hand, science and the computer represent knights in shining armor come to the rescue.

Osborn makes the point that high-speed information retrieval may be necessary in clinical and defense-related situations, but that in the typical university library context, time-consuming study and reading of source material makes rapid retrieval unnecessary.[13] Although this same criticism—that is, that information is only very rarely needed "immediately" has been leveled at full-scale information systems oriented toward direct access and time-sharing capabilities, it certainly does not mean that no benefit would be reaped from applying certain principles of information retrieval to library reference work. Few would deny that there are shortcomings in the number and structure of access points to the information contained in a conventional library; and, although an increase in the number of access points would mean a corresponding increase in the difficulty of both generating and maintaining them, more effective access to the information would thereby be provided to the user. Thus, not speed, but accessibility, becomes a prime consideration.

One of the first experiments in automating a reference service was made at the Institute for Computer Research at the University of Chicago. Two hundred and thirty-four biographical books were categorized as to types of subjects included and as to the contents of the uniform entries they contained. Cherie Weil, the author, believes that by automating this phase of reference work the reference librarian could be freed for more intellectual activities. In so stating, she is recognizing one of the most powerful applications of the computer in library automation of this type: the computer and the human intellect can operate as a team, with complementary tasks resulting in optimum use of the library collection.[14]

Once again Project INTREX is providing valuable insights into library operations and into the possibilities of improving their effectiveness. The augmented catalog portion of the system, referred to earlier, is used in an experimental library storage and retrieval system, in which catalog requests can be made by specifying subject terms, authors, or titles, or any combination of these. The items retrieved by this initial inquiry may be narrowed further by requiring specific matches to be made on additional fields of the catalog records. Thus, a distinct parallel exists between library access and the development of search strategies of the type found in full-blown information retrieval systems. An additional feature permits dialogue between the user and the computer, which makes available to him a user's guide for instructional purposes. In this way his method of gaining access to the file can be made more effective.[15]

CIRCULATION

One of the most prolific areas of development in the use of the computer and other mechanized devices in the university library is circulation control—a quite understandable circumstance since the circulation activities in a large library are likely to number several thousand a day and present a management-control problem of considerable magnitude. This is especially true in a library that supports a wide variety of users, with different circulation procedures for undergraduates, graduate students, and faculty members. Whereas circulation control is accomplished by the use of a variety of equipment, most applications are performed on the IBM 357 Data Collection System. In this system, a book is charged by requiring the borrower to present it to the circulation attendant along with his plastic identification badge. This card contains a punched code representing the student's identification number. In the book the pocket contains a pre-punched master book card, which is removed from the book pocket and inserted, along with the borrower's identification badge, into the 357 input station. The master book card furnishes the call number and accession number for each book charged. The input station punches the charge card, which contains all the necessary information.

A variation of this process is represented in the two-card system, in which a cartridge containing a pre-set due date is inserted into the 374 cartridge reader. The system then produces two cards, which include the information outlined above plus the due date. One of these cards functions as a charge card and keeps the circulation files up to date, and the second becomes a due-date card to be inserted into the book pocket. When the book is returned to the library, the due-date card then becomes the discharge card.[16]

The IBM 357 Data Collection System is currently operating in nearly fifty college and university libraries. Not only is it performing a creditable job in controlling the circulation activities of libraries, but it is supplying important additional information that otherwise would not have been made available. For example, as a guide to more effective library management, an automated circulation system can provide information concerning the scheduling of personnel who staff the various public service desks. It can also be used to discover which areas of the collection are used most heavily, and it can find some of the characteristics of the patrons of the library as well as the proportion of faculty to student users.[17] Much of this information can be directly related to budget projections of the university, as well as to its acquisitions policy.

Libraries utilizing automated circulation systems differ as to their economic advantages. Many feel that little gain is made in personnel economies; the initial cost of the equipment itself, they believe, has to be considered. However, the advantages over a manual system must be recognized. Not only do automatic systems provide more efficient service to the users of the library, they also tend to be much more accurate in keeping records of the locations and due dates of books charged. Bruce Steward, in describing the circulation system at Texas A & M University Library, has suggested that "perhaps most significant of all is the fact that the present system can accommodate double or triple the present volume of circulation with only a minimum increase in personnel."[18] The significance of this statement cannot be overemphasized, in view of the tremendous continuing growth that is being experienced by the typical American university. It is incumbent upon systems planners, in designing automated library systems, to anticipate this growth and to accommodate it either by installing systems that can handle ever increasing workloads or systems that can be expanded in a modular fashion, without redesign and reprogramming.

Ideally, a circulation system should be capable of keeping immediately up to date, so that the location of all holdings of the library can be determined at any given moment. Essentially this means immediate updating of the master file upon the completion of each individual transaction. Such techniques have been developed at several libraries, notably the Illinois State Library, which uses a disc file in conjunction with an IBM 1710 computer.

As a matter of fact, several operations which are performed by the conventional non-automated library are by nature real-time (that is, constantly current) in their systems characteristics. Many of these real-time characteristics have been lost, Audrey Grosch has pointed out, when various operations of the library have been mechanized.[19] However, there is no reason why a mechanized system cannot retain this characteristic, rather than the common system of depending on batch mode processing, with its coincident delay in turn-around time. Yet although this may be true from a systems standpoint, from the standpoint of economics, computing equipment that provides real-time capability costs significantly more than simple devices that operate strictly in batch mode.

NETWORK APPLICATIONS

A typical library is unable to develop an exhaustive, infinitely comprehensive collection of materials. Except in the areas of most common use, such as general reference works, the typical college and university library tends to grow more vigorously in specialties represented most strongly in the curriculum and research programs at the institution. This situation, added to the problem of increasing costs, has stimulated libraries to develop forms of cooperation that either amplify existing systems or depart completely from traditional methods of interlibrary loan. In this way materials can be shared more effectively, and the existence and location of specialized collections can be made known more effectively. Outstanding progress has been made in the development of networks connecting various campuses of a single university as well as in providing interchange among different universities. Certainly, in the latter case, the problems are more difficult, if for no other reason than that the participants do not function under the aegis of a single administration. Yet it is precisely in this area that the most spectacular work has been done.

One of the most extensive communications networks in the university library field is that of Biomedical Communication Network of the State University of New York, which was conceived in the fall of 1965. The SUNY Network is an on-line real-time system, which links all three State University of New York Medical Center Libraries with each other and with the University of Rochester Medical Center Library and other university medical libraries in the area.[20] On 30 August 1968 the National Library of Medicine began experimental on-line computer communication with the SUNY Network, so that cataloging information could be exchanged with the participating libraries. An additional link is also being developed with a specialized information center, the Parkinson's Information Center at Columbia University, which is a part of the National Institute of Neurological Diseases and Blindness Specialized Information Center.[21]

Another significant advance in networks among university libraries is NELINET, the New England Library Information Network. Conceived in 1964, NELINET is designed to provide automated technical processing services to various libraries in the New England area. At present it is serving five state-university libraries—the universities of New Hampshire, Vermont, Massachusetts, Rhode Island, and Connecticut—and it is expected to extend to other university libraries in New England. It is designed to provide real-time access to the catalog information provided by the Library of Congress MARC Project, to produce catalog cards, book labels, and book pocket labels, and to provide automated order control for acquisition.[22]

Project INTREX is probably one of the most ambitious of the projects linking university library facilities by networks. Project INTREX was conceived at the Summer Studies Center of the National Academy of Sciences, at Woods Hole, Massachusetts, in a session held in September 1965. Its admittedly ambitious goal is to establish an information transfer system among a number of institutions "throughout the nation and perhaps the world." Based on work at Massachusetts Institute of Technology, Project INTREX "is expected to yield significant contributions toward the modernization of all large libraries and, indeed, toward the general improvement of information transfer." Providing some of the most advanced thinking in the field, the developers of Project INTREX recognize the value of intercommunication among university libraries by means of the sophisticated equipment needed to provide communications flexibility and convenience.[23]

Further reports of cooperation among university libraries for information interchange are encouraging. They indicate the growing awareness of the need of scholars for more effective dispersal of materials and information. A consortium of five universities in Washington, D. C., has been formed to study the practicality of various levels of intercooperation. A jointly operated computer, to function in batch mode, was recommended for implementation as soon as practicable. A sophisticated computer system for real-time applications, including the tie-in with remote terminals, was also considered for the future, since, although the cost was too great for present use, such a computer system could grow out of the system suggested for the present.[24]

In 1968, a consortium was formed by eleven colleges within a thirty-five-mile radius of the University of Dayton. A computer was installed at Dayton to serve these colleges, which composed the Dayton-Miami Valley Consortium. The system is designed to store records on all volumes currently in the University of Dayton's libraries, as well as to provide research capabilities for the various student bodies. This action represents still another effort directed toward the sharing of facilities and collections. Network interchange also aids in the elimination of a great deal of technical services duplication.

Another significant method of interchange provided by modern technology is the facsimile transmission of materials. Facsimile transmission has reduced tremendously the turn-around time between request and receipt of materials, and it has caused a decrease in the amount of administrative procedure that otherwise would have been required.

Several university libraries have become interested in facsimile transmission systems, such as those connecting the campuses of Pennsylvania State University. Yet there seem still to be considerable problems in terms of resolution, lack of flexibility, and high cost. Such equipment as the Xerox Telecopier was designed for use over ordinary telephone lines. It has several advantages, including those of convenience and cost. The Alden Company has developed a book scanner that seems to present the advantages of relatively high resolution and flexibility in speed.

The apparent difficulties in telefacsimile processing are suggested by the fact that, according to one source, only one working interlibrary facsimile system is in operation today—at Pennsylvania State University, among eight of its twenty campuses.[25] A major advantage of telefacsimile transmission is the rapid turn-around time it provides. However, research conducted at several universities, including The Massachusetts Institute of Technology, the University of Nevada, and the University of California, has indicated that an insufficient number of users need the turn-around time that telefacsimile can provide. A report discussing this research, published in 1968, indicates that emphasis should be placed on the improvement of existing manual systems, rather than on the attempt to develop faster turn-around techniques.[26] Naturally, in evaluating such findings, cost is not an insignificant criterion. The industry promises that it will not be long before it can provide inexpensive teletransmission. When it does become generally available for library applications, the consideration of fast turn-around may be seen in a different light—that is, in terms of economic feasibility.

## Problems in University Library Automation

It was stated earlier that the university library, for various reasons, presents a fertile field for research and development of mechanized techniques. Those involved in systems design and development for libraries will find themselves facing many problem areas not encountered elsewhere. The following problems often appear in all stages of the development of automated processes. They should be clearly recognized by library administrators and systems planners.

### SYSTEMS PROBLEMS

The overwhelming majority of the applications of automation within the university library environment have taken either one of two patterns: Either a single function has been automated to the exclusion of all others, or a function has been automated prior to the others, with uncertain plans to extend automation to other areas. In the latter case, particularly, problems are likely to arise. The library is often seen as an aggregate of functions, each of which is highly compartmentalized in nature. In all too many cases, the interrelationships among these functions are overlooked, and a single operation is automated with total disregard for other library activities.

The pitfalls of such an attitude have been recognized through bitter experience and have made the concept of a "total systems approach" a somewhat hackneyed and overused term in the library automation field. As a matter of fact, there is nothing inherently wrong in mechanizing only one activity at a time—in many cases, this may be the only economical and practical method of proceeding with library automation. The University of Chicago Library is a good example of a university library, as are those at Washington State and Stanford, committed to the total systems approach. Yet they are libraries that implement their systems in modules. Other universities, such as Yale and Harvard, are using the evolutionary approach, which implies moving through various stages of development from the manual to increasingly complex machine systems. Such implementation is applied to the entire library complex, so that the services and operations of the library can be continued with a minimum of disruption.[27] There are, however, certain disadvantages to the evolutionary approach. It does mean that procedural changes could well be taking place simultaneously in all departments. Further, it implies several levels of system development—all too often we mistakenly assume that changeover from one system to another can be made on a one-to-one basis. Experience has shown, however, that without special consideration being given to file re-formatting and procedural restructuring to facilitate the use of the newly selected equipment, such a procedure is wasteful of the capabilities of computing equipment. Further, lack of such consideration leads to general discouragement and an unwillingness to support further automation. Although making the big jump from manual to completely automated systems all at once has its own risks, it can successfully be accomplished through proper systems planning; we must realize that each operation within the library involves a relationship with all others, and that adherence to a "total systems approach" is vital to success.

A novel shortcut to library automation is outlined by Dougherty and Stevens in their report of an experiment using computer programs and data banks generated at one university and transferred to a second.[28] Specifically, the library of the University of Colorado transplanted the computer programs and data developed and generated at the University of Illinois libraries. Policy decisions as well as the inappropriateness of some of the computer programs seemed to present such problems that the process proved unpracticable. This experience is worth noting, however, on two counts. First illustrates the need for a process of systems design and development suitable to a particular situation. Although the operations of various libraries are often quite similar, it must be recognized that there are differences in procedure and policy, and that procedures and programs have not yet become so standardized that they can be readily transferred to different institutions. Dougherty's report, moreover, is worthwhile for a second and perhaps much more significant reason: it is a report of an attempt at library automation that was made *in an experimental context.* As a matter of fact, some areas of library automation have progressed so insignificantly that there is little justification for taking any steps to move directly into operational automation. Furthermore, in more than one case a library has gone ahead with ambitious plans for implementing automation programs (for either one or many library functions), and has found only after the expenditure of vast sums of money that the system was, in the final analysis, inoperable.

These experiences, in fact, are likely to have a chain effect: library planners sometimes seem to be transfixed by the glamour of the computer; they then describe impending or current attempts at implementation in somewhat optimistic, if not downright misleading, terms. Subsequently, if the system does not live up to expectations or, in fact, fails altogether, no further mention of it is made in the literature, since the attempt was made not as an experiment, but with a personal and professional commitment to its success. Other organizations, however, swayed by the tone of enthusiasm in initial reports, may well be misled, follow in their footsteps, and experience failure too. Evidence of the use of the scientific method, therefore, is often refreshing, because research was performed and acknowledged and because it was applied in the design of the systems. The setting up and testing of hypotheses, the construction of pilot systems, the use of modeling and simulation techniques and other such devices are powerful means of evaluation of systems before they are adopted widely.

A necessary prelude to systems design is an analysis of the existing system. A possible pitfall may be the conversion of the existing system to the mechanized system on a one-to-one basis; a thorough understanding of the goals of an operation and the methods by which it achieves those goals is essential. In too many cases the attempt to automate is made either by a librarian who has little knowledge of the equipment with which he is to be dealing, or by a computer expert who has slight insight into the problems of library operation and administration. Ideally, these two sets of skills would be combined in a single individual; rarely, however, is this the case. On the other hand, teams composed of librarians working with systems analysts have been successful. For example, Becker has reported the experience at Penn State in 1963 where, while in the course of automating its Acquisitions Department, the library used a team that included a professional librarian and an industrial engineer. The resulting new system was able to accommodate additional work load, reduce errors and time delays, and cause a significant reduction in unit costs.[29]

With all the talk of total systems, it appears that no completely automated library system is yet in existence. This objective has been achieved only partially.[30] Thus, information is lacking on the efficacy of total systems. One can only assess those instances in which individual operations or groups of operations have been automated and speculate whether the success of the whole, when automated, will be greater than that of its component parts.

PROBLEMS OF DATA INPUT

In many applications areas, computer technology has far outstripped our ability to use it effectively. Particularly in one area—that of input of data—little practical change has been seen since the initial development of the computer itself. This is especially true in the context of the input of non-numeric information, especially bibliographic material, which tends to be lengthy and sometimes difficult and tedious to transcribe. The technology of optical character recognition is still embryonic; it may yet be several years before devices able to read accurately and quickly several fonts and type styles achieve full operational status. Until then, we will continue to be limited in our means of input of documentary material.

The most widely used conversion technique of written records to machine-readable form is keypunch. Other techniques have been used, such as paper tape typewriting and optical scanning of preprepared forms. The costs of various methods seem to be almost the same; one author points out, however, that input cost is, after all, relatively inexpensive when it is compared to the total cost of the automated library program.[31] But these costs seem to be estimated without regard to the larger questions of logistics and materials handling, although the author stated that in considering conversion of shelf lists to machine-readable form, the need of sending the material to a service bureau would probably not be a problem, since a library can continue to function for limited periods without portions of the shelf list.

To the three usual techniques for converting bibliographic information to machine-readable form are being added other methods showing considerable promise. The use of on-line input terminals in various forms has considerable potential for maintaining a consistently accurate and up-to-date library file, as well as for providing greater convenience for library personnel. This technique is in use in the libraries of the State University of New York at Buffalo. In the conversion of the card catalog to machine-readable form, the IBM Datatext system was selected, and it proved to be quite flexible in both its editing capability and in its provision for upper and lower case character input.[32] Such on-line capability can be especially advantageous when considerations of editing and immediate turn-around of material are important.

COSTING

Experience has shown that cost projections for prospective areas of automation are often faulty.The tendency, unfortunately, to underestimate implementation and operating costs occurs so frequently that the library administration finds itself saddled with a system that has far exceeded its projected initial and operating costs. There are several reasons for this, not the least of which is the lack of systems planning that will allow the smooth, effective meshing of various areas as each is implemented. This point is made effectively by Johnson, in discussing the implementation of a mechanized book catalog system at Stanford University:

The determination of actual costs is a difficult undertaking and a meaningful comparison of costs estimated during the planning process is filled with problems, uncertainties, questions of definition, etc. In a sense, it is impossible to make a meaningful comparison. An element measured during planning is not the same as the element actually achieved.[33]

Closely linked to this problem is that of justification of expenses incurred—a problem encountered not only in the university, but by almost every library in operation. Certainly, use statistics can be important in determining the effectiveness of a library in meeting its objectives. Yet there is no direct way, similar to industry's procedures for cost-benefit analysis or measures of return-on-investment, to determine whether an expense the size of that usually involved in library automation can be justified except, perhaps, in terms of greater efficiency and smaller staff. (The latter has generally not been the case.) These circumstances place the library administrator in a precarious situation and make adequate funding of research and development projects difficult to justify. Libraries are operations in which the public seems to be unwilling to invest significant amounts of capital for research and development. They seem to have fairly low priority when compared with such activities as chemistry, physics, and defense programs, into which corporate and government funds are being poured in vast quantities.[34]

## LANGUAGE PROCESSING

Even though a great many applications of library automation are oriented toward technical services, more and more attention is being given to information retrieval applications, including the input and processing of natural language. Bibliographic materials, to be sure, provide problems in many aspects of computer processing, if only because of their bulk and lack of precise format. A problem of another order exists, however, when the computer is expected to analyze natural language and to derive meaningful indexes therefrom for retrieval purposes. The automation of retrieval processes and the production of retrieved material has progressed a great deal further than that of pre-analysis of the printed document. The ambiguities inherent in language, both in terms of initial indexing and in terms of the user's dialogue with the system, need further analysis and resolution before effective information systems can work economically.

## NETWORK PROBLEMS

If it is sometimes difficult for a single library to maintain internal consistency and smooth flow among the various sub-systems within it, it is infinitely more difficult to provide the ease of interchange and communication so necessary among various separate libraries within a network complex. The lack of compatibility not only between systems and hardware, but between the varying forms material takes in component parts of a network, creates difficulties. Such difficulties may, indeed, offset any benefits that might accrue from such interchange.

Inexpensive transmission facilities among the various components of a network are needed. The usual means of communication between computer components is by telephone lines. It often happens that greater expense is incurred (in a remote time-sharing communications situation) by the use of long distance telephone lines than by the use of computer time. The Federal Communications Commission and other agencies, fortunately, are studying this problem. Solutions, one hopes, will soon be forthcoming.

## COMPLETENESS OF THE LITERATURE OF AUTOMATION

In planning for automation of one or more library processes, the administrator is likely to turn to the published literature for guidelines, and he is likely to seek information about those systems functioning most successfully. The literature, unfortunately, presents an imperfect picture of the experiences of many libraries in their attempts at automation.

It is too bad that library automation is undertaken so often not in a research or in an experimental context, but in one which expresses total commitment to the success of the project. If the former were more common, we would find in the literature a great many more reports revealing negative conclusions. Instead, we find such commitment to success that the literature is filled with accounts of pilot projects, descriptions of planned systems, and stories of automation that has progressed to one stage or another of operation. In many instances it is only by word of mouth that we learn that systems that were once reported as completely operational have since become defunct, that pilot projects have failed, and that plans for automation have not been carried through. In each case, the reasons for the breakdown should be openly discussed in the literature—negative results, in development as in research, are valuable and can lead to savings of time and effort. There are, of course, many college and university libraries successfully operating automated systems. The fact that more and more university libraries are turning to automation for solutions to their problems is ample justification for accurate reflection in the literature of the relative merits of innovative techniques.

*The Future*

When we review the progress toward library automation in the university during the sixties, we find important advances indeed. The common acceptance and wide availability of electronic data processing equipment, used both in batch and real-time modes, has been significant. Its use in business and industry has demonstrated its suitability for applications in which factors of volume, speed, and accuracy make special systems demands—factors relevant to many library operations.

To some, library automation has not proceeded as rapidly as it might have. Some of the problems discussed have deterred many attempts, and they have caused others to be stillborn. Such setbacks, however, have paved the way for the successful completion and operation of other automated systems, which in turn provide operations and management experience upon which even more efficient systems can be built. Others believe that conservative university library administrators have impeded progress in research and systems development. Although caution can be carried to extremes in some cases, careful planning for such expensive equipment must be recognized and applauded.

Yet strides have been made and will continue to be made. Technology promises to provide flexibilities and economies of a high order. Inexpensive communications media will vastly increase the practicality of remote access to centrally stored library files. Computer network technology and technique will allow more effective interchange of information between libraries. Indeed, long range plans are being made today for information networks that will link university libraries with other information facilities, such as industrial centers, public libraries, and government information centers. In this way the broadest range of information can be made available to as many people as possible. The improvement of image-transmission devices will contribute to the usefulness of such networks.

Thus "past is prologue to the future"; the successes of multi-library network complexes found in the university are encouraging similar efforts elsewhere. Similarly, automation within individual libraries is leading to more widespread application of techniques already developed and to increased systems effectiveness. The benefits are sure to outweigh the cost and effort in terms of service to students and faculty, and the benefits should lead to an overall enhancement of the educational process.

## NOTES

1. Eugene B. Jackson, "The Use of Data Processing Equipment by Libraries and Information Centers: The Significant Results of the SLA-LTP Survey," *Special Libraries* (May-June 1967): 317-327.
2. Carl C. Cox, "Mechanized Acquisitions Procedures at the University of Maryland," *College and Research Libraries* 26, no. 3 (May 1965): pp. 232-236.
3. Ralph R. Shaw, "Control of Book Funds at the University of Hawaii Library," *Library Resources and Technical Services* 11, no. 3 (Spring 1967): 380-382.
4. Ned C. Morris, "Computer-Based Acquisitions System at Texas A & I University," *Journal of Library Automation* 1, no. 1 (March 1968): 1-12.
5. Connie Dunlap, "Automated Acquisitions Procedures at the University of Michigan Library," *Library Resources and Technical Services* 2, no. 2 (Spring 1967): 192-202.
6. Jackson, "Data Processing."
7. David Bishop, Arnold L. Milner, and Fred O. Roper, "Publication Patterns of Scientific Serials," *American Documentation* 16, no. 2 (April 1965): 113-21.
8. Fred W. Roper, "A Computer-Based Serials Control System for a Large Biomedical Library," *American Documentation* 19, no. 2 (April 1968): 151-157.
9. Richard D. Johnson, "A Book Catalog at Stanford," *Journal of Library Automation* 1, no. 1 (March 1968): 13-50.
10. "The MARC Pilot Experience: An Informal Summary," Information Systems Office (Washington: Library of Congress, June 1968).

11. William J. Studer, "Computer-Based Selective Dissemination of Information (SDI) Service for Faculty Using Library of Congress Machine-Readable Catalog (MARC) Records" (Ph.D. diss., Indiana University, 1968).

12. Alan R. Benenfeld, *Generation and Encoding of the Project INTREX Augmented Catalog Data Base*, (Cambridge, Massachusetts: Massachusetts Institute of Technology, August 1968), p. 2.

13. Andrew D. Osborn, "The Influence of Automation on the Design of the University Library," *Library Planning for Automation*, ed. Allen Kent (New York; Washington: Spartan Books, Inc., 1965), pp. 57-59.

14. Cherie B. Weil, "Automatic Retrieval of Biographical Reference Books, *Journal of Library Automation* 1, no. 4 (December 1968): 239-249.

15. "Massachusetts Institute of Technology: Project INTREX Semi-Annual Activity Report, 15 March 1968 - 15 September 1968," *PR*-6 (Cambridge, Massachusetts: 15 September 1968).

16. "Three Systems of Circulation Control," *Library Technology Reports*, Library Technology Project, American Library Association, (Chicago: May 1967).

17. Floyd Cammack, and Donald Mann, "Institutional Implications of an Automated Circulation Study," *College and Research Libraries* 28, no. 2, (March 1967): 129-132.

18. Bruce W. Stewart, "Data Processing in an Academic Library," *Wilson Library Bulletin* 41, no. 4 (December 1966): 392.

19. Audrey N. Grosch, "Implications of On-Line Systems Techniques for a De-Centralized Research Library System," *College and Research Libraries* 30, no. 2 (March 1969): 112-118.

20. "New York Biomedical Communication Network," *Information Retrieval and Library Automation* 3, no. 9 (February 1968).

21. "National Library of Medicine On-Line With SUNY," *Information Retrieval and Library Automation*, vol. 4, no. 6 (November 1968).

22. William R. Nugent, *NELINET—The New England Library Information Network*, (Cambridge, Massachusetts: Inforonics, Inc., 1968).

23. Carl F. J. Overhage, and R. Joyce Harmon, ed. *INTREX, Report of a Planning Conference on Information Transfer Experiments*, (Cambridge, Massachusetts: M.I.T. Press, 1965).

24. "Automation for University Library Consortium," *Information Retrieval and Library Automation* 4, no. 7 (December 1968).

25. Harold G. Morehouse, "The Future of Telefacsimile in Libraries: Problems and Prospects," *Library Resources and Technical Services* 13, no. 1 (Winter 1969): 42-46.

*26.* William D. Schieber, and Ralph M. Shoffner, *Telefacsimile and Libraries: A Report of an Experiment in Facsimile Transfer and an Analysis of Implications for Inter-Library Loan Systems*, (Berkeley: California University, Institute of Library Research, 1968).

27. Richard DeGennaro, "The Development and Administration of Automated Systems in Academic Libraries," *Journal of Library Automation* 1, no. 1 (1968): 75-91.

28. Richard M. Dougherty, and James G. Stevens. *Investigation Concerning the Modification of the University of Illinois Computerized Serials Book Catalog to Achieve an Operative System at the University of Colorado Libraries*, (Boulder, Col.: University of Colorado Libraries, 1968).

29. Joseph Becker, "Systems Analysis: Prelude to Library Data Processing," *ALA Bulletin* 59 (March 1965): 293-296.

30. Grosch, "Implications of On-Line Systems Techniques," pp. 112-118.

31. Richard E. Chapin, and Dale H. Pretzer, "Comparative Costs of Converting Shelf List Records to Machine-Readable Form," *Journal of Library Automation* 1, no. 1, (March 1968): 66-75.

32. Frederick M. Balfour, "Conversion of Bibliographic Information to Machine-Readable Form Using On-Line Computer Terminals," *Journal of Library Automation* 1, no. 4 (December 1968): 217-226.

33. Johnson, "A Book Catalog at Stanford," pp. 13-50.

34. Louis A. Schultheiss, et al., *Advanced Data Processing in the University Library*, (New York: Scarecrow Press, Inc., 1962), p. iv.

35. Burton W. Adkinson, and Charles M. Stearns, "Libraries and Machines: A Review," *American Documentation* 18, no. 3 (July 1967): 121-124.

# PART FOUR

# National Libraries and Bibliography

# 8 / National Libraries and Bibliographies in the U.S.S.R.

IVAN KALDOR
State University of New York, College
of Arts and Science at Geneseo

> Look to the essence of a thing,
> whether it be a point of doctrine,
> of practice, or of interpretation.

(Marcus Aurelius, *Meditations*, VIII, 22)

The object of this paper is to discuss—in the best traditions of comparative librarianship—two aspects of the Soviet library world: national libraries and national bibliographies.

The success of any study of the institutions of a foreign nation largely depends on the sincere determination of the inquirer to explore and to understand the basic philosophical and practical considerations which represent the raison d'être of those institutions. Such a statement seems to be true especially in the case of the American scholar studying Soviet institutions—including libraries and national bibliographical services. Hence, it is appropriate to start out the discussion with a brief summary of the main premises this paper has adopted.

The Soviet library network, with its nearly 370,000 libraries, is a vigorous, driving force in the cultural, economic, and political life of the nation. The collections and services of the system reflect the ambitious aspirations of a new society which has become the trademark of the Soviet Union.

It is not by accident or choice that Soviet libraries promote one particular ideology and support its political and economic thrust. They do so because they were created for this purpose. It is their mission.

Thus, the recognition and acceptance of the fact that Soviet libraries are mission-oriented institutions or, if you will, agents of the Soviet state seem to be the key to understanding Soviet librarianship. It ought to be possible to consider this fact without getting entangled in a thankless argument with the political doctrines and beliefs that Soviet libraries and librarians are destined to promote.

The Soviet Union, its institutions, and, to some extent, the Soviet people are the products of a revolution. Successful revolutions are neither accidental nor spontaneous. They are planned, engineered, and led by one individual or by a small group of individuals. The ideology, strategy, tactics, and also institutions of the revolution inevitably carry the intellectual handprints of their architects. This seems to be the case especially in the early phases of revolutions.

Therefore, neither the obscure art of "Kremlinology" nor the analysis and interpretation of the words and lines of party resolutions can give a true insight into the essence of the Soviet institutions. Only a thorough familiarity with the lives, ideas, and experiences of the architects of the Soviet state carries a promise of such privity. Thus, any attempt to understand the basic principles of Soviet librarianship ought to begin with a diligent study of the lives and library-related experiences and writings of Lenin, Krupskaia, Lunacharskii, and others. As far as the time lapse of some fifty years is concerned, the built-in inertia of a political system which is anchored to a single doctrine would still validate this approach.

## National Libraries

### THE ORIGINS

The Soviet library system was developed on the rubble of about fourteen thousand antiquated public libraries of the old Russian

Empire.[1] The gigantic task of creating a modern and democratic public library system was relentlessly pursued during the trying years of civil war, political chaos, famine, and foreign intervention. Ignorance, apathy, hostility, and lack of funds and qualified personnel had to be overcome. A daily running battle had to be fought to maintain a priority position for libraries on the national agenda. In spite of these difficulties and the onslaught of World War II, the Soviet Union claims today a fine network of interwoven systems of about 370,000 libraries with a total collection of over 2.5 billion volumes.[2]

Some questions inevitably arise. Who was the driving force behind the Soviet library movement? Who developed the principles and philosophies for Soviet librarianship? Which national libraries and public library systems, if any, served as models for the Soviet undertaking?

To find the answers to some of these questions one has to go back to the early 1900s.

In western countries a number of unhealthy prejudices are widespread from which Holy Mother Russia is free. There, for example, they hold that great public libraries with hundreds of thousands and millions of books, ought not to be the property only of the scholars and pseudo-scholars who use them. There they have dedicated themselves to the strange, incomprehensible, barbaric aim of making these great, immense libraries accessible not only to scholars, professors and other specialists like them, but to the masses, the crowds, the man in the street.

What a profane use of librarianship! What a lack of that 'good order' we take such a justifiable pride in. Instead of rules discussed and elaborated by dozens of official committees, thinking up hundreds of petty restrictions on the use of books, they take care that even children can use rich book collections, they are anxious for readers to read books bought at public expense in their own homes; they see the pride and glory of the public library . . . in the extent to which books circulate among the people, the number of new readers enrolled, the speed with which requests for books are satisfied, the number of books issued for home reading, the number of children enrolled as readers and library users . . . Strange prejudices are spread abroad in western countries, and it is a cause for rejoicing that in their concern for us our superiors guard us with care and consideration from the influence of these prejudices, shielding our rich public libraries from the mob and the rabble.

Before me lies the report of the New York Public Library for 1911. In that year the New York Public Library moved from two antiquated buildings to a new one built in the city. The total stock is now about two million volumes . . . During the year 1,658,367 people visited the library, 246,950 readers used the reading room, and 911,891 books were issued . . . The New York Public Library has forty-two branches . . . It is a matter of policy that every inhabitant should have within half a mile of his home—that is, under ten minutes' walk away—a branch of the public library serving as the focal point of every kind of institution and organization in the field of public education.

In 1911 almost eight million—7,914,882—volumes were lent for home reading . . . . Each of the forty-two branches . . . is also a place where evening lectures, public meetings, and cultural entertainments can take place.

New York Public Library has about 15,000 books in Eastern languages, about 20,000 in Yiddish, and about 16,000 in Slavic languages. In the main reading room there are about 20,000 volumes on open access, for the use of everyone.

For children the New York Public Library has built a special central reading room, and is gradually opening others in the branches . . . . The number of children visiting the reading room was 1,120,915.

As far as the loss of books is concerned, New York Public Library estimates losses as 70-90 out of every 100,000 books issued on loan.

This is the position in New York. And in Russia?[3]

The full text of the article with these laudatory statements about the services of New York Public Library was printed in the journal *Rabochaia pravda* on 18 (5) July 1913. The author of the polemical piece was an émigré Russian politician named Lenin.

At first the text looks like a matter-of-fact summary or sampling of the statements of the annual report of the famed New York library. However, the selection of items such as tax support, free use, open access, continuing educational facilities, a network of easily accessible branches, children's services, and specialized research collections suggests that Lenin's paper is really parabolizing the underlying concepts for a future Russian library system—in the best traditions of underground journalism.

During their travels and exile abroad, Lenin and his wife N. K. Krupskaia,[4] both avid library users, had the opportunity to test various national library systems.

Lenin was favorably impressed by Switzerland where libraries were well organized, and the interlibrary loan system worked flawlessly. The learned libraries of German Switzerland had direct connections with libraries in Germany and, even in wartime, Lenin managed to obtain through his Swiss library the books he needed from Germany. When he lived in a remote Swiss village during the summer of 1915, Lenin received library books through the mail, free of charge.

Excellent service to readers, the complete absence of bureaucracy, first-rate catalogs, and open access to the collections were some of the features Lenin was impressed by. "Vladimir Il'ich was loud in praise of Swiss culture, and *dreamed of what libraries would be like in Russia after the revolution*," reminisced Krupskaia.[5]

Lenin's exposure to some of the great national libraries of Western Europe was even more intensive. In 1895, during his first stay abroad, he used the Imperial Library in Berlin; in 1902 and 1903, he was a registered reader and user of the British Museum Library[6] in London; and, in 1914, he went through the disappointing experiences that many fellow readers shared at the Bibliothèque Nationale in Paris.

During his daily research and reading at the British Museum Library, Lenin developed a full appreciation of the potentials of a national library. He was moved by the wealth of the collections and by the services of subject specialist reference librarians. The British Museum Library enabled him to use Russian sources which were not to be found in St. Petersburg or Moscow because they had been confiscated by the Russian censors. Lenin wrote " . . . for the sources in all languages which I shall need in the close future, I can not imagine a better place to work than the British Museum Library. Here the gaps will be fewer than anywhere else."[7] And indeed, having worked at the British Museum Library for two years, in 1902 and 1903, Lenin returned there in 1908 when he found that Swiss libraries lacked the primary source material for his research.

In France, Lenin used the collections of the Bibliothèque Nationale and some other libraries. He was unimpressed by the services of the French national library, to say the least. Referring to Lenin's frustrating experiences, Krupskaia reported "The Bibliothèque Nationale did not have catalogs for the most recent years, and there was a great deal of bureaucratic red tape in the issue of books. Generally speaking, librarianship in France was plagued by bureaucracy . . . . *Il'ich judged the cultural level by the way in which libraries were run; for him the stature of libraries was an indication of the standards of culture in general* [italics added] ."

These references and remarks leave no doubt that Lenin and Krupskaia, during their travels and work in Western Europe, carefully observed and critically evaluated some of the best public and national libraries, library systems, and collections. Beyond his unquestionable personal interest in books, libraries, and reading, Lenin the politician pursued his review of western cultural institutions in preparation for one of the gigantic tasks he knew he would have to cope with after a victorious revolution—that of educating and politically indoctrinating tens of millions of backward, illiterate, unskilled, and uneducated poor Russian workers and peasants.

For Krupskaia, the data gathering and review were parts of her preparation for the role of the "grey eminence" of Soviet librarianship.

When the stormy days of the 1917 revolution were over, Lenin, the Chairman of the Council of the People's Commissars and a man blessed with an extraordinary range of interests and powers of innovation and initiation, set his mind to developing a broadly based nationwide library system for the young Soviet Republic. His speeches, statements, writings, and the decrees he signed are parts of an almost single-handed effort to achieve that goal. Hence, they are the original building blocks of Soviet librarianship.

The following selective list of Lenin's measures and statements concerning libraries, library systems, and bibliography should enable the reader to identify the prefigurations and underlying principles of further developments which, in turn, resulted in nationwide systems of public and special libraries, in a unique network of national libraries, and in a highly efficient national bibliographical service. They should also help to pinpoint the foreign models and experiences which are clearly reflected and echoed in most of Lenin's measures and references.

*November 1917.* Lenin ordered an immediate and unconditional reorganization of the St. Petersburg Public Library (today the national library of the R.S.F.S.R.) "based on principles long in existence in free countries of the west, particularly in Switzerland and the United States of North America."[9]

The measures included the institution of a system for the exchange of books with all libraries supported by the public in Petrograd and in the provinces and with foreign libraries; free delivery of books sent through the interlibrary loan system; long opening hours (8 a.m. to 11 p.m.) every day, including holidays and Sundays "as it is done in civilized countries;"[10] and the strengthening of the library staff.

*April 1918.* Lenin signed the resolution of the Council of the People's Commissars (Sovnarkom) ordering Lunacharskii to convene a conference of the representatives of governmental and party organizations to work out a program for the reorganization of the whole library system on the Swiss and American pattern.

*June 1918.* Lenin issued a resolution in which the Sovnarkom brought to the attention of the People's Commissariat for Education (Narkompros) its lack of concern for the organization of libraries, and it ordered the Commissariat to take drastic measures to centralize the administration of libraries, and to introduce the Swiss and American system.[11]

*July 1918.* Lenin signed the decree of the Sovnarkom safeguarding the collections of nationalized private and society libraries and the libraries of the liquidated state establishments. The Department of

Libraries of the Narkompros was made responsible for placing the collections at the disposal of the people.[12]

*November 1918.* The Sovnarkom decreed that the requisitioning (i.e., confiscation) of libraries, book shops, book depositories, and books in general could be done only with the knowledge and consent of the Narkompros.[13]

*February 1919.* In a letter addressed to the Narkompros, Lenin endorsed the idea of gathering library statistics and promoting competition among libraries, including innovative suggestions to cover all the improvements put into practice in Switzerland, America, and other countries.

*May 1919.* Addressing himself to the participants of the First All-Russian Conference on Adult Education, Lenin wrote "We must make use of the books which we have, and undertake the work of organizing a network of libraries ... ; we must not build parallel organizations, but one unified and planned organization."[14]

*September 1919.* Lenin signed the resolution of the Sovnarkom concerning learned libraries. The Sovnarkom ordered the Narkompros to transfer all valuable books of former private libraries to such state libraries as the Rumiantsev Library.

*January 1920.* Lenin signed a resolution of the Sovnarkom ordering various government organizations to deposit all white guard (i.e., antibolshevik) literature, Russian and foreign, with Narkompros for preservation and public perusal in state libraries.

*April 1920.* All stocks of books and other printed matter (with the exception of libraries) belonging to private individuals and to cooperative and other institutions were declared state property by the decree of the Sovnarkom.

*June 1920.* The Narkompros was placed in charge of the supervision of the bibliographical work in the R.S.F.S.R.

The resolution made the Commissariat responsible for the registration of all printed matter published in the R.S.F.S.R. and for the compilation of lists of this material.

Furthermore, the resolution envisaged an improvement in bibliographical work by setting up local depositories, by opening bibliographical institutes and running courses in bibliography, by publishing books and journals on the problems of bibliography, and by coordinating and regulating the activities of all bibliographical institutions and societies.

The resolution also ordered the Narkompros to publish "compulsory regulations on the free deposit of new publications in state and other depositories and to determine what depositories were to receive the free copies."[15]

The resolution laid the foundations for the Soviet system of dépôt légal established the depository rights of the state libraries, and also developed the framework for a more advanced national bibliographical system which was subsequently implemented by the All-Union Book Chamber, the Republic Book Chambers, and the national libraries of certain republics.

*November 1920.* This is the date of the most important library decree issued by the Sovnarkom under Lenin's chairmanship. The essence of the decree was that libraries within the R.S.F.S.R. were declared open to all and were organized into a single network under the control of the Chief Political Education Committee of the Narkompros.

A system of book distribution to libraries was organized. Central and local library distribution committees as well as a central library supply agency were brought into existence.[16] These are then the contributions to Soviet librarianship of Lenin, Krupskaia, Lunacharskii, Bonch-Bruevich, and their fellow revolutionaries. Some of the measures may seem rudimentary, haphazard, or even capricious. Whatever the case may be, they are the true origins of Soviet librarianship and represent the genesis of the Soviet library and bibliographical systems.

No study of Soviet librarianship can succeed without considering them.

THE SYSTEM OF NATIONAL LIBRARIES

The multi-national Soviet state is a federation of fifteen union and twenty autonomous republics.[17] Most republics are unique national, linguistic, historical, and cultural entities. The federation is based on a highly centralized political system and has a planned economy Thus, the sovereignty of the individual republics finds its expression mainly in the autonomy of such cultural institutions as national language, literature, arts, and customs. There have been numerous indications that this peculiar autonomy is becoming an issue of paramount importance, and its impact is felt in all walks of Soviet life.

Libraries are part of the republican cultural scene. Their role as agents of the autonomous national cultures has been recognized by both the planners of the federation and the leaders of the member republics. This is especially true in the case of national libraries which were created with the full backing of the supranational and national authorities.[18]

The unanimous support, however, does not preclude some differences between the central and local authorities as to their views of the primary mission of these libraries. The supranational authorities prefer to consider them as the local agents of a federationwide network of public libraries—agents in charge of the implementation and expert guidance of a library system designed in Moscow. Leaders of the republics seem to look at their national library as a unique treasure house of the intellectual products of their particular nation—a link with the national past and an assurance of the future. Furthermore, they view the national library as a clearinghouse helping the nation's best intellectuals to keep abreast with new developments in other republics and throughout the world.

However, these two points of view have never been considered totally incompatible, and today the Soviet Union claims a fully developed and operational network of national libraries.

The network consists of thirty-six member libraries. Two of them—the Lenin State Library of the U.S.S.R. in Moscow and the Saltykov-Shchedrin State Public Library in Leningrad—are considered to be the main central libraries of the system. The membership includes thirty-five republican national libraries—one for each of the fifteen union republics and one for each of the twenty autonomous republics.

The mathematics of this statement should become more acceptable by mentioning the fact that the Saltykov-Shchedrin State Public Library fulfills a peculiar double role by being one of the main central libraries of the network and also by serving as the official national library of the Russian S.F.S.R.[19]

The development of the network of Soviet national libraries followed the growth of the Soviet Union. Individual national libraries were established between 1921 and 1940 by legislative action of the respective republics.

The Armenian S.S.R., the Azerbaidzhanian S.S.R., the Belorussian S.S.R., and the Georgian S.S.R. led the way. Their national libraries were enacted in the years 1921-1923. The Central Asian republics followed suit; after the establishment of the new state boundaries, national libraries were set up by the legislatures of the Tadzhik S.S.R., the Turkmen S.S.R., and the Uzbek S.S.R.

The early 1930s were marked by the founding of national libraries in the Buriat A.S.S.R., the Kazakh S.S.R. (1931), the Kirghiz S.S.R., the Mordvinian A.S.S.R., and the Turkmen S.S.R. (1932). The mid-1930s brought national libraries to the Chechen-Ingush A.S.S.R., the Komi A.S.S.R., the Kabardino-Balkar A.S.S.R., the Mari A.S.S.R., the North-Ossetian A.S.S.R., the Udmurt A.S.S.R., and the other new autonomous republics.

Following the annexation of the Baltic states in 1940, the largest collections of the Estonian S.S.R., the Latvian S.S.R., and the Lithuanian S.S.R. were promoted to national library status. Another relatively recent addition to the network is the national library of the Moldavian S.S.R.

While the system of national libraries, just like any other Soviet institution, cannot claim a long and venerable past, some of its member libraries proudly look back at a history of one hundred or more years. For instance, the national library of the Uzbek S.S.R. was founded in 1870 and was known as the Tashkent Public Library. The national library of the Ukrainian S.S.R. was formerly the Kiev

Public Library and was founded in 1866. The old public libraries of Tbilisi (1846), Petrozavodsk (1860), and Kazan (1865) function now as prominent national libraries of their respective republics. Similarly, one of the two main central libraries of the system, the Saltykov-Shchedrin State Public Library, was known since 1795 as the first public library in Russia.[20] The other, the Lenin State Library, traces its origins back to the Library of the Rumiantsev Public Museum (1862).

However, most Soviet national libraries were organized in the 1920s and 1930s. In fact, many of them serve the population of union and autonomous republics which simply did not exist prior to those dates.

NATIONAL LIBRARY FUNCTIONS

The functions of the Soviet national library are basically fivefold: it fulfills the mission of the largest and, in most cases, the richest public library of the republic; it is designated to serve as the curator of library materials received by the republic under the dépôt légal; it serves as a national bibliographical center, mainly in the areas of recommending bibilography; it acts as a base for library instruction, research, and experimentation with the specific mission to develop methods which are most suited to satisfy the peculiar needs of the local library scene; and it is the natural center of the national public library system.

By and large, these five areas include most of the activities suggested for national libraries by K. W. Humphreys in his paper presented to the National and University Library Section of IFLA at Rome in 1964.[21] Some other functions, such as an international exchange service or the systematic provision of foreign literature within the country, are centralized and are performed mainly by the two main libraries of the system.[22]

The vastness of the geographical area covered by the Soviet Union and the relatively light use by libraries and readers of the interlibrary loan facilities warrant the ever growing drive toward self-sufficiency on the part of the national libraries. An agressive acquisitions policy together with the provision of the dépôt légal were instrumental in driving the holdings of most national libraries over the million volume mark. In January 1967,[23] three of the Soviet national libraries had collections counting over 3 million volumes; eight had between 2 and 3 million volumes; seven reported collections between 1 and 2 million; and eight were positioned between the half million and million mark. The total collection of the network amounted to more than 50 million volumes—not counting the holdings of the two main central libraries.[24] The public library services performed by the national libraries are very similar to those offered by any sizable public library in the United States. They include reference services, lending of materials, interlibrary loan facilities, bibliographic services "tailor made" for the individual reader, displays, exhibitions, lectures, and so on.

In 1967, the thirty-four member libraries of the network reported 682,000 registered readers, and the number of books borrowed during that year surpassed the 26 million mark.[25] The circulation figures for the two main central libraries have been omitted here because they are not typical for the network.

The readers are mainly high school and college students and blue- and white-collar workers living in the area. The number of scientists, research workers, and specialists among the users is conspicuously low—less than 10 percent.[26]

The functions of the national library as the curator of the books deposited with the republic under the dépôt légal arrangement on one hand and as a national bibliographical center on the other, are closely related. In some respects, they even overlap.

The national library receives depository copies of all works published within the republic. It is also responsible for storing and processing all material published in other republics of the Soviet Union and distributed to the national libraries by the All-Union Book Chamber. The distribution of dépôt légal copies is based on a 29 September 1948 decree of the U.S.S.R. Council of Ministers. Publications of the United Nations and UNESCO are also received by the national libraries.

The national library, in its capacity of the national bibliographical center, works in close cooperation with the All-Union Book

Chamber which registers all Soviet publications. It also participates
in the bibliographical activities of the Book Chamber in its own
republic. The national libraries of the Belorussian S.S.R., the
Estonian S.S.R., and the Latvian S.S.R. are directly involved in
supranational and national bibliographical activities because the
Book Chambers in these three republics are attached to the national
libraries.[27]

The essence of the participation by the national library in the
supranational or all-union bibliographical work will be discussed
later in this essay.

A major bibliographical contribution offered by Soviet national
libraries to the population of the republic is the compilation of
special bibliographies, mostly on local issues and often in the native
language used in the republic. A few national libraries also put out
lists of recommended bibliographies for members of the national
public library system.

Each national library has a special branch or department in charge
of local library instruction, research, and experimentation. The
expert staff of the department is responsible for developing and
popularizing advanced methods in librarianship, writing and publishing library manuals and texts, and organizing conferences where
problems peculiar to the particular state or area are discussed.
Another, though much less interesting, duty of these departments is
the systematic promotion of the ideas and directives, and quite often
just slogans, that are handed down to them by their counterparts at
one of the main central libraries of the system in Moscow or
Leningrad.

The role of the national library as a center of the local public
library system is expressed mostly in the administrative, guidance,
and instruction aspects of its work. Certainly, the most significant
asset of the center is the wealth of its collections which are
constantly tapped by the member libraries.

## ADMINISTRATIVE AND FINANCIAL STATUS OF NATIONAL LIBRARIES

Soviet national libraries are under the direct jurisdiction of the

Library Departments of the Ministry of Culture of their respective republics. The republican Ministry of Culture, in its turn, reports to the republican Council of Ministers.

Another line of command subordinates the Ministry of Culture of the republic to the Ministry of Culture of the U.S.S.R.

Soviet national libraries and other member libraries of the public library systems of the republics are financed from the federal budget of the U.S.S.R.

TWO NATIONAL LIBRARIES—TWO PORTRAITS

The following brief narrative description of the Lenin State Library of the U.S.S.R.[27] and the National Library of the Uzbek S.S.R. is offered here as a summary and illustration of what has been said about Soviet national libraries in general. The selection of these two libraries—one from each end of the spectrum—was intentional; it will help the reader to sense the endless variety of characteristics encompassed by the total system.

*THE LENIN STATE LIBRARY OF THE U.S.S.R. (MOSCOW)*

The Lenin State Library of the U.S.S.R. is the largest and most significant library in the Soviet Union. Its history can be traced back to the private collection of Count P. N. Rumiantsev, or, subsequently, to the Library of the Rumiantsev Museum which opened its doors to the public 1862. In 1925, the library was renamed after V. I. Lenin and became the State Library of the U.S.S.R. Thus, its traditions, pedigree, collection, sizes, and the variety of services performed place the Lenin Library in the same category with the Library of Congress, the British Museum Library, or the Bibliothèque Nationale.

As a result of a generous Russian and later a Soviet depository system as well as aggressive acquisitions and exchange policies, the Lenin Library claims a collection of about 25 million items, including about 10 million volumes of books. Eleventh-century manuscript codices, incunabula, rare books, endless runs of magazines and newspapers, private papers of statesmen and men of letters, deeds, maps, dissertations, films, monographs, and pamphlets in more than 170 languages, microfilms, and photographs—all are part of the huge collection which, reportedly, includes 90 percent of all Russian and Soviet publications.

The library maintains separate author catalogs for Russian books (3.177 million cards) and for books in major European (1.563 million cards) and other languages. The classified catalog, which was started in 1919, has over 3.5 million cards. The library also has developed over 60 separate classified catalogs of publications in the Near and Far Eastern languages as well as in the languages of the non-Russian nations of the U.S.S.R.

As far as its goals and functions are concerned, the Lenin Library is "the central library of the U.S.S.R., a depository for the publications of the entire Soviet Union as well as for foreign literature and manuscripts, it is the center of recommended bibliography, and a research center of national significance in the fields of library science, bibliography, and the history of books."[29]

The collections of the library are open to all, and the services are free. The twenty-two reading rooms easily accommodate twenty-four hundred readers who may use the library on any day of the week from 9 a.m. to 11 p.m. Specialized reading rooms and reference assistance are available to those interested in research. The library has over two hundred thousand registered readers, and the number of books issued for use in the reading rooms is close to 15 million per year.

Some other important functions of the Lenin Library are in the fields of international book exchange,[30] interlibrary loan services,[31] guidance, publishing, and advisory, technical and bibliographical services for the nation's public library system.

The library has a staff of over twenty-two hundred people, including about eighteen hundred librarians.[32]

In accordance with the 25 April 1953 decree of the R.S.F.S.R. Council of Ministers, the Lenin Library is under the jurisdiction and control of the R.S.F.S.R. Ministry of Culture. The annual budget for the Library is negotiated on the basis of plan projections, and the funds for the library are secured by the Ministry of Culture.

## THE NATIONAL LIBRARY OF THE UZBEK S.S.R. (TASHKENT)

The Alisher Navoi State Library of the Uzbek S.S.R. is the center of a public library system of 10,600 libraries with the impressive holdings of over 44 million volumes.

The history of the library goes back to 1870 when the Tashkent Public Library—the first public library in Central Asia—opened its doors to readers. For a short period, in 1919 and early 1920, the library was known as the Turkestan People's Library.

In May 1920, the Turkestan People's Library became the State Library of the Uzbek S.S.R., and in 1948 it was named after the famous Uzbek poet and statesman, Alisher Navoi.

In January 1967, the library had a collection of about 3.23 million volumes.[33] Such fields as local history, culture, economics, and ethnography as well as materials on Central Asia in general have found a uniquely strong representation. Rare books, technical literature, patents, standards, pictures, maps, recordings, Russian and foreign classics, and the works of Soviet authors indicate a drive for maximum self-sufficiency.

A yearly average of 35,000 readers is served by a staff of 200, including over 150 qualified librarians. The number of books borrowed surpasses the 1 million mark.

The publications of the library are issued in Uzbek and Russian.

In addition to the routine functions of a Soviet national library, the Alisher Navoi Library sponsors the Tashkent Popular University of Music, issues bibliographical indexes to the literature on Uzbekistan, and publishes a calendar of significant Uzbek dates.

## National Bibliographies

If there is any field of activity where planning, centralization, and tight control are desirable, it is the field of national bibliography. The Soviet Union has all the requisites for such a rigid approach: it has a planned economy; its publishing and printing trades are nationalized; and early Soviet attempts to centralize the bibliograph-

ical control of their output go back as far as the Leninian decree of
30 June 1920.[34]

It has become a consensus to distinguish three main forms of
bibliographical work as practiced in the U.S.S.R.: maintaining a
national bibliographical register of all publications; compiling and
circulating specialized bibliographies for the specialist; and compiling
and publicizing selective bibliographies and lists of recommended
readings for various categories of the general readership.

The first category unmistakably refers to national bibliography.
What is the purpose of the national bibliography in the Soviet
Union? Paraphrasing one of the Soviet authorities in the field,[35] one
could point out two major missions that bibliography is designed to
fulfill: one is to ensure that a national record is kept of everything
printed in the Soviet Union and to provide information about
current publications; the other is to constitute a basis both for
specialized bibliographies and lists of recommended works, and for
the bibliographical work and bibliographical reference services of
libraries.

It certainly sounds familiar. What then is the reason why Soviet
librarianship is probably best known all over the world for its
achievements in the field of national bibliography? The following
brief review of the Soviet national bibliographical apparatus is
intended to answer the question.

THE ALL-UNION BOOK CHAMBER AND THE REPUBLIC BOOK
CHAMBERS

In May 1917, a bibliographical center named the Russian Central
Book Chamber was founded in Petrograd, the temporary seat of the
young Soviet government. During 1920, two decrees[36] of the
Sovnarkom declared that the bibliographic registration of printed
matter was to become a prerogative of the state, and it put the Book
Chamber in charge of the administration of the Soviet dépôt légal.
The decrees also assigned to the Chamber the duties of a center for
national bibliography and mandated that it maintain complete
archives of Soviet publishing. After the Revolution, when Moscow

became the official seat of the government, the Book Chamber moved to the capital. By 1935, the growing territorial responsibilities of the centralized system were reflected in its new name: the All-Union Book Chamber. In 1936, the Central Executive Committee of the U.S.S.R. issued detailed regulations concerning the tasks, functions, direction, administration, structure, and funding of the organization.[37] It sanctioned the nationwide system consisting of one Book Chamber in each union republic and one for each of three autonomous republics.[38] The Book Chambers of the union and autonomous republics are independent institutions, guided and supervised only by the All-Union Book Chamber. However, three of them, the Book Chamber of the Belorussian S.S.R., the Estonian S.S.R., and the Latvian S.S.R., are directly attached to the national libraries of their respective republics.

Some of the basic functions of the All-Union Book Chamber can be identified as the official registration of all publications issued in the U.S.S.R. and the compilation of respective bibliographies; the gathering and publication of statistical data concerning the press of the U.S.S.R.; the issuing of annual bibliographical indexes of Soviet publications; the preparation and printing of standard cards for library catalogs and for special files; the guidance and coordination of the work of the Book Chambers throughout the Soviet Union; the administration of a central publishing house of bibliography; and the management and supervision of the Soviet dépôt légal.

Here we shall concern ourselves solely with those functions which are directly related to the Soviet national bibliography.

THE DÉPÔT LÉGAL AND THE NATIONAL BIBLIOGRAPHY

The legal deposit system is the solid foundation of Soviet national bibliography. The All-Union Book Chamber receives a specified number of copies of all publications printed within the Soviet Union. The Chamber has the authority to follow up on the fulfillment of the depository obligations by the printing establishments through field inspectors and to check the lists of new publications submitted by various publishing houses. The copies obtained under the dépôt légal are distributed by the Chamber to major libraries throughout the U.S.S.R., according to a formula prescribed by law.[39]

The All-Union Book Chamber uses its own depository copies for the compilation of a bibliographical register which is in fact the Soviet (All-Union) national bibliography. The processed materials are subsequently deposited in the archives of the Chamber.[40]

The bibliographical functions and procedures of the Book Chambers of the union and autonomous republics are basically similar to those of the central institution. In addition to fully supporting the All-Union Book Chamber, they compile bibliographical registers and publish national bibliographies for their respective states. These national bibliographies are mostly limited to publications printed in the particular republic, and the entries are in the native language.

The national bibliographical activities of the All-Union Book Chamber and the republican Book Chambers do not stop at the simple listing of new publications. They also include current analytical listings of periodical and journal articles and the centralized production and distribution of catalog cards for all publications cataloged in source.

Considering the tight control and reporting of the output of Soviet publishing as well as the excellent bibliographical apparatus designed to process the publications, one would be inclined to agree with Thomas J. Whitby[41] that the Soviet bibliographical system has been a success from the standpoint of organization and achievement. The listing of the publications seems to be "as complete as human ingenuity permits." Thus, Soviet bibliographers have attained their main goal—a complete and current supranational and national bibliography—and now they need concern themselves only with refinement.

CURRENT SOVIET NATIONAL BIBLIOGRAPHY

Using the data accumulated in the bibliographical register, the All-Union Book Chamber publishes several good bibliographical listings—all representing parts of the Soviet national bibliography.

*Knizhnaia letopis'* [Book chronicles] (1907- ) is the current national bibliography of the Soviet Union. This weekly bibliographical service lists all monographs of five or more pages published anywhere and in any language within the country.[42]

Each entry includes a full bibliographical description, the number of published copies, the price, and the language of the item—all in Russian. It also includes a D.C. class number and the Book Chamber registration number for the particular work. The entries are arranged in subject groups and, within these, in alphabetical order by author or title. An added list number facilitates references to entries from the index.

Serial publications are listed only by their titles and are analyzed in one of the sister publications of *Knizhnaia letopis'*.

Quarterly author, editor, illustrator, subject, and geographical area indexes to *Knizhnaia letopis'* are also available.

Each republican Book Chamber—with the exception of the R.S.F.S.R.—issues its own *Knizhnaia letopis'* or *Letopis' pechati* which concentrates on the reporting of local publications. Many of their titles are simultaneously listed in the supranational organ.[43] Complete runs of *Knizhnaia letopis'* on microfilm have been made available to U. S. libraries by the Library of Congress. A reprint of the complete set, beginning with 1907, is produced by a U. S. publishing house.

*Knizhnaia letopis'–dopolnitel'nyi vypusk* [Book chronicles—supplementary issue] (1961- ) is a monthly bibliography published by the All-Union Book Chamber. It lists items which are considered to be of little use and interest for the general public. Such categories include materials intended for internal use by political, administrative, or scientific organizations, advertising, standards, and so on. They are mostly free publications intended for limited distribution.

*Ezhegodnik knigi S.S.S.R.* [The annual of the Soviet book] (1927- ) is a two-volume cumulative listing of all commercially available books published in the Soviet Union during the preceding six months. The entries are shorter and simpler than those in *Knizhnaia letopis'* and are classified by subject. The subject subdivisions are more numerous than in the *Knizhnaia letopis'*. The first volume covers the social sciences and the humanities, textbooks, and children's books. The second volume is devoted to the natural sciences, medical sciences, technology, agriculture, and so on. Each entry carries a consecutive series number. The numbers are used as references in the index which is divided into Russian and non-Russian sections.

In the field of analytical bibliography and indexing, the All-Union Book Chamber offers a number of services which lend further depth to the national bibliographical activities.

*Letopis' zhurnal'nykh statei* [Chronicles of magazine articles] (1926- ) is a weekly bibliography of articles published in selected Soviet magazines.

*Letopis' gazetnykh statei* [Chronicles of journal articles] (1936- ) is a monthly listing of articles printed in major Soviet newspapers.

*Novye knigi* [New books] (1956- ) is a weekly bibliographical bulletin for small libraries and the general public about new, important titles which have been published during the previous week and also alerting them to new titles about to be published. As a bibliographical tool, it is of limited use. *Novye knigi* is published jointly by the Chamber and by *Mezhdunarodnaia Kniga*, a Soviet book export company.

*Letopis' periodicheskikh izdanii SSSR* [Chronicles of serial publications of the U.S.S.R.] (1933- ) is an exhaustive listing of new serials published in the Soviet Union. The period 1933-1950 was covered by one-volume annual issues. Since 1951, the annual volume has consisted of two parts: one lists new magazines and newspapers, titles of discontinued publications, title changes, and the like; the other is devoted to the reporting of numbered serials such as proceedings, transactions, and annuals, which are published at irregular intervals. The annual reports reflect the status of serials as of April 1 of the year.

Beginning in 1955, an ambitious venture further improved the reporting of serial publications; the All-Union Book Chamber published the first of a continuing series of five-year cumulations to the *Letopis' periodicheskikh izdanii*. This publication covers the period 1950-1954 and is a direct continuation of the multivolume project *Periodicheskaia pechat' SSSS: 1917-1949* [The periodical press of the S.S.S.R.: 1917-1949]. The second five-year cumulation was published in two volumes and has established the pattern for future quinquennial sets.

*Letopis' izobrazitel'nogo iskusstva* [Chronicles of pictorial art] (1934- ) is a quarterly index to printed reproductions, posters, drawings, picture postcards, portraits, visual aids, and the like. The material is presented in classified arrangement with biographical sketches of artists and indexes to illustrators and authors whose works have been illustrated.

*Letopis' muzykal'noi literatury* [Chronicles of musical literature] (1931- ) is a quarterly bibliographical listing of published musical scores. Each issue has an index of names, and the closing issue of the year carries an index of titles and beginning words of the lyrics.

*Letopis' retsenzii* [Chronicles of reviews] (1934- ) is a quarterly bibliographical record of Russian-language reviews and critical essays printed in the most important periodicals. The entries are arranged in classified order and indexes of the authors of the works reviewed, of titles and reviewers are added.

*Kartograficheskaia letopis'* [Cartographical chronicles] (1931- ; with gaps in publication from 1941-1945 and 1947-1950). After a rather irregular publishing pattern, annual volumes of the set started coming out in 1955. They list new maps and atlases. The indexes to this publication facilitate search by author and by the name of the geographical area in question.

*Literatura i iskusstvo narodov SSSR i zarubezhnykh stran* [The literature and art of the peoples of the U.S.S.R. and of foreign countries] (1957- ) is a fortnightly publication published jointly by the All-Union Book Chamber and the All-Union State Library of Foreign Literature. It helps the reader to locate Russian translations of belles lettres written originally in any non-Russian language. The publication also covers Soviet editions of works of pictorial art by the nationalities of the U.S.S.R. and by foreign artists. Indexes to authors, illustrators, and translators are appended.

*Bibliografia Sovetskoi bibliografii* [Bibliography of Soviet bibliographies] (1939- ) is an annotated annual list of all bibliographical compilations with more than thirty entries published separately as parts of books or Russian periodicals. The listing includes publications in the field of bibliography and library science.

### NATIONAL UNION CATALOG

In 1947, the Lenin State Library of the U.S.S.R., the Saltykov-Shchedrin State Public Library, the Library of the U.S.S.R. Academy of Sciences, and the All-Union Book Chamber began the formidable task of compiling a union catalog of Russian books. When completed, the printed union catalog will have about sixty volumes. The compilers took a rather unorthodox but definitely practical approach: the entries in the new union catalog are grouped by subject and—following the general Soviet bibliographical practice—within each subject section, they are subdivided into two chronological groups—that of the pre-revolutionary period and that of the Soviet era. The total number of entries in the union catalog is over 1.3 million.

The period from the fifteenth through the eighteenth century has been covered previously by a number of printed union catalogs.[44] -

As far as publishing in the non-Russian republics is concerned, the national libraries work on the production of union catalogs in the native languages. For example, the national library of the Georgian S.S.R. printed a two-volume bibliography of local publications entitled *Georgian Books: 1629-1945.*[45]

Finally, one should add that there are several other, mostly specialized, library networks and bibliographical services in the U.S.S.R. Some English language sources which offer information about them are included in the following bibliography.

NOTES

1.  O. S. Chubar'ian, *Obshchee bibliotekovedenie* (Moskva: Izd-vo "Sovetskaia Rossiia," 1960), p. 37; and A. A. Khrenkova, "40 let Sovetskogo bibliotechnogo stroitel'stva," in *40 let bibliotechnogo stroitel'stva v SSSR*, ed. F. S. Abrikosova (Moskva: Gosudarstvennaia ordena Lenina biblioteka SSSR imeni V. I. Lenina, 1958), p. 5.

2.  V. Serov, "Sosredotochim vnimanie na nereshennykh zadachakh," *Bibliotekar'*, no. 1 (1969): 3.

3.  S. Simsova, ed., *Lenin, Krupskaia and Libraries* ([Hamden, Conn.]: Archon Books, [1968]), pp. 15-17; with slight changes. The original article was entitled "Chto mozhno sdelat' dlia narodnogo obrazovaniia" and was reprinted in V. I. Lenin, *Sochineniia*, Izd. 4[Moskva] Gos. izd. polit. lit-ry. 1941-1950, vol. 19, pp. 247 ff.

4.  Librarian, library educator, and co-author of the text of the Sovnarkom decree "On the Centralization of Libraries in the R.S.F.S.R.," (November 3, 1920). Cf., K. Abramov, "Krupskaia i dekret o tsentralizatsii bibliotechnogo dela," *Bibliotekar'*, no. 1 (1969): 16-18.

5.  [V. I. Lenin], *Lenin of bibliotechnom dele* (Moskva: Gospolitizdat, 1960), p. 152.

6.  Krupskaia and Lenin arrived in London in early 1902. They registered under the assumed name of Richter. Soon after their arrival, Lenin applied for permission to use the British Museum Library. The application was supported by a letter of introduction from I. H. Mitchell, a trade union leader and member of the Independent Labor Party. On 29 April 1902 a reader's ticket was issued to Jacob Richter. See also P. Bogachev, "Lenin-chitatel' Britanskogo Muzeia," *Bibliotekar'*, no. 4 (1961): pp. 25-29.

7.  Ibid.

8.  [Lenin], *Lenin of bibliotechnom dele*, p. 151.

9.  Lenin, *Sochineniia*, vol. 26, p. 297.

10. Ibid.

11. *Leninskii sbornik*, vol. 21 (Moskva: Gos. izd-vo., 1925-1929), pp. 207-208.

12. [Lenin], *Lenin of bibliotechnom dele,* pp. 133-134.
13. Ibid.
14. Lenin, *Sochineniia,* vol. 29, p. 310.
15. *Sobranie Uzakonenii i Rasporiazhenii rabochego i krest'ianskogo pravitel'stva,* no. 65 (1920), p. 289.
16. Ibid., no. 87 (1920), p. 439.
17. The fifteen Union Republics of the Soviet Union are the Armenian S.S.R., the Azerbaidzhanian S.S.R., the Belorussian S.S.R., the Estonian S.S.R., the Georgian S.S.R., the Kazakh S.S.R., the Kirghiz S.S.R., the Latvian S.S.R., the Lithuanian S.S.R., the Moldavian S.S.R., the Russian S.F.S.R., the Tadzhik S.S.R., the Turkmen S.S.R., the Ukrainian S.S.R., and the Uzbek S.S.R. The twenty autonomous Republics are the Abkhaz A.S.S.R., the Adzhar A.S.S.R., the Bashkir A.S.S.R., the Buriat A.S.S.R., the Chechen-Ingush A.S.S.R., the Chuvash A.S.S.R., the Dagestan A.S.S.R., the Kabardino-Balkar A.S.S.R., the Kalmyk A.S.S.R., the Kara-Kalpak A.S.S.R., the Karelian A.S.S.R., the Komi A.S.S.R., the Mari A.S.S.R., the Mordvinian A.S.S.R., the Nakhichevan A.S.S.R., the North Ossetian A.S.S.R., the Tatar A.S.S.R., the Tuva A.S.S.R., the Udmurt A.S.S.R., and the Iakut A.S.S.R.
18. Any attempt to draw a parallel between Soviet and American federalism, a Soviet republic and an American state, or a republican national library and an American state library would be an exercise in futility. The Soviet Union still has to demonstrate its ability to act as a melting pot of nationalities. Unlike the American states, each of the republics strictly adheres to its national language, culture, history, and traditions.
19. Leningrad. Publichnaia biblioteka. *Ustav* (Leningrad: 1956), as cited in P. L. Horecky, *Libraries and Bibliographic Centers in the Soviet Union* (Bloomington, Ind.: Indiana University, 1959), p. 226.
20. Leningrad. Publichnaia biblioteka, *Istoriia Gosudarstvennoi ordena Trudovogo Krasnogo Znameni Publichnoi biblioteki imeni M. E. Saltykova-Shchedrina* (Leningrad: Lenizdat, 1963), p. 12.
21. K. W. Humphreys, "National Library Functions," *UNESCO Bulletin for Libraries* 20 (July-August 1966): 158-169.
22. It was not until April 1956 that the Saltykov-Shchedrin State Public Library was given permission to enter into direct

exchange agreements with foreign countries. See also Horecky, *Libraries and Bibliographic Centers*, p.92.

23. I. Nazmutdinov, "National Libraries in the Republics of the U.S.S.R.," *UNESCO Bulletin for Libraries*, 23 (January-February 1969): 50.

24. The Lenin State Library reported about the same time a collection of 25 million items, and the Saltykov-Shchedrin State Public Library was known to have on its shelves about 14 million books alone.

25. Nazmutdinov, "National Libraries," p. 50.

26. Ibid.

27. F. S. Abrikosova, "The Part Played by State Libraries in the USSR in the Bibliographical Work of the Country," in United Nations Educational, Scientific and Cultural Organization, *National Libraries: Their Problems and Prospects; Symposium on National Libraries in Europe, Vienna, 8-27 September 1958* (Paris: UNESCO, 1960), pp. 63-70.

28. For a more complete, though somewhat dated, description of the history, collections, and services of the Lenin Library, the reader is referred to such standard works as Horecky and Ruggles. Those who read Russian could consult the volume *Istoriia Gosudarstvennoi ordena Lenina biblioteki SSSR imeni V. I. Lenina za 100 let: 1862-1962* (Moskva: Izdanie biblioteki, 1962).

29. Ministerstvo kul'tury RSFSR, *Gosudarstvennaia biblioteka imeni V. I. Lenina* (Moskva: 1957), p. 4.

30. B. P. Kanevskii, "International Exchange of Publications at the Lenin State Library," *UNESCO Bulletin for Libraries* 13 (February-March 1959): 48-52.

31. S. A. Zerchaninova, "International Library Loan Service of the USSR Lenin State Library," *UNESCO Bulletin for Libraries* 14 (July-August 1960): 170-174.

32. M. J. Ruggles and R. C. Swank, *Soviet Libraries and Librarianship* (Chicago: American Library Association, 1962), p. 111.

33. D. Tadzhieva, "The National Library of Uzbekistan," *UNESCO Bulletin for Libraries* 22 (March-April 1968): 87-89.

34. For a summary of the text of the decree, see the entry under June 1920 earlier in this essay.

35. F. S. Abrikosova, "The Part Played by State Libraries in the U.S.S.R.," p. 63.

36. Of June 30, 1920 and August 3, 1920.

37. L. G. Fogelevich, comp., *Osnovnye direktivy i zakonodatel'stvo o pechati: sistematicheskii sbornik* (Moskva: 1937), pp. 156-158; as cited in Horecky, *Libraries and Bibliographic Centers.*

38. The Bashkir A.S.S.R., the Chuvash A.S.S.R., and the Tatar A.S.S.R.

39. The decree of the U.S.S.R. Council of Ministers "Concerning the Procedure of Supplying Free and Paid Depository Copies of Publications to the Most Significant Libraries of the U.S.S.R." was enacted on 29 September 1948.

40. In 1968, the archives stored over 30 million books, pamphlets, newspapers, magazines and other publications; see P. A. Chuvikov, "Vsesoiuznoi Knizhnoi Palate-50 let," *Kniga* 16 (1968), p. 6.

41. T. J. Whitby, "Libraries and Bibliographical Projects in the Communist Bloc," *The Library Quarterly* 28 (October 1968): 288-289.

42. Works printed in runs of less than a hundred are reported only if they are of exceptional significance.

43. For differing views concerning the usefulness of this partial duplication the reader is referred to Ruggles and Swank, *Soviet Libraries*, pp. 20-21; and L. Vladimirov, "Soviet Centralized Bibliography; Its Strength and Weaknesses," *College & Research Libraries* 27 (May 1966): 188-189.

44. There is, for instance, a published union catalog of the sixteenth- through eighteenth-century Russian books printed in *poluustav* type; and published in two volumes: Leningrad, Publichnaia biblioteka imeni M. E. Saltykova-Shchedrina, *Opisanie izdanii napechatannykh pri Petre I. Svodnyi katalog . . .*, vol. 1, *Opisanie izdanii grazhdanskoi pechati 1708-ianvar' 1725 g.* (Moskva: Izd-vo Akademii nauk SSSR, 1955); vol. 2, *Opisanie izdanii napechatannykh kirillitsei 1689-ianvar' 1725 g.* (Moskva: Izd-vo Akademii nauk SSSR, 1958). Finally, there is a union catalog of Russian books published between 1725 and 1800.

45. F. S. Abrikosova, *State Libraries*, p. 67.

## SELECTIVE BIBLIOGRAPHY

The available literature on Soviet national libraries and national bibliography is sadly repetitive. The titles listed here provide scattered information relevant to the topic. Some of the accounts tend to be biased one way or another. Hence, the reader is advised to peruse them critically.

Abrikosova, F. S. ed. *40 let bibliotechnogo stroitel'stva v SSSR; doklady nauchnoi konferentsii 23-26 dekabria 1957 goda.* Moskva: Gosudarstvennaia ordena Lenina biblioteka SSSR imeni V. I. Lenina, 1958.

Avicenne, P. *Bibliographical Services Throughout the World, 1960-1964.* Paris: UNESCO, 1968. Updated by UNESCO, *Bibliography, Documentation, Terminology* 8, (September 1968- ).

Berdnikova, K. and Krachek, R. "Catalogues of Children and Young People in the Lenin State Library of the U.S.S.R. " *UNESCO Bulletin for Libraries* 17 (March-April 1963): 65-69.

Beyerly, E. "Soviet Bibliographical Projects: Achievements in the USSR, Assessment in the USA." *American Documentation* 11 (January 1960): 44-54.

*Bibliotekar'* (the official organ of Soviet librarianship) issues for 1968 and 1969, with papers commemorating the Lenin and Krupskaia Centennials.

Chubar'ian, O. S. *Obshchee bibliotekovedenie.* Moskva: Izd-vo "Sovetskaia Rossiia", 1960).

Chuvikov, P. A. "USSR Book Chamber." *Indian Librarian* 22 (March 1968): 205.

———. "Vsesoiuznoi Knizhnoi Palate-50 let." *Kniga* 16 (1968): 5-9.

Cope, R. L. "Bibliography: a Major Preoccupation of Soviet Librarianship." *The Australian Library Journal* 16 (April, 1967): 62-70.

Dudley, E. "Libraries in the U.S.S.R." *The Library Association Record* 61 (May 1959): 111-115.

Horecky, P. L. *Libraries and Bibliographic Centers in the Soviet Union.* Bloomington, Ind.: Indiana University, 1959.

Humphreys, K. W. "National Library Functions." *UNESCO Bulletin for Libraries* 20 (July-August 1966): 158-169.

Kanevskii, B. P. "International Exchange of Publications at the Lenin State Library." *UNESCO Bulletin for Libraries* 13 (February-March 1959): 48-52.

Kent, D. "The Leningrad State Library." *Canadian Library Association Bulletin* 16 (September 1959): 67-70.

Klevenskii, M. M. *Geschichte der Staatlichen Lenin-Bibliothek der UdSSR Band I. Geschichte der Bibliothek des Moskauer Öffentlichen und Rumjancev-Museums.* Leipzig: Harrassowitz, 1955.

Kondakov, I. "The Chief Library of the U.S.S.R." *Indian Librarian* 21 (March 1967): 203-205.

Kuharkov, N. "Copyright Deposit and Related Services: The All-Union Book Chamber of the U.S.S.R." *UNESCO Bulletin for Libraries* 11 (January 1957): 2-4.

[Lenin, V. I.] *Lenin of bibliotechnom dele.* Moskva: Gospolitizdat, 1960.

Leningrad. Publichnaia biblioteka. *Gosuderstvennaia Publichnaia imeni M. E. Saltykova-Shchedrina v ...godu.* Leningrad: Izdanie biblioteki.

――――. Publichnaia biblioteka. *Istoriia Gosudarstvennoi ordena Trudovogo Krasnogo Znameni Publichnoi biblioteki imeni M. E. Saltykova-Shchedrina.* Leningrad: Lenizdat, 1962.

――――. *Ustav.* Leningrad: 1956.

Mach, O. "Lenin-Bibliothek und Saltykov-Scedrin-Bibliothek." *Zeitschrift fur Bibliothekwesen und Bibliographie* 9 (February 1962): 143-150.

Maichel, K. "The Listing of Scientific Literature in Soviet National Bibliographies." *Special Libraries* 50 (January 1959): 13-15.

Minkovich, M. "Half a Century's Progress in Bielorussian Libraries." *UNESCO Bulletin for Libraries* 22 (March-April 1968) 93-94.

Moscow. Publichnaia Biblioteka. *Bibliotechnoe delo v SSSR; sbornik statei.* Moskva: Gosudarstvennaia ordena Lenina biblioteka SSSR imeni V. I. Lenina, 1957.

――――. *Biblioteki RSFSR (bez Moskvy i Leningrada): spravochnik.* Moskva: Izd-vo "Kniga," 1964.

――――. *Istoriia Gosudarstvennoi ordena Lenina biblioteki SSSR imeni V. I. Lenina za 100 let 1862-1962.* Moskva: Izdanie biblioteki, 1962.

――――. Publichnaia biblioteka. *Gosuderstvennaia ordena Lenina biblioteka SSSR imeni V. I. Lenin v . . . godu,* Moskva: Izd-vo "Kniga."

Nazmutdinov, I. "National Libraries in the Republics of the U.S.S.R." *UNESCO Bulletin for Libraries* 23 (January-February 1969): 50-51.

Orlov, V. "USSR Technical Libraries in the Nation-wide System of Scientific Technical Information." *Libri* 18 (1968): 230-236.

Ranganathan, S. R. "VINITI: All-Union Institute for Scientific and Technical Information." In *Documentation and Its Facets*, edited by S. R. Ranganathan, pp. 90-113. Bombay: Asia Publishing House, 1963.

Rudomino, M. "The All-Union State Library of Foreign Literature in Its New Premises." *UNESCO Bulletin for Libraries* 22 (January–February 1968): 20-25.

Ruggles, M. J. and Swank, R. C. *Soviet Libraries and Librarianship.* Chicago: American Library Association, 1962.

Simsova, S., ed. *Lenin, Krupskaia and Libraries.* Hamden, Conn.: Archon Books, 1968.

Smirnova, B. A. *Deiatel'nost' Gosudarstvennoi biblioteki SSSR imeni V. I. Lenina v oblasti rekomendatel'noi bibliografii.* Moskva: Izd-vo "Kniga", 1964.

Tadzhieva, D. "The National Library of Uzbekistan." *UNESCO Bulletin for Libraries* 22 (March-April 1968): 87-89.

Tiulina, N. "The Foreign Librarianship Section of the V. I. Lenin State Library of the U.S.S.R." *UNESCO Bulletin for Libraries* 22 (May-June 1968): 141-143.

United Nations Educational, Scientific and Cultural Organization. *National Libraries: Their Problems and Prospects; Symposium on National Libraries in Europe, Vienna, 8-26 September 1958.* Paris: UNESCO, 1960.

Vasil'chenko, V. E. *Istoriia bibliotechnogo dela v SSSR.* Moskva: "Sovetskaia Rossiia," 1958.

Vladimirov, L. "Soviet Centralized Bibliography; Its Strength and Weaknesses." *College & Research Libraries* 27 (May 1966):

Whitby, T. J. "Libraries and Bibliographical Projects in the Communist Bloc." *The Library Quarterly* 28 (October 1968): 277-294.

———. "New Directions in Soviet Planned Bibliography." *College & Research Libraries* 21 (January 1960): 9-12.

Zerchaninova, S. A. "International Library Loan Service of the USSR Lenin State Library." *UNESCO Bulletin for Libraries* 14 (July-August 1960): 170-174.

# 9/The National Library in Latin America

ARTHUR E. GROPP

*Former Librarian*
*Columbus Memorial Library,*
*Pan American Union*

The national library in Latin America has played the usual role in the preservation of publications, documents, and other materials. To the extent of its activity in this role, the national library constitutes a substantial element in the cultural and intellectual heritage of the nation it serves. In a lesser degree the national library has participated in the development of libraries and library services, and in a number of cases has been a leader in the dissemination of national bibliographical and historical information.

The national library has been of particular value in the preservation of publications of national origin. Its collections of nationally published resources, in general, are unsurpassed in volume by any other library, at home or abroad, although the congressional library and the university library occasionally are close seconds. It has made a generous contribution in the issuance of published bibliographies that reflect national periodical and book publishing, general and specialized holdings, and information about persons, places, and subject matter of prevailing importance.

The national library, additionally, has undertaken to generate popular interest and pride in its national culture by organizing lecture series, radio programs, and exhibitions. These programs of popular interest emphasize publications pertaining to national history and significant commemorative dates, life and customs of the country, and prominent contributions by nationals in their specific fields of endeavor.

The national library, frequently, has gone beyond the physical library to promote cultural and intellectual endeavor. It has aided in the establishment of local libraries, and in lesser measure, to extending reading services to outlying communities. In several instances the national library has taken the lead in the training of librarians, who in turn have made, and are making, significant contributions to their respective communities.

In the countries of Spanish America, the national library emerged with the gaining of independence from Spain. The early desire to establish public libraries forms a part of the record of some nations in their movement for independent statehood. The possibility of libraries available for public use came as a natural consequence of earlier action, when the Spanish government in 1767 ordered the expulsion of the Jesuit Order from its dominions. The newly independent nations in America inherited the libraries of the Jesuits and transformed them into public libraries. Indeed, some had been opened to public use even before independence. These public libraries, subsequently, became the national library as the colonies gained their independence. Two countries, Guatemala and Mexico, used the collections of monasteries and convents for the foundation of their national libraries when they suppressed monasticism in the life of the nation.

Brazil, whose history is linked with Portugal, developed separately from the Spanish colonies. In brief, it became the seat of Portuguese royalty in 1807 during the Napoleonic rule in Portugal when the royal family fled to Brazil, and from exile João VI ruled the Portuguese kingdom until 1821 when he returned to the homeland, leaving his son, Dom Pedro, in charge of Brazil. Dom Pedro proclaimed the independence of Brazil from Portugal in 1822, with himself as emperor. Brazil became a republic in 1889. The Royal Library, established in 1810, is the National Library of today.

Among Spanish American countries, the oldest national library was founded in Bogotá, Colombia, in 1777, followed by Ecuador in 1792, both beginning as public libraries. The national libraries of Argentina, Chile, and Uruguay came into existence as public libraries during the period of struggle for independence, whereas that of Peru was founded within a month after the independence proclamation. Those of Bolivia and Venezuela were created before the middle of the nineteenth century, and those of the Central American countries, Mexico and Paraguay, date from before the end of the nineteenth century. The two remaining national libraries, of Cuba and Panama, were founded in the twentieth century.

Haiti declared itself independent from France in 1804. It remained without a national library until 1939. On September 10 of that year the cornerstone of the building was laid.

Today the only country in Latin America without a national library is the Dominican Republic. Here, functions usually ascribed the national library, such as the depository for nationally produced publications and the government agency in charge of international exchange of publications, are the responsibility of the Universidad de Santo Domingo.

The development of the national library to the present time, in Latin America, has taken place not without hardships. In general, the governments have been confronted with political and social unrest and turmoil throughout their history, thus interfering with continuous and consistent progress and growth of the national library. These conditions of turmoil and unrest likewise have impeded the creation and support of a national system of libraries. Furthermore, an adequate funding of the national library has seldom been forthcoming, particularly in those countries that have had to meet acute economic problems. It is, therefore, evident that fruitful fulfillment of its objectives has been irregular and that the national library, indeed, has been denied accomplishments possible under more normal circumstances.

Most of the materials received by the national library come without cost through the legal deposit of national publications, negotiated exchange, and solicited and unsolicited gifts. A lesser number of publications are purchased. However, on occasion, special provisions are made for the acquisition of private collections. But usually funds are insufficient to enable the national library to obtain materials, generally not available except by purchase, offered in local and foreign markets. It is, therefore, not surprising that important reference materials and periodical collections needed for consultation are lacking in most national libraries.

Among private libraries of outstanding research value acquired by national libraries are the José Toribio Medina library in Chile; the Gilberto Valenzuela library in Guatemala; the library of Pedro de Angelis, an Argentine collector, acquired by the National Library of Brazil; the library of Agustín P. Justo, also an Argentine collector, purchased by the National Library of Peru; the Gabriel René-Moreno library in Bolivia; the library of Cardinal Lambruschini, former librarian of the Vatican, purchased by the government of El Salvador; and more recently the Fernando Ortiz library acquired by the National Library of Cuba.

The national library, additionally, has invited the participation of foreign institutions and governments in important special events as a means for increasing the holdings. These events are in connection with such happenings as the dedication of a new building, the commemoration of the 100th anniversary of foundation, and in one instance, the rebuilding of a collection lost by fire. Responses have been generous. For example, the National Library of Colombia, on the occasion of the dedication of its new building in 1938, received over 6,000 volumes from twenty countries, and the National Library of Peru, after the disastrous fire in 1943, had received a total of 22,894 volumes by the time of reopening in 1945.

In some instances the national library has benefitted from a foreign cultural relations program in the course of which participant countries deposit select national collections in that national library.

The quarters of almost any given national library at the time of foundation were, at best, modest, usually a room in a government or university building. Sometimes an old convent, monastery, or church was conditioned for use. As the library outgrew these early quarters, various of them eventually constructed more suitable buildings for occupation. Most of the buildings were erected at the turn of the century, or soon thereafter. These have long since proved inadequate, and even the buildings constructed more recently, although adequate in size, have not always incorporated features best suited for administration and organization. There remain some Latin American countries that still do not have a building especially constructed for national library use. The National Library of Mexico is still quartered in the St. Augustine church. Plans are being developed for the construction of a new building for the national libraries of Panama and Costa Rica. Bolivia, Ecuador, Nicaragua, and Paraguay have not yet erected buildings especially designed for library purposes. Argentina, whose present building was inaugurated in 1901, has chosen a new site for the relocation of the National Library, and was developing plans for a modern building. Terms for the acceptance of bids for construction were published in the official government gazette.[1] No further action seems to have been taken.

The national library, in some cases, has suffered heavy physical losses. For example, the National Library of Uruguay, during the struggle for independence, and the National Library of Peru, during the conflict with Chile, were used for quartering invasion troops. Although in Uruguay the collection was stored in a basement, an apparently safe place, many valuable items nevertheless disappeared. In Peru most of the collection disappeared at the time of the conflict. Subsequently, only about fourteen thousand volumes of the fifty-five thousand volume collection were recovered. Then, tragically, in 1943 disaster struck this National Library again, when a fire completely destroyed the building and nearly all its contents.

It would be difficult to estimate damage to library materials credited to dampness and insects, losses particularly heavy in libraries and archives in tropical zones. The writer, in his survey of libraries and archives in Central America and the West Indies, 1937-1938, found evidence of dampness. In relation to Nicaragua he stated, "On the patio gallery the cases are placed along the wall and along the outer edge, facing each other . . . . The books in the outer row of cases are subject to dampness during the rainy season."[2] However, the current trend of concern for library materials is evident in the construction of modern buildings which assure control of dampness and insects, and security against losses by fire.

The national library disseminates information of its resources and activities through the media of publications. Most libraries, in greater or lesser degree, have published bulletins, journals, and catalogs of the collections and of exhibitions, current national and special bibliographies, reports of activities, commemorative leaflets, brochures, and historical documents.[3] They are important contributions to cultural and intellectual activities of the nation. Among the most valuable publications, particularly for those concerned with Latin American studies, is current national bibliography for which some national libraries have made themselves responsible. Greater effort and support should be given to this activity. The compilation of current national bibliographies has been carried on by the national libraries of Brazil, Chile, Costa Rica, El Salvador, Guatemala, Honduras, Panama, Peru, Uruguay, and Venezuela.[4] The National Library of Haiti is represented by a comprehensive bibliography, 1804-1950, compiled by the director of the National Library, but published commercially in the United States. Current national bibliography, however, is not up-to-date, and its continuing publication on a regular schedule is doubtful.

The publication record of any given national library is usually in direct ratio to the funds allocated for this purpose, the output ranging from creditable to disheartening.

The national library differs substantially from other libraries in emphasis on use of library materials. For instance, municipal and popular libraries emphasize liberal use of library materials and are administered in a manner that will produce maximum use in areas such as reading and consultation within the library, circulation of books to the home, provision of reading rooms and special services for children, in some cases bookmobile units, and in others a central library with branches. The national library on the other hand, in keeping with its primary objective—that of preservation of materials—generally restricts the use of its collections to consultation on the premises. Users of the national library, for the most part, are students, professors, and researchers.

Education for librarianship in Latin America is a recent development. In 1929, modern universally recognized techniques were introduced in a teaching program in São Paulo, Brazil.[5] In 1943 a similar program was initiated in Buenos Aires.[6] Earlier librarians in charge of administration and organization, more often than not, were highly individual, leading to the use of widely divergent practices from one library to another and from one country to another. Because library schools and courses for the training of librarians now are functioning in most of the Latin American countries, the younger generation of professional and resourceful librarians is able to operate from more standardized and interchangeable methods—from one library to another and from one country to another.

Two national libraries, Brazil (1946) with a reorganized course of study, and Peru (1944) with a newly established school, aimed for the training of their own personnel, but the courses were opened to personnel from other libraries. A library school, reported in 1957, for the training of librarians was being established in the National Library of Argentina.

The training of librarians has led to significant changes in patterns of library service, and in some instances the government has recognized librarianship as a profession. For example, in Uruguay the law creating the library school requires that all vacancies of technical positions in state and municipal libraries be filled by graduates of the school; more recently, the government added the category of librarian to the professions accorded minimum wages.

A consequence of training for librarianship is the formation of national, local, and special library associations. These associations have contributed considerably to the formulation of standards for the organization of libraries and for personnel qualifications, and they are setting the course of professional activity.

In 1948 the writer found eighteen associations on record in the Latin American countries. Only a small number of these had progressed beyond the organizational stage. However, by 1966 a total of fifty-six library and archival associations was listed.

*Argentina*

In 1796, at the time of his death, Bishop Manuel Azamor y Ramírez left his collection of books for the establishment of a public library. The provisions of the will were not carried out until the Junta Revolucionaria on September 7, 1810, authorized its establishment. The library of Bishop Rodrigo Antonio de Orellana and the books of other supporters of the opposition were added to the collection left by Bishop Azamor y Ramírez. Quarters were designated in the Colegio de San Carlos. Mariano Moreno was named protector of the library and Saturnino Segurola and Fray Cayetano Rodríguez became the librarians. On March 16, 1812, it was opened for use as the Biblioteca Pública de Buenos Aires.

The Library continued to function as a public library until September 9, 1884, when the government proclaimed it the National Library. The first director of the new administration was José Antonio Wilde, who was succeeded in 1885 by Paul Groussac, an eminent scholar, for the next forty years. During this period the library grew from 32,000 volumes to nearly 230,000 volumes, aided by the law, adopted in 1870, requiring the deposit of nationally published materials. The publications which had accumulated during the period 1870-1884, in the Library of the Oficina de Depósito y Reparto de Publicaciones, were incorporated in the National Library.

The present building of the National Library was dedicated on December 12, 1901. These quarters have become crowded, and a new building is projected. Land was acquired for this purpose, adjacent to the Facultad de Derecho y Ciencias Sociales, and the terms for bidding on the construction were opened in 1961. However, no further action seems to have been taken.

The National Library has a good record of publishing: reports of activities, regulations, explanation of the classification system; reproduction of documents; catalogs of its book collection and of manuscripts; catalogs of gift collections; lists of acquisitions; history of the library; several editions of the most used books; catalogs of documents related to the Río de La Plata region in the Archivo General de Indias in Spain; and a journal, published as *Revista* (1879-1882) of the Biblioteca Pública de Buenos Aires; *La Biblioteca* (1896-1898); *Revista* (1937-1951); and again as *La Biblioteca* (1951- ).

## Bolivia

On 30 June 1838 the president of Bolivia decreed the establishment of a free public library in the capital of each province, to be supervised by the national government and the director of the Instituto Nacional through a local literary society. At that time two such libraries were established, one in La Paz and the other in Sucre. The latter became the National Library, now administered under the Ministerio de Instrucción Pública. In 1936 the Archivo Nacional was merged with the Biblioteca Nacional.[7]

At the Third Pan American Scientific Congress, Lima, 1924, the Bolivian delegate reported that his government was establishing a second National Library at La Paz, but the plan was not carried out.

The initial collection of the National Library was formed from the library of Antonio José Sucre, first president of Bolivia. In 1907 it added the extensive collection of Gabriel René-Moreno, historian and bibliographer.

Editors, authors, and government offices are required to deposit two copies in the National Library of every publication printed in the country.

The Library published the *Revista* (1920, no. 1-2; 1932; 1936-1943).

## Brazil

In 1808 Dom João VI, fleeing from the Napoleonic invasion of his country, brought with him his library containing many rarities, Portuguese history, pamphlets, pictures, and maps. This collection became the foundation, in 1810, of the Real Bibliotheca do Palacio da Ajuda. It was housed in the Hospital of the Ordem Terceiro do Carmo. In 1811 it was opened to the public. When D. João returned to Portugal in 1822 he took a part of the collection with him.

From 1853 to 1870 the Library was housed in the Casa do Largo de Lala, where for the first time reading room space was provided. In 1910, on the 100th anniversary of its founding, the National Library was transferred to the present building, a granite and marble structure rising four stories above the basement.

In 1853 the government purchased the library of the Argentine bibliophile, Pedro de Angelis, which contained some 2,700 volumes and 1,300 manuscripts rich in the history of the Río de La Plata region. In 1886 the government established its office for international exchange, and in 1890 transferred the operation to the National Library. Additional acquisitions come from the requirement of deposit of any work registered in the copyright office, which is located in the Library.

In addition to the book collection, the Library has many pamphlets, periodical publications, newspapers, maps, and manuscripts. One of the largest single acquisitions by the library was the special collection of Dom Pedro II in 1889, numbering some 48,236 volumes. It possesses a Gutenberg Bible and other incunabula.

A library science course was made a part of the National Library in 1914, offering studies in bibliography, paleography, iconography, and numismatics. In later years cartography replaced numismatics. However, in 1946, with the reorganization of the Library under the direction of Rubens Borba de Moraes, the course was completely revised and modernized.

The National Library continually, throughout the years, particularly since occupying the present building, frequently has featured special exhibits of library materials.

It has a long list of publications, many of them catalogs of exhibits. However, in the series *Documentos históricos* (1928- ), already totaling 110 numbers, the Library has published numerous historical documents. Another series of outstanding note is *Anais*

(1876- ) formerly *Annaes,* in which it has published historical documents, catalogs, bibliographies, inventories of manuscripts, a history of the Library, and so forth. Many numbers of *Anais* have been reprinted as separates. The most recent issue contains a 208 page catalog of newspapers and journals published in Rio de Janeiro, 1808-1889, in the collection of the National Library. In 1951 the Library began publication of manuscripts from the Pedro de Angelis collection, of which six volumes have appeared. Among other publications are the regulations governing the Library, reports of the director, and courses of study of the Library School. It publishes *Boletim bibliográfico* (1918-1921; n.s., 1951- , semiannual). Issues of the *Boletim* appeared for the years 1931, 1938, and 1946, in which only Brazilian imprints were listed.

## Chile

The Junta Revolucionaria, on August 19, 1813, proclaimed the founding of a public library in Santiago, which eventually became the National Library. As an aid to its establishment it solicited funds and books from the citizenry. Library materials acquired in this way were added to the old library of the Jesuits, which had been housed, since 1767, in the Universidad Real de San Felipe. Manual de Salas was chosen to organize the collection.

Government action in passing the copyright law in 1834 stimulated growth of the Library. Provision of the law required the deposit of two copies in the National Library of publications submitted for registration. Subsequently, the printing law, passed in 1846, required all printers to deposit two copies of every publication in the Library.

The National Library, in 1886, was relocated in a building remodeled from the former Congreso Nacional quarters. On the 113th anniversary, in 1926, the library moved to its present building, erected on property purchased from the Monasterio de Santa Clara. The Historical Museum and the General Archives also moved into the same building.

The Library, during the course of its existence, added a number of important collections to the original donation from citizens and the library of the Jesuits. One of the early acquisitions, in 1846, was the Mariano Egaña collection of some 9,000 volumes. Other collections include the Diego Barros Arana library of some 15,000 volumes, the library of the Instituto Nacional which contained 13,519 volumes, and a donation from the Carnegie Corporation of 3,000 volumes by North American authors. Acquisitions also came from the libraries of Andrés Bello, José Ignacio Eyzaguirre, and Benjamín Vicuña Mackenna. However, the most outstanding single private library added to the collection came from José Toribio Medina, who donated 30,000 volumes and some 500 manuscripts. The contributions by Medina to the history of printing in the Spanish Americas remains unsurpassed.

The publishing program of the National Library began early. In 1854 it published a catalog of holdings, and followed in 1860 with the publication of the catalog of the Mariano Egaña collection, acquired in 1846. In 1886 it started *Anuario de la prensa chilena,* devoted to national publications. It continued with regularity until 1927 with publication of the *Anuario* listing national production for the year 1916 at which time publication was suspended. In 1963 Guillermo Feliu Cruz, director of the Library, renewed publication, and by 1965 Chilean national bibliography was up-to-date. He added a publication in 1952 listing national publications from 1877 through 1885, when the *Anuario* first began.

The National Library has issued numerous catalogs covering donations and special collections. Among them are the *Catálogo breve* (1926, 2 vols.) of printed materials and *Catálogo breve* (1928- ) of the Medina library. Two supplements, 1953-1954, were added to the catalog of printed materials. By 1951, four volumes had appeared of the manuscript collection. The Library also is publishing a series of historical documents, one related to the independence period and the other to the national period. A companion series to the *Anuario de la prensa chilena* is the *Anuario de publicaciones periódicas chilenas* (1915 ) under various titles. The Library has issued a *Boletín* (1901-1913; 2a. ép., 1929-1938) and the *Revista chilena y extranjera* (1913-1918). Currently it is publishing *Revista de bibliografía chilena* (1927- ). A complete record of the publications of the National Library was reported by Guillermo Feliu Cruz in *Las publicaciones de la Biblioteca Nacional, 1854-1963* (1964).

## Colombia

In Colombia, after the Jesuit Order was expelled from the dominions of Spain in 1767 and its libraries confiscated, the libraries were combined to form the Biblioteca de la Real Audiencia. On January 9, 1777, it opened for use in the old Seminario of the Jesuits. It remained in this spot until 1822 when it was relocated in the Colegio de San Bartolomé. It was closed during the independence movement until December 25, 1823, when it reopened as the National Library with a collection of about ten thousand volumes.

In 1938 a new, modern, five-story building was erected at a cost of a million pesos. The new building contains reading rooms, a map room, a room for the blind, children's library quarters, lecture and exhibition space, offices, and book storage areas. In connection with the inaugural ceremonies, the National Library sponsored an Exposición del Libro commemorative of the fourth centenary of the foundation of the city of Bogotá. Twenty countries were represented in the six thousand volume exhibit which became the property of the National Library at the close of the exhibition.

The National Library in the 1930s directed the establishment of popular libraries in municipal centers throughout the country. These libraries were referred to as the Bibliotecas Aldeanas in which, as a base, the National Library deposited the 101 volume set of a series representative of Colombian thought and literature, selected and published under the guidance of Daniel Samper Ortega, director of the Library.

A summer school to train librarians was held in 1942 directed by Rudolph H. Gjelsness, head of the Library School of the University of Michigan. Classes were held in the National Library. Further short courses were given in the Library in 1957 and 1958.

In 1957 the government obtained the services of two Spanish librarians and an archivist to study the reorganization of the National Library. They were followed in 1960 by a librarian from the United States to advise on an in-service training program for the staff of the Library.

The National Library has published a *Catálogo* (1855-1897, 6 vols.) of the book collection; a catalog (1897) of the Hispanic American books in the collection; two issues of the *Catálogo* (1917; 1935, 2 vols.) of newspapers published in Colombia; *Catálogo del "Fondo Anselmo* Pineda" (1935, 2 vols.); *Catálogo del "Fondo José María Quijano Otero"* (1935); the first edition of *Bibliografía de bibliografías colombianas* (1954) by Gabriel Giraldo Jaramillo; two editions of an adapted Spanish translation (1944; 2a. ed., 1948) of the Dewey decimal classification system; and *Revista* (1923-1930).

## Costa Rica

The National Library was founded on September 13, 1888. In 1890 the 536 volume library of the discontinued Universidad de Santo Tomás was incorporated in the National Library. The resources of the Library have been augmented from the deposit of government publications established by law in 1889, of which duplicates are used for exchange purposes. The deposit requirement has been extended to non-official presses. Of the five copies they must deposit, one remains in the collection of the National Library.

The present building was constructed in 1907 and has suffered from frequent earthquakes. The construction of a new building is reported underway for which the government of Venezuela has donated the sum of $150,000, estimated at a million colones Costa Rican currency.[8]

The National Library has published two editions of its *Catálogo* (1900; 1920-1929, in parts) and *Anuario bibliográfico costarricense* (1956- ) previously issued with titles, *Boletín bibliográfico* (1938-1945, typewritten) and *Publicaciones nacionales* 1946-1955). It published a *Boletín* (1898-1927) in sixty issues.

## Cuba

The National Library was established on October 18, 1901, by order of General Leonard Wood, United States Military Governor of Cuba. Its first quarters were in the La Fuerza fortress with Domingo Figarola-Caneda as director. Later it was moved to the second floor of the Maestranza building. By 1938 these quarters had become cramped, and in 1939, the Library was returned to the fortress until permanent quarters could be found.

The new location is in the Plaza Martí, a development in which the departments of government are being centralized. Here an ample modern building was dedicated on February 21, 1958. The new quarters have a capacity of a million volumes.

In 1960, the government purchased the Fernando Ortiz library of about 30,000 volumes, rich in Cuban history and literature and in anthropology and ethnology.

The National Library opened an Escuela de Capacitación Bibliotecaria in 1963 for the training of its personnel.

Among the publications of the National Library are: a catalog (1917) of the collection on international law, donated by Antonio Sánchez de Bustamante y Sirvén; *Los 120 años de la imprenta en Cuba, 1723-1843* (1951), catalog of an exhibit; *Impresos relativos a Cuba editados en los Estados Unidos de Norteamérica* (1956); *Bibliografía del teatro cubano* (1957) by José Rivero Muñiz; an index of documents in the Antonio Bachiller y Morales collection; *Revista* (1909-1912; 2a. ép., 1949- ) in which have appeared significant articles, special bibliographies, manuscripts in the Library, reports, and library statistics; and, quite recently, monographic bibliographies pertaining to agricultural and industrial products.

## Ecuador

The National Library, formerly the Biblioteca Pública, derives its original collection from the library of the Jesuit Order, suppressed during the colonial period. The Council of the Indies, in 1772, approved the opening of the Biblioteca Pública, then located in the Colegio de Quito. However, not until May 25,1792, after its transfer to the Universidad de Santo Tomás, was the library opened to the public. Eugenio Santa Cruz y Espejo was appointed the first librarian.

On October 7, 1912, the Archivo de la Presidencia was incorporated in the National Library. In the same year the Library was placed under the direction of the Consejo Superior de Educación, and legislation was adopted requiring the deposit of copy of nationally printed publications in the National Library.

In May 1922 the government purchased the Coliseum and relocated the National Library in these quarters.

Among the publications of the National Library are: a centennial anniversary volume (1922) in memory of Antonio José Sucre, the Gran Mariscal de Ayacucho; *Bibliografía geográfica ecuatoriana* (1927) by Luis Telmo Paz y Miño; several catalogs of its exhibits, one on journalism (1941) and one on Ecuadoran imprints, 1930-1940 (1940); and *Incunables y libros raros y curiosos de los siglos XV, XVI, XVII* (1959). The Library also published *Boletín* (1918-1919; n.s., 1920-1922; 1925-1927). It was continued in the one issue of *Revista* (1936) and in *Mensaje* (3a. ép., 1936-1940).


*El Salvador*

The National Library dates from July 5, 1870, when the government purchased the library of Cardinal Lambruschini, former librarian of the Vatican. It was located in the quarters of the Universidad Nacional and administered by it. In 1887 it became a dependency of the Ministerio de Instrucción Pública. On March 15, 1888, its services were extended to the public.

For a period of time, until May 1, 1938, the Library was housed in a series of rooms at the rear of the National Theater, when it was relocated in the building vacated by the Círculo Militar. The new quarters were modified in 1954 to provide more space for the shelving of books. Plans were presented in 1958 for a new building, and construction of it was completed quite recently.

The National Library opened four library stations to extend services to the more populated centers of San Salvador. Similar services are also extended to cities outside the capital. An in-service staff training program was started in 1955.

By a 1933 decree two copies of every national imprint must be deposited in the National Library.

The Library has published four editions of its *Catálogo* (1887 and *Apéndice*, 1890; 1896-1897, 3 vols.; 1905; 1930-1932, 2 vols.). It issued the *Bibliografía salvadoreña* (1952) a preliminary listing of a national retrospective bibliography; *Bibliografía salvadoreña, 1945-1946* (1948); and *Anuario bibliográfico salvadoreña* (1952) of which previous compilations, 1947-1951, had appeared in issues of its *Revista* and *Anaqueles*. A library bulletin with varying titles has appeared consecutively since 1920, except for the years 1922-1928, 1947, and 1950: *Boletín* (1920-1921; 2a.-3a. ép., 1932-1946), *Revista bibliográfica científica literaria* (1929-1931), *Revista* (1948-1949), and *Anaqueles* (1951- ).

*Guatemala*

The National Library, established by presidential decree on October 18, 1879, was formed by the libraries of religious orders suppressed by the government; the library of the discontinued Sociedad Económica; the several libraries of the Universidad de San Carlos; the library of the Escuela Politécnica; and the library of the Escuela de Artes y Oficios. It was originally quartered in a room of the Sociedad Económica headquarters, but on April 25, 1881 it was given space in the Asamblea Nacional for more convenient access to the public.

After the 1917-1918 earthquakes, which devastated the city and the quarters of the Asamblea Nacional, the collection of the National Library was moved into the building that became the Facultad de Ciencias Físico-Matemáticas of the University. In 1925 it was installed in a new building that gave the Library little room for growth. In September 1957, the government dedicated a new modern building in which the National Library now is located.

Since 1957, the National Library has the responsibility for the national publications exchange program, and is the distributor of the publications of the Ministry of Education. It extended services through the creation of a Biblioteca Circulante in Guatemala City and helped establish others in the faraway province of Petén.

In 1963 the National Library acquired the extensive library of Gilberto Valenzuela, particularly rich in Guatemalan imprints, from which Valenzuela compiled *Bibliografía guatemalteca* (1821-1860). His son Gilberto Valenzuela Reyna, continued the compilation through 1960.

The National Library published a *Catálogo* (1932) of its holdings; *Indice bibliográfico guatemalteco* (1951-1959) continued as *Anuario bibliográfico guatemalteco* (1960- ); and its *Boletín* (1932-1941; 1945) with varying titles, *Boletín de museos y bibliotecas* (1941-1945) and *Revista* (1962- ).

## Haiti

On September 10, 1939, the president of the Republic laid the cornerstone of the building of newly established Bibliothéque Nationale. On the occasion, M. Léon Leleau, Secretary of the Direction Générale des Travaux Publics, addressed the assembly.

While he was director of the Library, Max Bissainthe compiled a comprehensive bibliography of Haiti, *Dictionnaire de bibliographie haitienne* (Washington, D.C., 1951, 1052 pages).

## Honduras

The National Library was founded by decree, February 11, 1880, as a section of the National Archives and Library and was dedicated on August 27, 1880. It opened for use in a first floor room of the University building. During the civil strife of 1893 to 1895, the collection was partially destroyed. A new building was completed in 1905 and occupied by both sections, the National Archives and the National Library.

During the period of February through November 1967, a library science and archives management course was given at the Library. The National Archives and Library publishes the *Revista* (1904- ). The *Revista* is also the organ of the Sociedad de Geografía e Historia de Honduras. The Library published a *Boletín* (1939-1947); *Anuario bibliográfico* for the year 1961; and *Catálogo metódico* (1915). Several inventories of records in the archives section were published. The Mobile Unit of UNESCO microfilmed records of which the National Library and Archives published *Lista de materiales microfilmados* (1958).

## Mexico

The government of Mexico supports three libraries that are national in scope: the Biblioteca de México with 80,000 volumes, directed by María Teresa Chávez, the Hemeroteca Nacional with 116,000 volumes, directed by Gustavo A. Pérez Trejo, before 1944 a department of the National Library; and the Biblioteca Nacional.

The National Library was founded in 1857, after several unsuccessful attempts. Over 80,000 books from the suppressed religious orders and 10,600 volumes from the University formed the basic collection. Fernando Ramírez was named director. During the European intervention, 1861-1867, the Library closed and the books were stored in the Museum. In 1867 it was opened for service in the same locale in which it still functions, the church of St. Augustine. Systematic organization of the collection began under the administration of José Vigil who took charge in 1880.

The National Library is under the administration of the University. When the University was relocated in Ciudad Universitaria, only the working collections of the University Library were transferred, whereas the older historical and research materials of the National Library remained in the quarters of the church of St. Augustine, although preparations had been made also to move the entire Library to Ciudad Universitaria.

When it became evident that the National Library would remain in the same quarters, steps were taken to remodel the building to improve services and to make better use of space for the shelving of books.

A new copyright law was put into effect requiring authors, publishers, and printers to deposit two copies of all nationally produced publications in the National Library and in the Congressional Library. Failure to do so makes the producer liable to a fine of from 50 to 500 pesos.

The National Library has an active Instituto Bibliográfico Mexicano and issues the publications of the Institute, as for example *La literatura jurídica española del Siglo de Oro en la Nueva España* (1959) by Javier Malagón Barceló; *Léxico bibliográfico* (1959) Juan Bautista Iguíniz; *Catálogo descriptivo de los libros impresos en la ciudad de Salamanca en el siglo XVI* (1961) to be found in the Biblioteca Pública, Guadalajara, Mexico, compiled by Robert Duclas; and *Antonio Espinosa* (1962) biography and imprints of the second printer in Mexico, by Alexander A. M. Stols. It publishes a series, *Bibliografías mexicanas contemporáneas* in which one may find bibliographical information on such Mexican personalities as Alfonso Reyes, José Vasconcelos, Elías Nandino, and Jaime Torres Bodet. The Library published its *Catálogos* (1889-1908, 9 vols.) with *Suplemento* (1895; 1903) to some sections of the *Catálogos;* the *Catálogo* (1897) of the Biblioteca Nocturna; and *Catálogo especial de obras mexicanas o sobre México* (1911). It issued *Biblos* (1919-1922 in 198 numbers; 2a. ép., 1925-1926 in fifteen numbers). It continues to issue its *Bolétin* (1904-1929; 2a. ép., 1950- ). In 1967 it published *Anuario bibliográfico* (1958- ), and its Instituto Bibliográfico began issue of Bibliografía mexicana (en./feb. 1967- ).

## Nicaragua

The National Library was established in 1881 as a dependency of the Ministerio de Instrucción Pública. Fortunately, its location was outside the area of the fire that followed the 1931 earthquake. In 1937 the Ministry authorized the classification of the collection by the Dewey decimal system. On December 11, 1939, the government annexed the Archivo Nacional to the National Library.

In 1937, in his survey of libraries and archives in Central America and the West Indies, the writer found the National Library housed in a former private residence with noticeable lack of space, with those books shelved on the patio gallery subject to dampness during the rainy season. This has been corrected with a move into more suitable quarters in a new government building.

In 1965 the second Curso de Capacitación para Auxiliares de Bibliotecas was given in the National Library under the sponsorship of the National University and the Library Association of Nicaragua.

The National Library has in its record of publications only its *Catálogo* (1882) with a new issue in 1906.

## Panama

The government of Panama by executive decree, February 2, 1942, established the National Library with Ernesto J. Castillero Reyes as director. The basis for the collection was the Biblioteca Colón, a municipal library in Panama City, founded on September 17, 1892 and inaugurated on October 12 to commemorate the four hundredth anniversary of the discovery of America by Columbus. The present quarters are too small, and studies have been made relative to cost of land, building plans, and needs to 1980.

In 1959 the National Library offered a four-week Cursillo Intensivo de Capacitación Bibliotecaria which was repeated in 1960.

In its *Circular,* the National Library has issued a series of informative leaflets on services and plans for extension. In another series, *Publicaciones,* it has published *Introducción a la bibliografía panameña 1618-1945* (1946) by Juan Antonio Susto; *La Universidad Interamericana* (1943) by Ernesto J. Castillero Reyes; *Bibliotecas juveniles* (1952) a bibliography of books for children, issued on the occasion of inaugurating a service for children; and various reports of the director. In addition to the above mentioned work by Susto on national bibliography, the Library published *Bibliografía panameña (1954).* It has published *Catálogo de libros panameños* listing the books of two exhibits sent, one to Rio de Janeiro in 1946 and the other to Artemisa, Cuba, in 1948.

## Paraguay

According to José Segundo Decoud, Paraguayan statesman, the National Library was founded in 1871, but the first law relative to it, recorded in the *Registro oficial*, was promulgated on September 21, 1887. It provided for a commission of five members to direct the Library and to administer its funds. On April 25, 1901, the Library was placed under the Ministerio de Instrucción Pública.

In 1915, the Library opened a section of Paraguayan works of some 4,460 volumes, among them old Spanish documents on the history of the River Plate region and of the Jesuits from 1534-1600 who had established active missions in Paraguay.

Three publications of the National Library are on record: *Catálogo* (1904); *Bibliografía paraguaya* (1906), a catalog of the Biblioteca Pública "Solana López" to which Jones refers as "acquired in part by the government from Enrique Solano López, now a public *library in Asunción*",[9] and a report, 1933, on the organization of the Library.

## Peru

The National Library was founded in Lima by a decree of José de San Martín on August 28, 1821, placing it under the Ministerio de Gobernación. It opened for service on February 8, 1822, with Mariano Arce as director. A further decree, August 31, 1822, extended services to the public for which opening ceremonies were held on September 17, 1822. At that time the collection numbered 11,256 volumes. By 1880 it had reached 55,127 volumes, of which some 7,777 volumes came as a legacy in 1830 from Miguel Fuentes Pacheco.

On February 28, 1881, the invading Chilean army used the National Library as quarters for soldiers. When peace was restored between the two countries, the books of the National Library numbered scarcely 700 volumes. However, through the diligent efforts of the director, Ricardo Palma, over 14,000 volumes were recovered. At the reopening on July 28, 1884, a total of 27,894 volumes was available for use.

Further disaster followed the Library. On the night of May 9, 1943 the National Library and the Sociedad Geográfica de Lima, housed in the same building, suffered irreparable loss by fire. An inventory taken after the fire revealed that only twenty-nine rarities and some 1,009 other items of the 130,000 volume collection were saved.

A sympathetic response was immediate to the call for help. By 1945, 22,894 volumes had been donated from twenty-two countries for the purpose of reconstituting the collection. The government also purchased, in 1945, the 28,000 volume library collected by Agustín P. Justo, an Argentine bibliophile, of which about 90 percent was Americana. At the same time the construction of a new building was undertaken, planned for a capacity of a million volumes.

On August 8, 1962, the government transferred the Departamento de Fomento de Bibliotecas Populares y Escolares to the National Library, thus enabling the Library to develop public and school libraries in the nation through purchase and distribution of books. In Lima, services are extended by bookmobile to four library stations.

Under law 10847, the proceeds from a special tax on sales of jewelry and luxury items were set aside for (1) construction of an annex building to the National Library, and (2) the creation of the San Martín Fund, dedicated to the improvement of library extension services of the Departamento de Fomento de Bibliotecas Populares y Escolares.

The National Library established its Library School in November 1943 with assistance from the American Library Association. During the first year of the School, librarians from the United States and Cuba, supplemented by local librarians, formed the teaching staff. The Library was unable to continue the full teaching program of the first year and admitted for the second year only personnel of the National Library and reduced instruction to procedures in cataloging and classification. Subsequently, the School enlarged its program of studies and admitted persons who wished to follow the profession as a career.

The Library offered short courses in technical processes to personnel of libraries in Lima and in the provinces in 1963 and in 1964.

The Library published *Anales del Cuzco, 1600-1750* (1901); *Apuntes históricos del Peru* (1902); *Catálogo de libros* (1891) of books in the Salón América by Ricardo Palma; a 617 page manuscript, *Memorias histórico-físicas-apologéticas de América Meridional* (1904) by José Eusebio de Llano y Zapata, donated by the author to Carlos III of Spain and now in possession of the National Library; and reports of the director of the National Library (1888- ). It publishes the *Anuario bibliográfico peruano* (1943- ); *Fénix* (1944- ), a journal of excellent quality; and *Boletín* (1919-1920; 1943- ).

## Uruguay

Under terms of his will, January 10, 1814, José Manuel Pérez Castellano left his house, books, and special funds for the establishment of a public library. He named José Raymundo Guerra as librarian, but since he could not serve, Dámaso Antonio Larrañaga, also named in the will, became librarian. On May 26, 1816, the library opened for service in upper rooms of the Fuerte de Gobierno.

The library suffered the ravages of war when on January 21, 1817, the invading Portuguese general ordered it removed to provide accommodations for his troops. It was stored in the basement of the building for several months when permission was secured for its transfer to the homes of Pedro Berro and Larrañaga. The Portuguese general reestablished the library and even donated a number of volumes to the collection.

The Brazilian forces moved into Montevideo in 1824, causing

further damage to the book collection. It was removed from its quarters and left in a disorganized condition for some years.

The Constitutional Assembly in 1830 recommended that the library, originally opened for services in 1816, be reestablished, but no action was taken until 1837 when the government named a Committee to implement the recommendation of the Assembly, and in 1838, under the administration of the Committee, the Library was opened for services. In 1840 the Committee named Francisco Acuña de Figueroa director of the Library.

The administration of the National Library was placed under the Junta Económica on July 21, 1859, where it remained until July 22, 1872, when it was made a dependency of the Ministerio de Gobierno. However, in 1885 it was finally settled in the Ministerio de Justicia, Religión y Instrucción, today the Ministerio de Instrucción Pública.

Attempts to provide adequate quarters began as far back as 1881. In 1911 the Library was transferred to the building of the Facultad de Ciencias Jurídicas y Sociales of the Universidad de la República. On August 25, 1942, the foundation stone for a new building was laid, and on completion of the building in the early 1950s, it moved into the new quarters. Subsequently, bookstacks were enlarged in an area under the street.

The Library maintains the office, established in 1912, for the registration of copyright.

In the middle 1950s a new division was added, the Centro de Documentación Científica, Técnica y Económica, which as a first project gathered information on the holdings of scientific, technical, and economic periodicals in libraries of Uruguay.

The Centro has published a *Catálogo* (1954) of the scientific, technical, and economic periodicals published in Uruguay since 1850, and a *Catálogo* (1961) of similar periodicals published currently. In fulfillment of the above mentioned project, the Centro began publication of an *Inventario* and by 1965 had issued, in twenty parts, periodical holdings of thirty-seven libraries.

The National Library has published *Anales de la bibliografía uruguaya* for the year 1895; *Anuario de la bibliografía uruguaya,* *1946-  ; Biblioteca Nacional,* 1816 (1942); and *Biblioteca Nacional* *del Uruguay* (1946) detailing plans for reorganization. From time to time in recent years it has issued a listing of periodicals published in Montevideo and in the interior of the country, new titles of periodicals, and periodicals which have ceased publication. Among bibliographies of Uruguayan personalities are Carlos Vaz Ferreira, Eduardo Acevedo Díaz, José Artigas, Juan Antonio Lavalleja, Francisco Acuña de Figueroa, Pedro Figari, and José Enrique Rodó. It issued two numbers of its *Boletín* (1944-1945), and in 1966 published the first number of *Revista.*

*Venezuela*

The National Library, after unsuccessful attempts at establishment in 1811, 1831, and 1833, culminated in success on April 19, 1841, following the 1839 organization of the Liceo Venezolano by a group of young intellectuals whose objective was the creation of a national library. The Liceo succeeded in bringing together two thousand volumes and two thousand pesos in funds which were turned over to the government. Initially located in the Convento de San Francisco, it was relocated, December 17, 1852, in the Universidad Central, where it remained until it was moved into a separate building in 1903.

A new building was completed and occupied in 1912, which together with an annex building, begun in 1938, was to give the National Library a capacity of approximately 800,000 volumes. However, on March 13, 1958, the government authorized the construction of a new building in order to facilitate the modernization of library services, enlargement of the program of cultural events, and development of popular libraries on a national level.

In 1939 and 1940 the Library contracted Annita M. Ker from the Library of Congress to assist in the reorganization of the collection; and in 1946, Mrs. Anne V. Gard, also from the Library of Congress, was contracted as a consultant.

The Rudolph Dolge collection of some twenty thousand volumes was added to the Library through purchase in 1941. It contained mostly Venezuelan imprints, books on Venezuela, and a large collection of newspapers and periodicals dating from about 1810, among them a complete file of the government gazette. In 1958 the Library acquired the Víctor M. Arcaya collection.

The National Library maintains an active international exchange program through its Servicio de Canje y Propaganda.

The National Library is responsible for the *Anuario bibliográfico venezolano, 1942- .* It published *Bibliografía de don Arístides Rojas* (1944); at least four editions of the *Catálogo* of its Biblioteca Circulante; a series, *Catálogo analítico* (1956- ) in which have appeared a bibliography of Andrés Bello (no. 1), an index to the *Revista nacional de cultura* (no. 3, 1956; no. 5, 1961), and an index to Venezuelan periodicals (no. 4, 1959). The donations of books to the National Library of Colombia and to the National Library of Peru were listed in *Libros venezolanos* (1945, 1946). It published *Escritores venezolanos fallecidos entre 1942 a 1947* (1948) and various catalogs of exhibits. It publishes its *Boletín* (1923-1933; 2a. ép., 1936; 3a. ép., 1959- ) and *Indice bibliográfico* (1956- ).

NOTES

1. *Boletín oficial,* Buenos Aires 69, no. 19,534 (mayo 18, 1961):1.
2. Arthur E. Gropp, *Guide to Libraries and Archives in Central America and the West Indies,* p. 522.
3. For a listing of the publications of national libraries, the following publication may be consulted: *Bibliografía sobre las bibliotecas nacionales de los países latino-americanas y sus publicaciones,* compiled by Arthur E. Gropp, 1960.
4. The *Bibliografía brasileira* is compiled by the Instituto Nacional do Livro, an independent body, located in the National Library.
5. Adelpha Silva Rodrigues, *Desenvolvimento da biblioteconomia em S. Paulo* (Rio de Janeiro: Impr. Nacional, 1945), pp. 9-10.

6. Arthur E. Gropp, "Education for Librarianship in Latin America," *Library Quarterly* 18, no. 2 (April 1948): 110.
7. Arthur E. Gropp, *Bibliography of Latin American Bibliographies* (Metuchen, N. J.: Scarecrow Press, 1968), p. 338, item 5723.
8. *La Nación,* San José, mar. 1, 1969.
9. C. K. Jones, *Bibliography of Latin American Bibliographies.* 2d ed. (Washington, D.C.: Government Printing Office, 1942), item 2641.

BIBLIOGRAPHY

Argentina. Biblioteca Nacional. *Biografía de la Biblioteca Nacional.* Crónicas argentinas, no. 1. Buenos Aires: 1957.
Babcock, Charles Edwin. "The National Library of Honduras". *Bulletin,* Pan American Union, Washington, D. C., 61 (Nov. 1927):1106-1108.
Basadre, Jorge. "La Biblioteca Nacional de Lima, 1943-1945". *Fenix,* Biblioteca Nacional, Lima, 2 (1er. sem. 1945): 312-52; 3 (2.º sem. 1945):642-658.
Castillero Reyes, Ernesto de Jesús. *La Biblioteca Nacional de Panamá; su origen, su inauguración y su futuro desarrollo.* Publicaciones de la Biblioteca Nacional, 1. Panamá: Impr. Nacional, 1942.
"Coleccion de leyes, decretos y demas resoluciones concernientes a la Biblioteca Nacional". *Revista,* Biblioteca Nacional, La Habana, año 1, no.3/6 (sept./dic. 1909):66-69.
Coronado, Francisco de Paula. "La Biblioteca Nacional: su historia y propósitos". *Revista,* Biblioteca Nacional, La Habana, 2ª. ép., 1 (feb. 1950):7-12.
Cruzat Vera, Manuel. "The National Library of Chile". *Bulletin* Pan American Union, Washington, D.C., 62 (Sept. 1928):998-1002.
"Datos históricos sobre la Biblioteca Nacional de Venezuela." *Boletín,* Biblioteca Nacional, Caracas (nov. 1923):5-7.
Escobar, Julio César. "Reseña histórica de la Biblioteca Nacional". *Revista,* Ateneo de El Salvador, San Salvador, año 21, no. 146 (1933):80-82.

Esdaile, Arundell James K. *National Libraries of the World.* 2d ed. completely rev. by F. J. Hill. London: Library Association, 1957.

Feliu Cruz, Guillermo. *Las publicaciones de la Biblioteca Nacional, 1854-1963.* Santiago: Dirección de Bibliotecas, Archivos y Museos, 1964.

Forero, Manuel José. "Apuntaciones para la historia de la Biblioteca Nacional". *Boletín de historia y antigüedades,* Bogotá, año 30, no. 342-343 (abr./mayo 1943): 509-516.

Gonzalez Obregon, Luis. *La Biblioteca Nacional de México, 1833-1910.* México, D.F.: 1910.

Gonzalez, Luis Felipe. *La obra cultural de Don Miguel Obregón.* Publicación, Escuela Normal de Costa Rica, no. 2. San José, C.R.: Impr. Nacional, 1919.

Gropp, Arthur Eric. "Asociaciones de bibliotecarios en los países latinoamericanos". *Boletín* Asociación de Bibliotecarios Diplomados del Uruguay, Montevideo, año 1, no. 2 (agosto 1948): 2-8.

―――. *Bibliografía sobre las bibliotecas nacionales de los países latinoamericanos y sus publicaciones.* Bibliographic series, Columbus Memorial Library, 50. Washington, D. C.: Unión Panamericana, 1960.

―――. *Guide to Libraries and Archives in Central America and the West Indies.* Publication, Middle American Research Institute, 10. New Orleans, La.: Tulane University of Louisiana, 1941.

―――, and Ker, Annita M. "Notes on Library Events and Trends". *Handbook of Latin American Studies,* 4-12 (1938-1946).

Groussac, Paul. *Noticia histórica sobre la Biblioteca de Buenos Aires (1810-1901).* Buenos Aires: Impr. de Coni Hermanos, 1901.

Inter-American library relations, Columbus Memorial Library, Pan American Union, Washington, D.C., no. 1- , Apr./June 1955- .

Levene, Ricardo. *El fundador de la Biblioteca Pública de Buenos Aires (estudio histórico sobre la fundación y formación de la Biblioteca Pública en 1810 hasta su apertura en marzo de 1812).* Buenos Aires: 1938.

Mello, José Alexandre Teixeira de. "Resumo histórico da Biblioteca Nacional do Rio de Janeiro". *Annaes,* Biblioteca Nacional, Rio de Janeiro, 19 (1897): 219-242.

"Para la historia de la Biblioteca Nacional". *Boletín,* Biblioteca Nacional, Lima, 1 (en. 1944): 151-154; (abr. 1944): 264-269; (jul. 1944): 383-388.

Quesada, Vicente Gaspar. *La vida intelectual en la América española durante los siglos XVI, XVII y XVIII.* Buenos Aires, La Cultura Argentina, 1917. Contains information on the history of the National Library of Colombia.

Sandy, Gerald B. "An Account of the National Libraries of the Spanish Speaking Countries of South America". Thesis, University of Illinois, 1932.

Scarone, Arturo. *La Biblioteca Nacional de Montevideo; reseña histórica con motivo del primer centenario de su fundación.* Montevideo: Tall. Graf. del Estado, 1916.

Silva Castro, Raúl. "Biblioteca Nacional y biblioteca pública". *Anales,* Universidad de Chile, Santiago, 108 (3°-4° trim. 1949): 238-252.

————. "Los primeros años de la Biblioteca Nacional de Chile (1813-1824)". *Revista de historia de América,* México, Quinto." D.F., 42 (dic. 1956): 355-407.

Teran, Enrique. "Fundación de la Biblioteca Nacional de Quito". *Mensaje,* Biblioteca Nacional, Quito, 8-9 (oct. 1938): 154-160.

Vela, David. "Historia de la fundación de la Biblioteca Nacional." *Boletín,* Biblioteca Nacional, Guatemala, año 1, no. 10 (agosto 1934): 347-353.

# 10 / National Libraries and Bibliographies in Africa

### HANS E. PANOFSKY
*Northwestern University*

Today's scholarly research on Africa has come to rely increasingly on information generated in Africa. This material consists of the publications of the various governmental agencies and private publishers. There has been an increasing volume of publishing in African languages for a number of years, some of which has been issued by missionary presses. Significant in both content and quantity is the material published by voluntary associations such as trade unions, women's groups, and agricultural organizations. However, a great deal of the literature relevant to Africa is still published outside the African continent, including that written by Africans. Most African publishing concerns are small; some European publishers have branches in Africa with varying levels of African control. The book trade, with few exceptions, is more concerned with the distribution of imported products than with the handling of national publications. The nature and function of national libraries in Africa must be viewed against this background of bibliographic complexity. Together with the national archives, national libraries have the basic function of keeping the national records and of retrieving them. In Africa, with its many demands for trained manpower, the effective operation of these organizations presents a difficult task indeed.

This paper attempts to describe briefly the present state of national libraries and national bibliographies in Africa, as well as bibliographical work pertinent to Africa performed elsewhere. One

should perhaps stress here that because of the extremely wide
dispersal of African material and the necessity for efficient retrieval,
the need for worldwide cooperation has been acute, and only in part
has this need been met. One of the few functioning arrangements is
the Cooperative African Microform Project (CAMP), administered
by the Center for Research Libraries (CRL).[1]

National libraries are institutions that may or may not carry that
name, for example, the Bibliothèque Nationale, the Library of
Congress, or the British Museum. They strive to acquire all
publications issued within a country, usually by means of a
depository clause in a copyright law. They try to collect whatever is
published about a country irrespective of place of publication. They
collect not merely monographs and serials, (published privately or
by governments) official and unofficial documents, (including all
forms of ephemera) but also such material as maps, posters, motion
picture films, and sound recordings. Frequently they function as
national archives, and may also serve as research or public libraries.

The national library is responsible for issuing lists, that is,
bibliographies, of material it receives. It may strive to coordinate the
work of other libraries within the country by maintaining a national
union catalog. The national library may lend from its own collection
to other libraries or individuals, and it sometimes arranges for a loan
from within the country or from abroad. The national library is
frequently concerned with questions of training and for the setting
of professional standards. It is usually the main link between
libraries within the nation with libraries abroad. The national library
may be the only library in a country, or it may be one of many,
although it is not necessarily the strongest institution in any given
country. National libraries are usually the source of the most
comprehensive bibliographies prepared in a country. Indeed, the
most significant function of a national library is to prepare the
national bibliography.

The trend all over the world is to have national libraries, although
Canada established one only in 1953. In broad perspective, the
rational solution, because of shortages of trained manpower and

funds, would be to have regional libraries to serve groups of small states. In practice, national pride does not make this possible. It should, however, be possible to have one effective multi-purpose library in each country. This one library could be labeled National Library at one entrance, Public Library at another, University Library at a third, and perhaps Government Archives on a fourth side. The tendency in Africa and elsewhere is to set up too many libraries where only one can function effectively.

Let us now examine the national libraries, regardless of their names, in the different countries of Africa, taking a more or less geographical approach; and let us also examine the national bibliographies and other bibliographical tools that permit access to retrospective and current literature.

The United Arab Republic (Egypt) has, of course, a long and distinguished history of libraries. In fact, one of the very first libraries in the world was established in Alexandria. Among the many retrospective bibliographies one can recommend Ibrahim-Hilmy, *The Literature of Egypt and the Sudan from the Earliest Time to the Year 1885,* originally published in London between 1886 and 1888, and recently reprinted by Kraus.[2] The national library to turn to more modern times, issues an annual bibliography that includes books and pamphlets, new serials, and government publications, an accessions list rather than a national bibliography.[3] Another useful accessions list is the one issued by the Library of Congress' Public Law 480 office in Cairo, *Middle East.*

Turning from the plenty of Egypt, although much of the material cited is hard to locate even when one has mastered Arabic, we move to Libya. The government libraries in Tripoli and Benghazi perform the functions of a national library. At the end of 1966 work on a national library building was begun in Benghazi. There the national bibliography will be issued.[4] Two retrospective bibliographies, although now old, are useful. Roy Wells Hill has prepared *A Bibliography of Libya,* issued by the Department of Geography of the University of Durham.[5] Mohammed Murabet's *A Bibliography of Libya,* is one written with particular reference to sources available in libraries and public archives in Tripoli, was published in Valetta, Malta, by the Progress Press in 1959. It is a classified bibliography containing 710 entries. Great credit is due to Philip Ward and the Oasis Oil Company of Libya for issuing a *Survey of Libyan Bibliographical Resources* (2d ed., Tripoli, Libya Publishing House, 1965).[6] This short guide, in English and Arabic, describes the main governmental and commercial libraries, and it includes a guide to the Libyan press and even discusses sources of supply and library classification.

Henry Spencer Ashbee compiled *A Bibliography of Tunisia from the Earliest Times to the End of 1888.* (London, Dulau, 1889.) It is available in the United States at the Library of Congress and at Harvard University. Tunisia does have its Association tunisienne des Documentalistes, Bibliothecaires et Archivistes that in 1966 began to issue the quarterly *ATD Bulletin.*[7] A national bibliography is in preparation.[8]

Algeria has a university library that enjoys the rather large scale support of the Ford Foundation, administered through the American Library Association. This library contains material mainly in French.

A fine retrospective bibliography is R. L. Playfair's *Bibliography of Algeria and Supplement* (London, 1888), and also Charles Tailliart, *L'Algérie dans la littérature francaise* (Paris, Champion, 1925). The latter work, as may be inferred from the title, is a scholarly essay rather than a bibliography in the restricted sense of that term. In 1964 the Bibliothèque Nationale issued the first section of its *Bibliographie de l'Algérie,* which unfortunately ceased after five or six of the classified sections were issued.[9]

Finally, among the North African states, we shall mention Morocco. Here again there are ancient libraries and another *Bibliography* compiled by Playfair and published in London in 1892. *Bibliographie marocaine 1923-1933* (Paris, Larose, 1937) consists of reprints from *Hesperis* and has been continued to be undated in that journal.[10]

The National Library in Rabat has a mimeographed list of the more than 500,000 pages of manuscripts and books, microfilmed by the UNESCO Mobile Microfilm Unit, at the National Library and Archives.[11]

There is, although now rather dated, a bibliography prepared at the Library of Congress in 1957: *North and Northeast Africa,* a selected and annotated list of writings, 1951-1957, compiled by Helen F. Conover.[12] Highly recommended is the *Annuaire de l'Afrique du Nord,* prepared by the Centre de Recherche sur l'Afrique Mediterranéene (CRAM) and published by the Centre de la Recherche Scientifique (CNRS).[13] This annual has been issued for the years 1961 onward. Each volume discusses scholarly work and contains a chronology and an excellent classified bibliography on Libya, Algeria, Morocco, and Tunisia. Very useful also is the *Maghreb Digest* (the first volume, covering 1963, was known as the *Maghreb Labor Digest*), a quarterly journal issued by the Middle East and North African Program of the University of Southern California, containing abstracts, a chronology, and reviews.[14]

We turn now to the countries of former French West Africa. Mauritania, large in area and small in population, contains several fine private scholarly libraries. The Ministry of Education has appointed librarians to operate libraries in three of the cities.[15] There are at least two useful retrospective bibliographies: Charles Toupet, "Orientation bibliographique sur la Mauritanie" in Institut français [now Fondamental] d' Afrique Noire (IFAN) *Bulletin,* (series B, volume 21, numbers 1-2, January-April 1959, pp. 201-239, and volume 24, numbers 3-4, July-October 1962, pp. 594-613) and France, Service des affaires sahariennes, *Etude de bibliographie du Sahara français et des régions avoisinantes* written by Bernard Blaudin de Thé ([Algiers] 1959). There is, however, no current bibliographical service.

Mali has numerous libraries, including a national one, which, however does not issue any bibliographies.[16] A new building was under construction for the national library at the end of 1967.[17] An excellent retrospective bibliography was recently compiled by Madame Paule Brasseur, titled *Bibliographie générale du Mali . . .*

(Dakar, IFAN, 1964, IFAN catalogues et documents no. 16).[18] This work is somewhat supplemented by: Charles H. Cutter, "Mali: A Bibliographical Introduction." (*African Studies Bulletin*, vol. 9, no. 3, December 1966, pp. 74-87.)

The main library in Upper Volta is that of the former IFAN Center, now the Centre Voltaique de la Recherche Scientifique.[19] Françoise Izard has just issued, in the *Recherches* series no. 7, "A Bibliography of Upper Volta, 1956-1965."

Nigèr is truly ill supplied with libraries and bibliographies. The IFAN-CNRS Centre does have a scholarly library, however, of some 3,000 volumes and occasionally issues *Etudes nigèriennes.*

The coastal countries of franco-phonic West Africa have better developed library systems. Senegal's libraries are many and distinguished. It is necessary to visit them to gather bibliographical and, of course, other information on the country's past and present. There are, however, some exceptions: The *Bulletin bibliographique des archives du Senegal* lists the receipt of government publications. The *Bulletin,* issued with varying frequency, started to appear in 1963. Useful also is Laurence Porges, *Elements de bibliographie senegalaise, 1959-1963* (Dakar, Archives Nationales, Centre de Documentation, 1964), a classified, selective bibliography of official and quasi-official publications found in the Archives Nationales and other depositories of Senegal. The IFAN library and the one at the University of Dakar, as well as the one at the national archives, are impressive indeed.[20]

The Ivory Coast, which is making giant strides economically, has likewise increased the number of volumes published each year. It is, however, a country that is not yet very advanced bibliographically, nor in the size or quantity of its libraries. Useful is *Essai d'une bibliographie sur la Cote d'Ivoire*, (Paris, Organization for Economic Cooperation [OECD], 1964) an alphabetical list of 661 references largely pertinent to questions of socioeconomic development. There is no national library, and no national bibliography is being issued. The new University Library has some 25,000 volumes. Students of Africana are likely to find more useful material among the 6,000 volumes at the Centre National de Documentation of the Centre des Sciences Humaines (formerly IFAN).[21]

Dahomey, Guinea, and Togo have national libraries. A bibliography of books published in Guinea since independence, 1958-1963, has appeared in *Rechèrches africaines.*[22] There is also an OECD bibliography on Guinea, issued in Paris in 1965, a work similar to the one on the Ivory Coast.

For those who have access mainly to French scholarly publications indispensable is Edmond A. Joucla's *Bibliographie de l'Afrique occidentale française* ... (Paris, 1937) containing almost 10,000 entries. Excellent too is the working document prepared by Paule Brasseur and Jean-François Maurel, "Les sources bibliographiques de l'Afrique de l'Ouest d'éxpression Française" (Dakar, 1967). Everyone, but particularly North Americans, will find most helpful: *French-Speaking West Africa*, a guide to official publications, compiled by Julian W. Witherell (Library of Congress, 1967)[23] A North American location, or if need be another one, is given for the 2,431 items listed.

From French-speaking West Africa we turn to English-speaking West Africa, excluding in our discussion the university libraries which are the subject of chapter 6.

The sovereign state of The Gambia, or just Gambia, has, considering its size, a surprisingly large volume of publications, both governmental and private. Six independent journals are published in Bathurst, none of which has a circulation of more than 250-300 copies.[24] The second edition of David P. Gamble's *Bibliography of the Gambia* (Bathurst, Government Printer, 1967) contains 1,649 entries.

Library service in Sierra Leone, besides that given at Fourah Bay College and at some special government libraries, is the function of the Sierra Leone Library Board, a statutory body, financed by the government to provide a national library service to individuals, schools, and government. The Board must direct a collection of about 100,000 volumes by now. One of the functions of the Board has been to issue, since 1962, an annual list of English language books and pamphlets received by the Board. Other languages in which publications take place are Mende and Bo.

Some retrospective bibliographies deserve special mention. One such is P. E. H. Hair's "A Bibliographical Guide to Sierra Leone, 1460-1650; 1650-1800," *Sierra Leone Studies* (new series no. 10, June 1958, pp. 41-49). There is also the work of a former Colonial Secretary, Harry C. Luke, *A Bibliography of Sierra Leone* (second edition, London, Oxford University Press, 1925). Its 230 pages contain 1,103 titles under seven headings. Hans M. Zell has compiled *A Bibliography of Non-Periodical Literature on Sierra Leone, 1925-1966,* (excluding Sierra Leone government publications; Sierra Leone, Fourah Bay College Bookshop , 1966) a classified list of 239 items. Zell also notes G. J. William's *A Bibliography of Sierra Leone, 1925-1965*, as being in preparation and records that it was scheduled to be published in 1967 as a special supplement to *Sierra Leone Studies*. The Williams bibliography is to include some 2,000 references, including periodical literature. Audrey A. Walker, formerly of the African Section of the Library of Congress has compiled *Official Publications of Sierra Leone and Gambia* (Washington, D.C., Library of Congress, 1963).[25]

Turning to Liberia, and excluding its university and colleges, we may mention the National Public Library, which in 1963 had two branches and some 12,800 volumes.[26] Liberia is tricky, bibliographically speaking. There are few aids indeed. One of them, compiled by Marvin D. Solomon and Warren L. d'Azevedo, is called *A General Bibliography of the Republic of Liberia* (Evanston, Illinois, 1962, Northwestern University. Working papers in social science, no. 1.)[27] Over 2,000 entries are reproduced from cards of what was intended to be a working draft for the publication of a revised and amplified version. Note also Svend E. Holsoe of DePauw University in Indiana who has published "A Bibliography of Liberian Government Documents." (*African Studies Bulletin,* Volume 11, no. 1, April 1968, pp. 39-62 and no. 2, September 1968, pp. 149-194.) At least one location, usually reasonably accessible, is given for almost all of the documents, in the United States, Liberia, or England.

Ghana is in many ways a model for library development and bibliographical control anywhere in the world. The Ghana Library Board (starting as the Gold Coast Library Board in 1950) has established a strong central library in Accra with regional and branch libraries. In the absence of branches the Book Box Service and bookmobiles have begun to give library service in all parts of this thinly settled country.[28] An attempt is being made to maintain a national union catalog. The first volume of the annual national bibliography has appeared: *Ghana National Bibliography 1965.* (Accra, Ghana Library Board, 1968.)

Ghana is also well supplied with retrospective bibliographies. Only the most important ones will be mentioned below. They are: Allan Wolsey Cardinall, *A Bibliography of the Gold Coast.* (Accra, Government Printer, 1932, issued as a companion volume to the Census Report of 1931.) Cardinall went to the Gold Coast in 1914 and spent eighteen years there as a District Commissioner and managed to collect over 4,600 references to the Gold Coast, some of which, while referring to West Africa, have little bearing on that country. The volume contains spare pages for "Addenda" and also some unallocated numbers.[29] Cardinall is updated by Albert Frederick Johnson's *A Bibliography of Ghana, 1930-1961.* (Evanston, Illinois, Northwestern University Press, 1964.) The book was published on behalf of the Ghana Library Board and consists of a classified listing of more than 2,600 items.[30] This fine tradition has been continued by David Brokensha and S. I. A. Kotei, "A Bibliography of Ghana: 1958-1964." (*African Studies Bulletin*, Vol. 10, no. 2, September 1967, pp. 35-79.) *Ghana, A Guide to Official Publications, 1872-1968* has been compiled by Julian W. Witherell and Sharon B. Lockwood of the African Section of the Library of Congress.[31]

It is hard to discuss Nigeria bibliographically without mentioning the University of Ibadan (see chapter 6). Attention here will be given to the National Library of Nigeria in Lagos and the public library systems. The National Library was opened, after a lot of preliminary study, in 1964 and is still in a temporary building in

Lagos.[32] The library serves Nigerian government officials, officials of foreign embassies, scholars, and authors; in fact, it serves all members of the public over sixteen years old. "The National Union Catalogue . . . represents holdings in the National Library and all the University Libraries in Nigeria except the University of Ibadan."[33] The National Library has published *Lagos Past and Present, an historical bibliography.* (Lagos, 1968.) This is a short, unpaged, illustrated pamphlet with an introduction by the military governor of Lagos, a foreword by the Oba, and a preface by the acting deputy director of the library. Locational symbols in Nigeria are given for most of the items cited. Recently the first issue, also prepared by the National Library, of the *Index to Nigerian Periodicals* has appeared.

It is amazing, but no one in Nigeria has to date issued any significant retrospective bibliographies. The work abroad is largely confined to that of Sharon Burdge Lockwood, compiler, of *Nigeria, A Guide to Official Publications*, (Washington, Library of Congress, 1966)[34] containing 2,451 entries, and two modest publications, Howard Wolpe's *A Study Guide for Nigeria,* (Development Program. African Studies Center. Boston University, 1966, mimeographed), and J. O. Dipeolu's *Bibliographical Sources for Nigerian Studies* (Evanston, Illinois, Program of African Studies, 1966). Perhaps John Harris will one day turn his *Books about Nigeria: A Select Reading List* (4th edition, Ibadan University Press, 1963) into a full retrospective bibliography.

As a result of the Ibadan seminar on public library development in Africa, a pilot project, supported in part by UNESCO, was set up in Enugu in 1955.[35] The Enugu library has been remarkable, especially with regard to the rate of its development. In 1965 the Enugu library loaned about as many books per registered reader as did the Federal Republic of Germany or the U.S.S.R.[36]

It was, however, the Northern Region that was the pioneer in Nigerian public library development, a result of the pioneering labors of Joan Allen.[37] Even the Western Region had more volumes in the early 1960s than the Eastern Region Library Board, whose librarian may still be Kalu Okerie.[38]

We shall now complete, in brief, our survey of French-speaking Africa—first, former French Equatorial Africa, then the Congos, Burundi and Rwanda, and last, Madagascar. Cameroon has a university with some 2,000 students, a library of 26,000 volumes and 500 current periodicals, 25 of which are published in Cameroon.[39] Important is the library of the former IFAN Center, now the Institut de Rechèrches Scientifiques du Cameroun (IRCAM).[40] There is little other library or bibliographical activity to report.

Chad does have its Centre National de Documentation.[41] Its purpose is to raise standards of teachers by giving them access to the State National Library.[42]

Congo (Brazzaville) contains a number of libraries, including a public one in the capital. There is, however, no national library or bibliography.[43]

In spite of a fair level of governmental and economic activity in Gabon, there is hardly a library nor is there any bibliographical activity. An excellent volume is Brian Weinstein's *Gabon: Nation Building on the Ogooué* (Cambridge, Mass., M.I.T. Press, 1966, bibliography pp. 257-279).

Once again there is a useful guide by the Library of Congress for the *Official Publications of French Equatorial Africa, French Cameroons and Togo, 1945-1958*, compiled by Julian W. Witherell, 1964, listing 405 items.[44]

We turn now to areas formerly under Belgian colonial administration. The Congo (Kinshasa), Burundi and Rwanda benefited from the bibliographical labor of Théodore Heyse. *Bibliographie du Congo Belge et du Ruanda-Urundi, 1939-* and *Documentation Générale sur le Congo et le Ruanda-Urundi, 1953-1960,* are the most significant.[45] For many years Olga Boone prepared the *Bibliographie ethnographique de l'Afrique sud-saharienne* (formerly the *Bibliographie du Congo Belge et des regions avoisinantes*) (Tervueren, Belgiun, Musée Royal de l'Afrique Central, 1932- ) which is of great interest to those particularly concerned with ethnology and linguistics.

The Congo does have a Bibliothéque Centrale,[46] and the

Université Iovanium has more than 100,000 volumes.[47] There are other university and special libraries. Most of these institutions produce periodic accession lists.

Rwanda has few libraries and the main retrospective bibliography is now ten years old. It was written by Joseph Clement and is called *Essai de bibliographie du Ruanda-Urundi.* ([Usumbura] 1959.)[48] Some bibliographical work may be expected from the Université Nationale du Rwanda[49] and the Institut Nationale de Recherche Scientifique.[50]

Burundi is much better off bibliographically and otherwise than Rwanda. The Université Officiel du Burundi has a collection of 25,000 volumes. There is no law of legal deposit.[51]

Madagascar, or the Malagasy Republic, is well supplied bibliographically. There is first of all the monumental three-volume work of Guillaume Grandidier, *Bibliographie de Madagascar* (Paris, Comité de Madagascar, 1905/6-1957), covering the period from European discovery in 1500 to 1955.[52] This is supplemented by Jean Fontvielle's work for the years 1956-1963.[53] An annual national bibliography has to date been issued for 1964 and 1965. These are impressive volumes that list, according to the Universal Decimal Classification (UDC), books and journals and journal articles published in and about Madagascar. Besides the university library, which together with the national library issues the national bibliography, there are many governmental and special libraries in Madagascar, and even a small public library in Tananarive.[55]

Two published American bibliographies on Madagascar should be noted: *Madagascar and Adjacent Islands: A Guide to Official Publications,* compiled by Julian W. Witherell, (Library of Congress, 1965, 927 entries)[54] and Peter Duignan, *Madagascar*, a list of materials in the African Collections of Stanford University and the Hoover Institution on War, Revolution, and Peace (1962, 257 entries Hoover Institution, Bibliographic series, no. 9).[56]

Little can be usefully said about the Portuguese colonial territories in Africa: Portuguese Guinea, São Tome and Principe, Mozambique and Angola. The main libraries—governmental, special, and even public—are described in the UNESCO *Handbook*.[57] The most useful retrospective bibliography was compiled by Mary Jane Gibson. Her study is called *Portuguese Africa, A Guide to Official Publications* (Library of Congress, 1968) and within 217 pages there are 2,831 references.[58] On a more modest scale is *Angola; a Bibliography*, compiled by Margaret Jean Greenwood and published by the School of Librarianship of the University of Capetown in 1967. The Instituto de Angola has since 1964 issued *Boletim bibliográfico* monthly.[59] Each issue contains about one hundred items. In Mozambique ever since 1935 *Documentario trimestral* has been issued. (Lourenco Marques, Impressa nacional.) The final section of each issue of this journal lists books and other publications deposited, under the copyright law, during the previous four months.

Let us now move to the Sudan, before going to the Horn of Africa and Eastern and Southern Africa.

The Sudan, like many other Anglo-phonic countries, is well supplied with retrospective bibliographies and a fine journal: *Sudan Notes and Records*, 1921- , which until 1956 carried regularly a comprehensive "Sudan Bibliography." The retrospective bibliographies are: Richard Leslie Hill's *A Bibliography of the Anglo-Egyptian Sudan from the Earliest Times to 1937*, (London, Oxford University Press, 1939) and a volume by the librarian of the University of Khartoum, Abdel Rahman el Nasri, *A Bibliography of the Sudan, 1938-1958* (London, published on behalf of the University of Khartoum by the Oxford University Press, 1962, listing 2,763 books and periodical articles).[60] The role of public libraries has largely been played by active information libraries maintained by the British Council, the Centre Culturel Français, and the United States Information Service.

Ethiopia has two classical bibliographies, one compiled by Giuseppe Fumagalli for the period from the fifteenth century until 1891, and the other by Silvio Zanutto for the period from 1891 until 1936.[61] For 1963/64 and 1965 have appeared *Ethiopian Publications: Books, Pamphlets, Annuals and Periodical Articles*, compiled by S. Chojnacki and Ephraim Haile Selassie. (Addis Ababa, Institute of Ethiopian Studies, Haile Selassie I University.)[62] This very useful bibliography, which excludes official publications, can hardly be classified as a national bibliography.[63]

Addis has impressive libraries, particularly the one at Haile Selassie I University and the one at the United Nations Economic Commission for Africa (ECA). There is a national library that is a storehouse indeed. It recently issued Stephen Wright's *Bibliography to Ethiopian Incunabula*, 1967, from the collections in the National Library of Ethiopia and the Haile Selassie I University.

The Somali Republic has a retrospective bibliography prepared for the Chamber of Commerce, Industry and Agriculture in Mogadiscio and published in 1958.[64] Another, compiled by Helen F. Conover, is called *Official Publications of Somaliland, 1941-1959.* (Library of Congress, 1960, containing 169 entries.)[65]

Kenya has the fine retrospective bibliography compiled by John B. Webster and others: *A Bibliography of Kenya.* (Syracuse, New York, Program of Eastern African Studies, containing no less than 7,210 entries.)[66] There are many special and governmental libraries and one well-established new public library, the Macmillan Library in Nairobi.[67] There is, however, no coordinated bibliographical service in Kenya.[68]

Tanzania lacks retrospective bibliographies. Since March 1966, *Tanzania Notes and Records* has carried a bibliographical section semi-annually.

The situation in Uganda is similar. *Uganda Journal,* also semi-annual, has included, since 1963, a bibliographical section. B. W. Langlands of the Department of Geography of Makerere University College in Kampala, Uganda, compiles both the Uganda and Tanzania bibliographies. Makerere University College library dates from 1948. Although it still plays an important role in Uganda, it may well already be surpassed by the much younger libraries at the other colleges of the University of East Africa, those in Dar es Salaam and Nairobi.[69] Many other libraries are listed in a now rather outdated compilation of E. J. Bolton's called *Directory of East African Libraries.* (Kampala, Makerere College Library, 1961, Makerere Library publications no. 1.)

There is a fine *Bibliography of Malawi*, compiled by Edward E. Brown and others. (Syracuse, Program of Eastern African Studies, 1965,[70] an unnumbered, classified series of references to book and periodical material.)[71] John B. Webster and Paulus Mohome compiled *A Supplement to a Bibliography of Malawi*, 1967 (Program of Eastern African Studies, Occasional bibliography no. 13). *A List of Publications Deposited in the National Archives of Malawi* has begun to be issued annually, starting with the year 1965.[72]

On 4 October 1967 the Malawi Parliament set up a National Library Service. Its "basis is the centralizing of all the existing library services to provide a national coverage, at the same time providing economies through the provision of a single executive body."[73]

Zambia has a great potential. It is possible that the new university library may also become the national library.[74]

The Library of Congress, as part of the National Program for Acquisitions and Cataloging (NPAC), has since January 1968, from the Library of Congress' Nairobi office, issued a quarterly *Accessions List, Eastern Africa*. The December 1968 issue reports receipt of publications from Angola, Ethiopia, French territories of the Afars and Isaas (formerly known as French Somaliland), Kenya, Malagasy, Malawi, Mauritius, Mozambique, Seychelles, Rwanda, Sudan, Uganda, Zambia, Zanzibar, and the East African Common Services Organization. The Library of Congress certainly needs offices in other parts of Africa and elsewhere. Perhaps one will be established in Dakar before too long.

Southern Rhodesia has several fairly large libraries, including the ones at the University, the National Archives in Salisbury, and public libraries there and in Bulawayo. In 1961 an annual *List of Publications Deposited in the National Archives* was started. This has begun to be called the *Rhodesian National Bibliography*, effective for 1967, and, no doubt, will continue thus. This eight-page list, classified according to the Dewey Decimal classification, reports publications received in terms of the Printed Publications Act.

South Africa has two current national bibliographies. *Africana*

*Nova,* published quarterly since 1958 by the South African Library in Cape Town, lists publications of and about South Africa, and the *South African National Bibliography* (SANB), published since 1959 by the State Library at Pretoria, cumulated annually, is restricted to South African publications.[75]

There is a distinguished retrospective bibliography: *Sidney Mendelssohn's South African Bibliography.* (London, K. Paul, 1910.)[76] The first volume has 1008 pages and the second 1139. This work has been reprinted by the Holland Press, London, in 1968. Since 1960 Mendelssohn's work has been revised and supplemented.[77]

The library scene in South Africa is too vast, complex, and, segregated for rapid treatment. Fortunately, readers may turn to a recent book in comparative library studies, Loree Elizabeth Taylor's *South African Libraries.* (Hamden, Conn., The Shoe String Press, 1967.)

With regard to South West Africa, the library scene is one of centralization under a director of library services who rules over governmental and non-governmental libraries, including the Windhoek Public Library.[78] Although South West Africa has been incorporated, not only bibliographically, into the Republic, the following bibliographies may be found useful: Florette Jean Welch, compiler, *South West Africa: A Bibliography* (Cape Town, University of Cape Town, School of Librarianship, 1967) and Samuel Delca, *South-West Africa; 1960-1968 An Introductory Bibliography* (Kingston, University of Rhode Island, 1968).

As for the former High Commission Territories, we can benefit from retrospective bibliographies compiled by the Bibliographical Section of the Program of Eastern African Studies of the Maxwell Graduate School of Citizenship and Public Affairs of Syracuse University. For Botswana, formerly Bechuanaland, there is Paulus Mohome and John B. Webster, compilers, *A Bibliography on Bechuanaland* (1966, Occasional bibliography no. 5), supplemented by Webster and Mohome (1968, Occasional bibliography no. 15).

What should be the function of a national library? It must be an efficient operation of governmental activity. Any government needs a library, although not necessarily a separate one for each government office. A library, or national archive, is best equipped to service the records of government, except perhaps the current ones, and to give information to civil servants and politicians for the performance of their duties. The national library as a public library can serve students and teachers in preparing their texts and assignments, and it can assure that literacy, once gained, will be retained.

We have surveyed national libraries as well as bibliographical work. Some of the latter, if not actually performed in Africa, is at least related to specific African countries. Although libraries everywhere are only in part concerned with the publications that emanate from and pertain to their countries, the comments that follow are particularly concerned with Africana—that is, with anything that facilitates a greater understanding of Africa's past and present and with anything that may even allow us to speculate about the future of that continent. Through the cooperative approach of area studies the future may provide ever greater satisfaction of man's universal quest for knowledge.

At present only a small proportion of bibliographic work pertaining to Africana is carried out on the most obvious continent for such work. International bibliographic work is largely performed in Europe and the United States, and the subject bibliographies that refer all or in part to Africa tend to be prepared in countries bordering the northern Atlantic Ocean. Only the most important work will be mentioned.

Highly significant for a better understanding of mankind is the work issued, with the support of UNESCO, by the International Committee for Social Science Documentation. Annual classified bibliographies are issued in political science, economics, sociology, and social and cultural anthropology. These volumes index the global literature, both monographic and serial, of the social sciences.

With regard to anthropology, and until the 1940s or so, most scholarly work on Africa was performed by anthropologists. We first must mention the work of the International African Institute (IAI)

in London which since 1928 has published a quarterly, *Africa,* with
a broadly classified bibliography in each issue, and since 1950,
another quarterly, *African Abstracts,* with an annual index.[79] Both
of these publications are mainly anthropological and linguistic.

An ambitious and promising indexing and abstracting organization
that may, however, not have survived recent academic reorganization
in France is CARDAN, after its French initials, the Center for
Analysis and Documentary Research for Black Africa.[80] CARDAN
has analyzed and abstracted a large volume of periodical and
monographic literature and has experimented with the development
of a standardized language, opening the way to automated retrieval.
The all too many other bibliographical card services have been
discussed by René Bureau in "Les services de Fiches bibliographiques" in Pearson and Jones (forthcoming).

Of more practical significance is the African Bibliographical
Center's *Current Bibliography on African Affairs* (New York,
Greenwood Periodicals, Inc., monthly). Each issue contains references to monographs and journal articles arranged by broad general
subjects, and a geographical section, and it includes features
pertaining to forthcoming publications, the book trade, bibliographical tools, as well as an annotated book review section.

The African Department of Northwestern University Library in
Evanston, Illinois, has issued every other month the *Joint Acquisitions List of Africana* (JALA) since January 1962. Some 950 cards,
representing current Africana, cataloged by some of the most
important libraries concerned with Africana in the United States, are
reproduced photographically.

*United States and Canadian Publications on Africa* is an annual
published by the Hoover Institution of Stanford University. The
most recent annual available (in March 1969) is the volume for
1965, with 2,312 entries including, for the first time, doctoral
theses. A similar work is issued in Britain and Germany.

Of the many one-volume bibliographies that strive to cover either
the entire African continent or just sub-Saharan Africa, just a few of
the most useful ones will be mentioned. *Africa: Classification*

*Schedule, Classified Listing by Call Number, Alphabetical Listing by Author or Title, Chronological Listing* (Widener Library shelflist no. 2, Cambridge, Harvard University Library, 1965);[81] and Helen F. Conover, compiler *Africa, South of the Sahara*, a selected annotated list of writings (Library of Congress, 1963 2,173 entries, arranged geographically and by subject, usually indicating the Library of Congress call number). It is a real bargain for $2.25 from the Superintendent of Documents of the U.S. Government Printing Office. The Library of Congress' *Serials for African Studies* is currently under active revision before the publication of a second edition.

A more up-to-date bibliography, concentrating on subjects of particular interest, is that compiled by Peter C. W. Gutkind and John B. Webster, *A Select Bibliography on Traditional and Modern Africa.* (Syracuse, Program of Eastern African Studies, 1968, Occasional bibliography no. 8, almost 3,000 references.) Nearly half that number can be found in Edith Ehrmann's *Bibliography of Africa South of the Sahara for Undergraduate Libraries.* (New York, Foreign Area Materials Center, forthcoming probably in 1969.)

For a bibliography aimed at the high school and junior college level, note the one compiled by Daniel C. Matthews, *African Affairs for the General Reader: A Selected and Introductory Bibliographical Guide 1960-1967.* (Washington, African Bibliographical Center for the Council of the African-American Institute, 1967; African bibliographic center: Special bibliography series, vol. 5, no. 4)

The *African Experience* may prove useful too. (Northwestern University, Program of African Studies, four volumes.)[82] Volume 2 contains bibliographical references and an essay (pp. 1-16), "Reference Sources for African Studies," which, among other matters, mentions the most important subject bibliographies for Africana. All scholars of Africa are eagerly awaiting the long promised *Handbook of African Library Resources*[?] , edited by Helen F. Conover and Peter Duignan.

It should perhaps be stressed that the preparation of suitable reading material and the operation of effective libraries is an

---

important part of socioeconomic development. The main function of one of the libraries in each county is the compilation of a national bibliography. Subject bibliographies can be prepared as the need for them arises in the particular country or elsewhere.

Once the need for libraries has been accepted by the political leaders of African countries, they will ensure that libraries, the proper training of librarians (which is just as important) and the supply of reading and reference material is sufficiently stressed in development plans.

### NOTES

1.  5721 Cottage Grove Avenue, Chicago, Illinois 60637; telephone: (312) 955-4545; teletype: CG1516.
2.  Constance M. Winchell, *Guide to Reference Books,* 8th ed. (Chicago: American Library Association, 1967), p. 510, no. DD 43.
3.  Robert C. Greer, "National Bibliography" in Robert B. Downs and Francis B. Jenkins, eds. *Bibliography: Current State and Future Trends* (Urbana: University of Illinois Press, 1967), p. 25.
4.  United Nations Educational, Scientific, and Cultural Organization (UNESCO), *Bibliography, Documentation, Terminology* 8, no. 5 (September 1968):197.
5.  Winchell, *Guide*, p. 511, no. DD55.
6.  Post Office (P.O.) Box 395, Tripoli, Libya.
7.  UNESCO, *Bibliography, Documentation, Terminology* 7, no. 5 (September 1967):115. Boite Postale (B.P.) 575, Tunis.
8.  Ibid. 7, no. 6 (November 1967):143.
9.  Ibid. 4, no. 5 (September 1964):124.
10. Winchell, *Guide*, p. 511, no. DD 60.
11. UNESCO, *Bibliography* 3, no. 2 (March 1963):33.
12. Available at the Photoduplication Service of the Library of Congress for $4.50 microfilm, $11 electrostatic print (xerox) or a Greenwood Press reprint at $12.
13. C.R.A.M. Faculté du Droit, Chemin des Fenouillères, Aix-en-Provence, France.

14. Los Angeles, California 90007.
15. E. W. Dadzie and J. T. Strickland, *Directory of Archives, Libraries and Schools of Librarianship in Africa,* (UNESCO Bibliographical Handbook no. 10) (Paris: UNESCO, 1965), p. 63.
16. Ibid., pp. 61-63.
17. Julian W. Witherell, *A Publication Survey Trip to West Africa, Ethiopia, France and Portugal* (Washington: Library of Congress, General Reference and Bibliography Division, Reference Department, Africa Section, 1968), p. 19. (Unpublished report available at the Library of Congress.)
18. Winchell, *Guide,* p. 511, no. DD 58.
19. B.P. 6, Ougadougou, Upper Volta.
20. J. Rousset de Pina, "Bibliothèque de l'Universite de Dakar," Standing Committee on African University Libraries (SCAUL) *Newsletter,* no. 5 (1968), pp. 238-244. See also his "La nouvelle bibliothèque central de l'Universite de Dakar," *Bulletin des bibliothèques de France* 11, no. 8, pp. 293-304.
21. Witherell, *Publication Survey* p. 13.
22. Fanny Lelande-Isnard, "Ouvrages publies en Guinédu 2 octobre 1958 au 31 decembre 1963," *Rechèrches Africaines: Etudes guinéennes* [nouvelles serie] (1964), pp. 167-169.
23. For sale by the Superintendent of Documents, U.S. Government Printing Office, Washington, D.C. 20402; price $1.25.
24. Witherell, *Publication Survey,* p. 2.
25. The U.S. Government Printing Office will supply a copy for $.55.
26. Dadzie and Strickland, *Directory of Archives,* p. 57.
27. No further papers have been issued or are likely to be in that series.
28. Evelyn J. A. Evans, *A Tropical Library Service: The Story of Ghana's Libraries* (London: Andre Deutsch, 1964). Note particularly "The Rural Areas," pp. 98-105. See also Evans' "Library Legislation in the Developing Territories of Africa," *Libri* 18, no. 1 (1968):51-78.
29. H. A. Rydings, *The Bibliographies of West Africa* (Ibadan: 1961), pp. 24-25. (Published on behalf of the West African Library Association by the Ibadan University Press)
30. Winchell, *Guide,* p. 510, no. DD 52.
31. U.S. Government Printing Office; $1.25.
32. Carl M. White, *National Library of Nigeria: Growth of the Idea,*

Problems and Progress (Lagos: Federal Ministry of Information, 1964.)

33.   National Library of Nigeria, *A Guide to Its Use* (Lagos: 1967), unpaged folder (National library publication no. 4).

34.   U.S. Government Printing Office; $1.

35.   *Development of Public Libraries in Africa, the Ibadan Seminar,* (UNESCO Public Library Manual, no. 6)    (Paris: UNESCO, 1954).

36.   Fanny Lalande Isnard, "The Development of Libraries in Africa," *UNESCO Bulletin for Libraries* 22, no. 5 (September-October 1968): 245. See also: "Regional Seminar on the Development of Public Libraries in Africa," *UNESCO Bulletin for Libraries,* supplement to vol. 17, no. 2 (March-April 1963), pp. 106-122.

37.   Joan Allen, "Early Days in the Northern Regional Library, Kaduna," *Northern Nigeria Library Notes,* nos. 2 and 3 (1964/65): 71-74. See also: D. H. Gunton, "A Library in the Tropics: A History and a Blueprint," *Library Association Record* 63 (May 1961):149-154.

38.   Simeon B. Aje, *Backgrounds, Status and Plans for Library Development in Nigeria* (University of Chicago, Master's thesis, 1963), especially pp. 76-92 dealing with the Western Region.

39.   Samir M. Zoghby, *A Publication Survey Trip to West Africa, Equatorial Africa, Tunisia, France and Belgium* (Washington: Library of Congress, 1968), p. 20.

40.   B. P. 193, Yaoundé.

41.   B. P. 731, Fort-Lamy.

42.   UNESCO, *Bibliography, Documentation, Terminology* 8, no. 5 (September 1968): 188; "Library Statistics for West Africa," *Wala News* 4, no. 3 (June 1962):116-117 may be of some interest. (Bulletin of the West African Library Association)

43.   UNESCO, *Bibliography* 6, no. 4 (July 1966):121-122.

44.   U.S. Government Printing Office, $.50.

45.   Winchell, *Guide*, p. 509, nos. DD 39 and 40.

46.   B.P. 3090, Kinshasa-Kalina.

47.   Zoghby, p. 4.

48.   Winchell; *Guide*, p. 511, no. DD 62.

49.   B.P. 117, Butare.

50.   B.P. 131, Butare.

51.   Zoghby, p. 10.

52.   Winchell, *Guide*, p. 511, no. DD 57.

53.   Not yet seen by this writer.

54. B.P. 908, Tananarive.
55. U.S. Government Printing Office, $.40.
56. Winchell, *Guide*, p. 511, no. DD 56.
57. Dadzie and Strickland, *Directory or Archives*, pp. 85-89.
58. U.S. Government Printing Office, $1.50.
59. P.O.B. 2767, Luanda.
60. Winchell, *Guide*, p. 509, nos. DD 37 and 38.
61. Ibid., p. 510, nos. DD 49 and 50.
62. P.O. Box 1176, Addis Ababa.
63. This is done in *College and Research Libraries* 30, no. 1, January 1969, p. 75.
64. Somaliland, Italian. Camera di Commercio, Industria ed Agricultura. Winchell *Guide*, p. 511, no. DD 65.
65. Available from Photoduplication Service, Library of Congress for $3 positive microfilm and $8 electrostatic print (xerox).
66. Syracuse University Press, Box 8, University Station, Syracuse, New York; $7.50.
67. The Macmillans were Americans who settled in Kenya.
68. UNESCO, *Bibliography, Documentation, Terminology* 8, no. 2(March 1968):61.
69. Glenn L. Sitzman, "Uganda's University Library," *College and Research Libraries* 29, no. 3, p. 212.
70. Winchell, *Guide; Supplement* (Chicago: American Library Association, 1968), p. 78, no. 1, DD 8.
71. Available from Syracuse University Press, $4.50.
72. P.O. Box 62, Zomba.
73. A.M. Nyasulu, Malawi Minister of Education as reported in the Rhodesia Library Association *Newsletter*, new series, vol. 1, no. 4 (December 1967):83-84.
74. Sharon B. Lockwood, "A Publication Survey Trip to West, Central and Southern Africa." Library of Congress, 1966, p. 7. (Report available at the Library of Congress.)
75. C. Parma, ed., *The South African Library: 1818-1968* (Cape Town: Balkema, 1968).
76. Winchell, *Guide*, pp. 511-512, no. DD 66
77. For details about the South African bibliographical scene note the useful articles by Reuben Musiker of Rhodes University Library in Grahamstown, South Africa, in the *African Studies Bulletin* and elsewhere and his contribution to the forthcoming *The Bibliography of Africa*, edited by J. D. Pearson and Ruth Jones.
78. South West Africa, Commission on Libraries in South West

Africa, *Report* mimeographed (Windhoek: The Administration,
79.  The IAI with the support of the Ford Foundation convened in
     December 1967, in Nairobi, a conference on the *Bibliography
     of Africa*. To date, the fullest report is in *Africa* 38 (July
     1968): 293-331, 337-339.
80.  René Bureau and Francois Izard, *African Studies Bulletin* 10,
     no. 3 (December 1967):66-81. CARDAN's current address is:
     Centre d'Analyse et de Recherche documentaires pour l'Afri-
     que noire (C.A.R.D.A.N.), c/o Institut d'etudes politiques, 2,
     rue de Rouen, 92-Nanterre, France.
81.  See this writer's review: *The Library Quarterly* 37, no. 1
     (January 1967):131-132.
82.  Final Report Africa Curriculum Project, compiled for the U. S.
     Department of Health, Education and Welfare. Project no.
     6-2863. Contract no. OEC-3-7-062863-1661. Completely re-
     vised edition is to be published by Northwestern University
     Press in 1970.


## ANNOTATED SELECTIVE BIBLIOGRAPHY

Publications cited in text or footnotes of this chapter are not
repeated, nor are items cited in Helen F. Conover's *African Libraries,
Book Production and Archives,* an annotated list of 341 references.
Washington, D.C: Library of Congress, 1962. (Available from the
Card Division, Library of Congress, $.60.)

*African Studies Bulletin,* 1958- . This is the official organ of the
     African Studies Association, 622 West 113th Street, New York,
     New York 10025, published three times a year and six - nine
     times a year supplemented by:
*African Studies Newsletter,* 1968-
*Africana Newsletter,* 1962-1964. The Hoover Institution, Stanford
     University. Unfortunately only six issues were published before
     it merged with the *African Studies Bulletin.*
Asheim, Lester. *Librarianship in the Developing Countries.* CM
     16.25 Phineas L. Windsor series in librarianship. Urbana:
     University of Illinois Press, 1966.
Avicenne, P. *Bibliographical Services Throughout the World,*

*1960-1964.* Paris: UNESCO, 1968. Updated by: UNESCO, Bibliography, Documentation, Terminology 8, no. 5 (September 1968).

Bogaert, Jozef. *Sciences humaines en Afrique noire,* guide bibliographique (1945-1965). Brussels: Centre de Documentation Economique et Sociale Africain (CEDESA), 1966. (Enquêtes bibliographiques no. 15).

Bousso, A. and others. "A Library Education Policy for the Developing Countries." *UNESCO Bulletin for Libraries* 22, no. 4 (July-August 1968): 173-188.

University of Cape Town, School of Librarianship. *Bibliographical Series, Consolidated List, 1941-1966.* Cape Town: University of Cape Town Libraries, 1966. (Lists 288 bibliographies submitted for the diploma of librarianship.)

Conover, Helen F. and Duignan Peter. *Handbook for African Studies.* Stanford: Stanford University, The Hoover Institution on War, Revolution and Peace, forthcoming.

Crossey, John M. D. "Notes on Bibliographic Aids and Dealers Necessary for Building a Working Collection on Africa." *African Studies Bulletin,* in press.

Gardner, Frank. "UNESCO and Library and Related Services in Africa." *UNESCO Bulletin for Libraries* 20, 5 (September-October 1966): 212-218.

Garling, Anthea, comp. *Bibliography of African Bibliographies.* (Occasional papers, no. 1.) Cambridge, England: African Studies Center, 1968.

Gelfand, M. A. *University Libraries for Developing Countries.* UNESCO Manuals for Libraries, no. 14. Paris: UNESCO, 1968.

Matthews, Daniel G. "African Bibliography Today: Selected and Current Bibliographical Tools for African Studies, 1967-68." *A Current Bibliography on African Affairs,* new series, vol. 1, no. 11 (November 1968): 4-17.

Molnos, Angela. "Whither African Bibliographies, an Observer's Afterthoughts to a Recent Conference." *East Africa Journal* 5, no. 2 (February 1968): 17-25.

Newsletter of the Archives-Libraries Committee and Cooperative African Microform Project (NLAL/CAMP). Evanston, Illinois, Northwestern University Library, no. 1, April 1967. (The only one issued to date.)

Panofsky, Hans E. "African Studies in American Libraries." In Tsuen-Hsuin Tsien and Howard W. Winger, eds. *Area Studies and the Library.* Chicago: The University of Chicago Press (1966): 96-105. (The thirtieth annual conference of the Graduate Library School, 1965.)

──────. "Cooperative Acquisitions Efforts in Africana." In Annette Hoage Phinazee, ed. *Materials by and about American Negroes.* Atlanta: Atlanta University, School of Library Services (1967): 55-61. (Papers presented at an institute sponsored by the Atlanta University School of Library Service with the cooperation of the Trevor Arnett Library, 1965.)

Plumbe, Wilfred J. *The Preservation of Books in Tropical and Subtropical Countries.* Kuala Lumpur, etc. Oxford University Press, 1964.

South African Library, Cape Town. *A Bibliography of African Bibliographies,* covering territories south of the Sahara. 4th ed. Cape Town: South African Public Library, 1961.

Standing Committee on African University Libraries (SCAUL) *Newsletter,* no. 1, 1965; no. 5, 1968. Library, University College, P.O. Box 9184, Dar es Salaam, Tanzania.

Standing Conference on Library Materials on Africa (SCOLMA) *Library Materials on Africa,* 1961-, three times a year. Mrs. M. R. Kettle, African Studies Unit, University of Leeds, Leeds 2, England.

Taylor, Alan R. *African Studies Research.* Westport, Conn.: Greenwood Press, forthcoming.

──────. "Library and Archival Resources for African Studies: Present State and Future Needs." Paper presented at the eleventh annual meeting of the African Studies Association, Los Angeles, 1968.

Varley, Douglas Harold. "Conference of University Libraries in Tropical Africa," *UNESCO Bulletin for Libraries* 19, no. 2 (March-April 1965): 73-76.

──────. "University Library Co-operation in Tropical Africa," Libi 15, no. 1 (March 1965): 64-71. (The Proceedings of the Leverhulme Conference on University Libraries in Tropical Africa held in 1964, which among other matters gave birth to the Standing Committee on African University Libraries (SCAUL), have not been published to date.)

──────. The Role of the Librarian in the New Africa. London: Oxford University Press, 1963. (An inaugural lecture given in the University College of Rhodesia and Nyasaland, 1962.)

Wallensius, Anna-Britta. *Library Work in Africa.* Uppsala: Scandinavian Institute of African Studies, 1966. (Proceedings of a conference held in 1965.)

Webster, John B. "Toward an International Automated Bibliographic System for Africana." Paper presented at the eleventh annual meeting of the African Studies Association, Los Angeles, 1968.

Willemin, Silvère. "The Training of Librarians in Africa." *UNESCO Bulletin for Libraries* 21, no. 6 (November-December 1967): 291-300.

*World Guide to Libraries.* Internationales Bibliotheks-Handbuch. 2d ed. New York: Bowker, 1968, pt. 2: Africa, America, Asia and Oceania. (Handbuch der technischen Dokumentation und Bibliographie, Bd. 8, 2.Ausg.)

# PART FIVE

# Special Libraries, Classification, and Information Retrieval

# 11/ Classification and Information Retrieval in Europe

ROBERT COLLISON

*University of California, Los Angeles*


The stimulus of national and international competition in the commercial and industrial fields is increasingly making both librarians and documentalists scrutinize every process of their classification and information retrieval operations. The emphasis is naturally concentrated on science and technology, though there have been some developments in the social sciences. The scant attention paid to the humanities reflects the almost universal attitude that there is little money to be made in this direction. Indeed, even the Dainton Report on National Libraries in Britain makes it fairly plain that it feels that more and more of library resources must in the future be devoted to scientific and technological purposes. In some respects it is clear that the Middle Ages were more enlightened.

The importance for the communications industry of a pattern of some definable shape has long been known. That pattern is usually regarded as internal only, but parallel with it there is also an external pattern that is becoming increasingly obvious. In the first place, individual efforts are growing into national cooperative efforts. For example, the Council of Ministers of the German Democratic Republic has decreed and is now implementing the establishment of information and documentation centers for some thirty-six areas of natural sciences, technology, and economics, in addition to some twenty areas of the social sciences. West Germany has created one Documentation and Information Commission responsible for coordinating all federal as well as interregional activities, including

*259*

specialized data centers and international documentation projects and research. In France, the National Association of Technological Research (ANRT) in Paris is concentrated on promoting all activities contributing to information development, including research into the automation of documentation, the compilation of thesauri, and the elimination of delays in information retrieval. Together with the Committee of Documentation Studies and the National Center for Scientific Research, the Association is attempting to coordinate all French activities in the field of information and documentation. In the Soviet Union—where all publications must include bibliographical descriptions and classification numbers—the All-Union Standards and Specifications Reference Library (VIFS) has been set up to supply organizations throughout the Union with copies of Soviet and foreign standards. And in the United Kingdom the book-numbering system has become firmly established, thus making exact identification of specific documents a very much easier job than it has ever been in the past. In fact, national effort and national cooperation have developed rapidly in the past four years or so, and the old hesitation to think on national lines is beginning to vanish.

Even more encouraging is the considerable amount of international effort that has not only been initiated but has mostly been sustained. For example, the ESRO/ELDO Space Documentation Service (SDS) now provides computerized literature searches for some dozen member states, thus constituting an extension of the NASA documentation system. A computer-based information retrieval system, covering nuclear energy and employing coordinate indexing, has been established at Euratom's Centre for Information and Documentation. And the Scandinavian countries are collaborating in a joint study of their problems in the communnication of information within industry.

The evidence of international collaboration could of course be elaborated indefinitely; what, however, is of far more interest are the renewed attempts at world coverage in information storage and retrieval within fairly wide subject groups. Ever since FID's attempts more than fifty years ago to establish a universal bibliography, the striving after comprehensive records has manifested itself from time to time, echoing the efforts of Robert Watt and the other great bibliographers of the past. The present projects are based more scientifically and appear to have the solid and lasting support that is necessary for ventures of this kind. At Amsterdam, the Excerpta Medica Foundation—responsible for one of the largest abstracting services in the world—has set up an international system for monitoring, abstracting, translating, classifying, and indexing the world's output in biomedical literature. The Bundesanstalt für Landeskunde und Raumforschung at Bad Godesberg has started the issue of *Documentatio geographica*—a new UDC-classified indexing service aiming at world coverage of all geographical documents, in which entries are sorted by computer. And the Committee for International Cooperation in Information Retrieval among Examining Patent Offices (CIREPAT) is cooperating in developing a new international patent classification.

By its very nature, classification must be an international effort if it is to survive. The sad fate of James Duff Brown's Classification is sufficient evidence of this. Most classifications, moreover, do not adjust themselves quickly enough, so that the few that do so will undoubtedly prevail. Nevertheless, the preoccupation with classification and its problems is peculiarly European (and Indian): there is no parallel to the extent and depth of the research effort in this direction in any other part of the world. Not only is there an International Building Classification Committee—not very surprising when one takes into account the remarkable progress in documentation in the architectural and building fields during the past twenty years—but FID has its classification research committee (CCC) and, in the United Kingdom, there is a very vigorous Classification Research Group (CRG) with a comparatively small membership comprising some of the most original thinkers in documentation.

It is true that throughout Europe there is a general reluctance to undertake the expense and to suffer the disruption inherent in any grand reclassification of a major library, and that therefore most libraries are likely to remain classified by the schemes—good or bad—with which they were originally arranged many years ago. On the other hand, there is still room for maneuver, particularly in the direction of the construction of new detailed classifications for special subjects, and the revision of individual parts of established classifications. Thus, in the immediate past, new classifications for such fields as Library Science, Law books, the Performing Arts, Engineering, and stores and samples, have been issued, these efforts reflecting the general discontent with existing schemes and the search for new means incorporating the ideas of such innovators as Ranganathan, Mills, Foskett, Lloyd, and Wells. It was the Classification Research Group—the body responsible for the new Library Science classification—which obtained a NATO grant to carry out research into the problems of a new general classification, and which appears to be tending toward the conclusion that there is probably a need for two schemes, one for library use, and the other for detailed information retrieval. This may reflect the general recognition that classification lends itself to machine exploitation but, in order to achieve the best results, it is therefore necessary to adhere rigidly to the schedules of faceted schemes and thus avoid "false drops." This, however, does not suit the operators of libraries who need a flexible scheme: one sufficiently pliable to take care of the interests of a locality or a special community, yet also flexible enough to cope with the vagaries of the book publishing industry, one which has never yet taken heed of the requirements of book classifiers.

A record of a classified document can certainly be stored satisfactorily in a machine, and the machine preparation of indexes to such material can be mechanically prepared in a satisfactory fashion, as in the case of *Documentatio geographica*. Nonetheless, there is no escaping the need for thesauri from which the index entries can be chosen. The activity in this field is remarkable: for example, the Excerpta Medica Foundation maintains at Amsterdam a thesauri of some 150,000 terms, controlled by computer. The Atomic Weapons Research Establishment at Aldermaston and the International Road Research Documentation are both compiling large computer-controlled thesauri. The Institute for Documentation and Information on Public Health at Bielefeld has issued its thesaurus, and there are others being prepared on Management and on Documentation. A large German nuclear research establishment, instead of developing its own thesaurus, is wisely using terms from the Euratom thesaurus, and the National Council of Scientific Research in Paris is planning the compilation of thesauri in its program of automated bibliographical services, with the consequent gradual modification of its outstanding abstract publication, the *Bulletin signalétique.* Within the past five years the Classification Research Group has held two conferences in Marseilles to try to secure international agreement on an intermediate lexicon for documentation, to be used in demonstrating conceptual equivalents between terms used in a number of indexing systems, both thesauri and classification schedules. FID plans to publish the preliminary document, embodying the main twenty-nine groups with their definitions.

Even if the thesauri are available, much depends on what kind of person chooses the terms for the index entries from the thesauri. It is clear that if an information scientist, an author, and a keypunch operator were asked to choose index entries for an article written by the author, it is quite possible that their selections would differ considerably. The whole of indexing is still in the evolutionary stage, and even recent attempts at its improvement are astonishingly naive. It is true that a KWIC-type index may help the searcher to recover the most relevant documents almost as well and as quickly as more elaborate indexes, but this is probably because such indexes are more elaborate than truly efficient. In a similar fashion, several independent simple indexes may give better results than a single more complex index embracing all the entries in one sequence, but here the real fault probably lies with the fiendishly difficult rules of arrangement that have now evolved for the vast indexes thought necessary for today's scientists and technologists. It is well, then, that Mr. J. Farradane—whose pioneer work in this field at City University, London, is widely known—should be pursuing research on information retrieval by relational indexing, for his system enables subtle differences to be conveyed by a simple form of notation that can be easily understood and applied. In the meantime, the machine expedients of KWIC and KWOC will continue to be widely employed—and with considerable success, as in the index of French nuclear information produced by the Centre for Nuclear Studies at Saclay.

In spite of the inevitable time lag in the publication of abstracts—a problem to which there is no satisfactory solution—the number of published abstracting services continues to increase. There are several reasons for this. In the first place, a glance at the *Yearbook of International Organizations* shows that the headquarters of the vast majority of international organizations are situated in Europe. The more effective of these bodies make a point of insuring that a good abstracting service in their field is operative either through their own staff and resources or under their auspices. Thus, a large number of abstracting services in important fields have come into being since World War II. Further, national governments, universities, professional associations, and so forth have tended to extend to the general public the use of abstracting services that they had long maintained for internal use. (In countries where foreign exchange is limited, this move has sometimes been prompted by the advantage of having something to offer in return for the publications badly needed from abroad.) In some cases the abstracting services are clearly prestige efforts; in a few definitely promotional. But whatever the motives behind their issue, their effect is invariably beneficial. It is true that this kind of uncoordinated effort carries with it some overlapping that could well be eliminated in favor of abstracting further material at present not covered. It is equally true that such overlapping has sometimes exposed weaknesses in individual services that have then been remedied.

Two recent studies have been published, one conducted by the Centre for Information and Documentation at Euratom, the other by the Abstracting Bureau of the International Council of Scientific Unions (ICSU), on the question of what Euratom calls "core journals." The International Council set out to get precise information on which journals provided the bulk of material for abstracting in the field of physics; Euratom made a similar study of nuclear material. The ICSU Abstracting Board made a statistical study of a single year's output by *Physics Abstracts, Physikalische Berichte,* and the physics section of the *Bulletin signalétique* of the [French] National Council of Scientific Research. The *Bulletin* yielded 97,772 abstracts, the *Berichte* 25,093, and *Physics Abstracts* about 31,000 abstracts. A scrutiny of these statistics revealed that about one-fifth of the journals were responsible for about four-fifths of the total abstracts, and that about one percent of the total number of journals provide about twenty-five percent of the abstracts. Euratom's investigation covered a narrower field, being restricted to the experience of *Nuclear Science Abstracts,* and this during a single quarter of 1965 only. Of the more than 21,000 abstracts surveyed, it was found that about two-thirds derived from about two thousand primary journals. About half the total number of abstracts came from only one-seventh of the journals under investigation. Thus, both surveys show what any experienced librarian or information scientist would expect: that not only the bulk but also most of the important abstracts derive from a very small number of journals, and that every abstracting service is probably conducting an uneconomic process in searching a great periphery of other journals in order to insure comprehensive coverage.

A glance at some of the leading abstracting services will show that there is an amazing amount of variation in almost every aspect of abstract publication. Probably the most obvious can be seen in the individuality of formats used in presenting the bibliographical references: an analysis of these shows that typography, punctuation, order of items, indication of place of publication and publisher, dates, volume and issue numbers, indication of presence of illustrations, bibliographies, charts, etc., are all presented in a variety of fashions, the explanation for which can only be judged to be the individual editor's preference. In some cases the abstract precedes the bibliographical reference, in others it follows. Sometimes the author is emphasized, sometimes his institutional affiliations are indicated, but more often the title is featured in capitals or bold face, and the author is less prominent. There are good reasons for all these differences, but none that can possibly outweigh the international advantages of dull uniformity. If the computer is to come into its own in this field, and if knowledge is to be increasingly automated, then abstracting services will need to conform to an acceptable mean in the interests of scholarship.

Far more important, however, is the apparent doubt concerning what constitutes an abstract. The very overlapping that has been criticized here lends force to the fact that there seems to be no universal agreement as to what constitutes an effective abstract. A brief and unpublished study conducted recently showed that in a case where three different people—the author, a professional abstractor, and a working contributor—had by chance abstracted the same article, from the abstracts alone it was by no means certain that they referred to the same original. In another case, where only two abstracts were available, each presented a significant amount of information that the other did not convey. Thus, with the many different surveys now being conducted concerning abstracting services, there appears to be room for at least one more on the *content* of abstracts and their relation to the originals.

The presentation of abstracts would also appear to warrant some examination in the interest of service to users. For example, the indexes to the individual issues of abstracting journals vary from the very elaborate to the almost nonexistent. The contents of these journals are also arranged by a surprising number of methods, ranging from simple alphabetical arrangement by title of journal, through alphabetical arrangement by author's name, to full-scale classified arrangement by means of an individual or an internationally known classification scheme. The reasons for all these variations are obvious and reasonable enough: each editor addresses his effort to the informed user who makes use of his journal month after month and can therefore be relied upon to be thoroughly familiar with the journal's methods and idiosyncrasies. No fault can be found with this, but at the same time it is clear that no provision has been made for the user who is unfamiliar with the abstracting journal, since he is likely to use it only infrequently for fringe material. Nor is there any provision for the librarian or information scientist who needs to use a large number of abstracting services every day and does not find it easy to adjust his mind to a new system of arrangement and presentation every time he refers to a new service. In particular, variations in index presentation and arrangement may result in an item being overlooked or missed. In addition, unusual— and unexplained—abbreviations may cause considerable delay while they are identified.

It is, in fact, time that an international conference on these and other aspects were held, and the right setting would still be Europe whence the majority of abstracts still originate. The problem is urgent, for not only are new abstracting services still coming into being, but established services are also increasing their coverage and producing more abstracts. With more international planning and some national willingness to make concessions in the interest of progress, a very much greater amount of material could be effectively covered without significant increases in cost, time, or staffs. Information retrieval would, in fact, gain immeasurably in its most important field.

Although mechanical translation has certainly not lived up to its promise so far, some progress has been made. The Autonomics Division of the National Physical Laboratory at Teddington appears to have reached a genuinely useful stage in the establishment of automatic translation of Russian scientific texts. It is gradually becoming clearer that automatic translation is most successful in small and very clearly defined subject-fields in science and technology, and that its effective application outside these areas may be subject to extensive delays. In the meanwhile, there are developments in the provision of non-automated translations: the Ingeniörsvetenskapsakademien (IVA) at Stockholm, in its work of facilitating loans from the Soviet Union, also arranges to supply Russian translations provided by the USSR. And the Technical Information Library at Hannover maintains an index of translations of scientific and technical literature from Slavonic and Far Eastern libraries, and collaborates with the European Translation Centre at Delft. The long-established translation sources at Aslib in London and the National Lending Library of Science and Technology in Yorkshire are well enough known to need no further elaboration here.

The present position of the UDC in Europe is quite astonishing: latest figures show that of a world total of some 110,000 libraries known to be using this classification, about fifty thousand of them are in the USSR and another forty thousand in Poland. Thus, a scheme that originated in the west of Europe is now mainly established in the east. Even more extraordinary is the fact that the Middle Edition of the UDC, prepared by the German Classification Committee, is published in German and intended to serve as a master edition for translations into other languages, whereas an English-language edition would stand more chance of drawing widespread international comment and criticism at a time when its increased adoption in libraries throughout the world is obviously very desirable. It is known that about 170,000 copies of the full edition of the schedules are in the hands of various libraries, and its continuing influence is therefore considerable. The vigorous efforts of such experts as Mr. J. E. Wright (Chairman of the British Standards Institution's Committee OC/20/4) in keeping the schedules up to date by informed revision need to be more widely known and recognized than they appear to be at the moment.

The mechanization applications of UDC were effectively demonstrated when the Centre Mechanized Documentation at Frankfurt-am-Main compiled the forty-thousand-entry alphabetical subject index to the 1967 Medium German edition of the schedules. FID hopes to install an automatic tape-type writing machine for use in preparing punched cards or paper-tape records of all UDC proposals, and offset masters or stencils for small office printing machines. Later the punched tape will be converted to magnetic form and used in computer operations. The FID's CCC subcommittee on mechanization is now engaged on compiling a standard code for converting UDC symbols into acceptable form for computer programming. The Soviet Union's adoption of the UDC dates back to 1921, though it was not until 1962 that it decreed that all material in the natural sciences and technology should be classified by UDC. This was followed by Czechoslovakia where, in 1965, the National Information System on Science, Technology and Economics (VTEIP) issued a directive making the UDC the standard classification for all information centers in that country. And in the United Kingdom, the British Standards Institution is making every effort to complete publication of the full English-language edition of the UDC in 1969. The remarkable thing about the UDC is that it is familiar to most librarians mainly through its scientific and technological schedules, and more needs to be known about the degree to which it has been found satisfactory in its application to the humanities and the social sciences. FID has certainly not been backward in its endeavors to take into account every point of view and every valid suggestion for improvement. For example, its Central Classification Committee has agreed to permit the use of the new Perrault Relator schema in the UDC for a trial period of five years, using the small-letter notation in conjunction with the colon by way of stressing the still experimental nature of the project.

The important part played by cataloging in the business of information retrieval is growing in recognition. For the past five years the School of Mines, in Paris, and the Bureau of Geological Research, in Orleans, undaunted by the fact that their catalogs are organized on different principles, have been exchanging cataloging information by teleprinter. In fact, France also shares cataloging among many libraries by means of Telex. In Britain, the *British National Bibliography* staff has insured that the United Kingdom MARC record is compatible with the Library of Congress MARC II. Centralized cataloging is increasingly a feature in several countries: the Soviet Union maintains a centralized cataloging system, the *BNB* provides a central cataloging service, and most European countries issue current national bibliographies from which cataloging detail can be drawn.

Standardization, the essential basis of modern bibliographical and information retrieval operations, is not as far advanced as it should be. Although there is fairly general recognition throughout Europe that standardization in library and information work is an essential preliminary to any schemes for practical international cooperation, the methods of preparing and establishing standards do not lend themselves to speedy adoption. The reasons are easily understood. To prepare a national standard it is necessary to secure the voluntary services of experts in the subject-field of that standard, and this means that each meeting needs to be arranged at a time when all or most can attend. The preparation of a single draft standard may involve as many as thirty or forty meetings, so that it is doubtful whether the preliminary drafts of many standards have been prepared in less than a year. The circulation of the drafts to the many interested bodies, the consideration of the innumerable points then put forward by those bodies for detailed consideration, and the finalizing of the text of the standard involve at least as long a period as the initial draft. The international aspects add considerably to the time element: whereas it is most desirable—if not essential—to get the widest international reaction to a national standard, the time needed to circulate and to gather comment can, in some cases, render parts of the original standard out-of-date. Thus, when one looks at the lists of standards in the field of information work, the titles are pitifully few—Bibliographical References, Indexes, Sizes of Periodicals, Alphabetical Arrangement, and so on and so forth—but significantly, not one on abstracts. That there is a move to establish such an abstract is a result of action in the United States, but how soon one can hope to see an internationally accepted standard on this very important subject is anyone's guess. This is not to detract in any way from the magnificent work performed by the ISO and the national standards bodies. It is simply to emphasize that in these days of jet transport and space satellites, geographical limitations are still in force to a certain extent.

In Europe—and, undoubtedly, throughout the world—cost consciousness is playing a greater part in the development of information retrieval processes. A French inquiry on SYNTOL, for example, revealed that the handling of an individual document averages forty-five francs. Other costing figures, established in connection with the interlending of books and periodicals, showed equally that costing on a realistic basis could materially affect policy in many information spheres. In all this, the impact of the computer is either immediate or imminent. The sterling pioneer work done at Newcastle-upon-Tyne in studying the computer's applications to handling bibliographical work has probably more significance in the area of test methodology than in the experimental results, but is nonetheless valuable. Not everyone likes the idea of automation, and there are too many tales that can be told of the ill-advised hasty adoption of mechanization for those interested in the progress of information work to believe that the changeover will at any time be easy. There is no point in automation for its own sake, still less in mechanizing something whose basic principles have yet to be grasped. Nevertheless, costing has shown that automation is essential, and therefore the provision of education in this area is all the more important. Thus, the courses at City University and Sheffield University and those at the Technical University in Budapest are only examples of some of the many training schemes now being initiated to cope with this problem.

What has proved a stumbling block in establishing these courses is that a sound mathematical background is essential in a sphere where Boolean algebra and the binary system are in daily use. This is an educational background not possessed by most of today's librarians and, although it has been proved that librarians with a background in the humanities can be very successful in information work in science and technology, the acquiring of sufficient mathematical skills is something that it is no longer possible to sidestep. Unfortunately, the essential prerequisite to attracting new entrants to the profession, with the kind of background that automation demands, is a better salary-and-prospects scheme than most European countries are now able to offer. After all, information retrieval depends on information storage, and in both of these operations staff of high caliber, of intelligence and initiative, are needed, and they are by no means available in sufficient numbers to the many establishments that could make use of them.

What the future may hold for Europe in this field is something that few would care to predict. One point is clear: that in spite of the national and international pressures of commercial competition and industrial challenge, there is no great sense of urgency in the steady and impressive progress being made in both classification and information retrieval. The policy is rather one of careful testing and trial experience before further steps are taken. On the other hand, there is an air of general involvement: Europeans favor all-round experience and every librarian and information scientist feels he has an interest and a right in every professional matter. Thus, detailed matters of classification are generally discussed and draw well-informed comment from a large audience. In fact, apart from India, where the Ranganathan theories are predominant, Europe provides the chief testing-ground for new throries and new classifications. Similarly, owing to the diverse natures of Europe's many nations, progress in information retrieval may equally well be influenced decisively by what emanates from Paris or Berlin, London or Moscow.

## BIBLIOGRAPHY

Abstracting Services in Science, Technology, Medicine, Agriculture, Social Sciences and Humanities. *(Report No. 372.)* The Hague; International Federation for Documentation, 1965.

Bohm, E. *Investigation on Nuclear "Core Journals."* Brussels: Euratom, 1968.

Bundesministerium für Wissenschaftliche Forschung. Bildung einer "Kommission Dokumentation und Information" des Interministeriellen Ausschusses für Wissenschaft und Forschung. 1965 (Pressedienst no. 22/65, 15 December 1965).

Cleverdon, Cyril William. *Report on the First Stage of an Investigation into the Comparative Efficiency of Indexing Systems.* Cranfield, 1960.

———. *Report on the Testing and Analysis of an Investigation into the Comparative Efficieny of Indexing Systems.* Cranfield, 1962.

Cleverdon, Cyril W., and others. *Factors Determining the Performance of Indexing Systems.* 2 vols. Cranfield, 1966.

Cockx, A. "Le centre national de documentation scientifique et technique." In *Industrie*. Bruxelles: February 1966.

Collision, Robert Lewis. *Indexes and Indexing*. 3d ed. London: Ernest Benn, 1969.

"Communication in the Biological Sciences." [summaries of papers presented at the December 1966 conference of the Institute of Biology] In *Journal of the Institute of Biology*, 14 (1967): 2-23.

The [Dainton]*Report on National Libraries*. London: HMSO, 1969.

deReuck, Anthony, and Knight, Julie, eds. *Communication in Science: Documentation and Automation*. London: J. & A. Churchill, 1967 (A Ciba Foundation volume).

Farradane, Jason. "Relational Indexing and Classification in the Light of Recent Experimental Work in Psychology," *Information Storage Retrieval* 1 (1963): 3-11.

Gardin, Jean Claude. "Document Analysis and Information Retrieval." *UNESCO Bulletin for Libraries* 14 (1960): 2-5.

*Government and Technical Innovation*. Report of the Organisation for Economic Co-operation and Development to the Second Ministerial Meeting on Science. Paris: January 1966.

Kent, Allen and Lancour, Harold, eds. *Encyclopedia of Library and Information Science*. Vol. 1. New York & London: Marcel Dekker, 1968.

King, Alexander. "Science Policy, Documentation and the Future of FID." In *Proceedings of the 1965 Congress of the International Federation for Documentation,* pp. 249-255. Washington, D.C: Spartan Books; London: Macmillan, 1966.

Lloyd, Geoffrey A. "The UDC in its International Aspects." *Aslib Proceedings* 21, no. 5 (May 1969): 204-208.

Needham, R. M. *The Place of Automatic Classification in Information Retrieval*. (Report no. ML 166). Cambridge, England: Cambridge Language Research Institute, 1963.

*Scientific Information*. Stockholm: The Swedish Government Research Advisory Board, 1963. (Promemoria, no. 4)

Vickery, Brian Campbell "Machines and Indexes," *UNESCO Bulletin for Libraries* 13 (1959):249-252.

Vickery, Brian Campbell and Simpson, D. J. "Future of Scientific Communication," *Science Journal* 2 (1966): 80-85

*World Literature in Physics as Seen through the Bulletin signalétique, 1964 Issues*. Paris, Conseil international des unions scientifiques, Bureau des résumés analytiques, 1967. 2 volumes.

Wright, J. E. "Steps in the Development of BS 1000," *Aslib Proceedings* 21, no. 5 (May 1969): 195-203.

# 12/ Special Libraries and
## Information Centers
### in Southwest Asia

JOHN F. HARVEY
*University of Tehran*

$B$efore presenting a picture of the special libraries and information centers in Southwest Asia, it is necessary to define several terms. Special libraries are those serving government ministries, private corporations, and university departments. Information centers are similar to special libraries, but they provide personalized, high quality reference service, usually pertaining to science and technology, and they often use punched cards for information storage and retrieval. Southwest Asia is that area bound by Turkey and the United Arab Republic on the West and Pakistan on the East.

This survey is presented on a country-by-country basis. Six of the countries were visited personally. Information stated about the others is often sparse because of the omission of a personal visit, the scarcity of relevant information available in Tehran, and the difficulties encountered in obtaining information by mail and in English. This survey is not complete; rather, it presents the initial outline around which more facts could be gathered. Also, it should be remembered that Southwest Asia is an area within which relatively few outstanding libraries can be expected.[1]

*Afghanistan*

The Kabul University Library is the leading library in this country with about seventy thousand volumes, but it has no well-organized

275

branches. Abdul Babury, its director, is an American-educated leader in Afghan library affairs. The new Russian-sponsored technical university library may also become important in future years. Recently the Higher Teachers College Library in Kabul has been expanded by H. V. Bonny, UNESCO expert. There are several small government ministry libraries, but they are without professional direction, the Press Department Library with twenty-eight thousand volumes being the largest. The Kabul Museum, The Royal Palace, and the National Bank have libraries also. Apparently, there are no corporate libraries in Afghanistan. None of the dozen or so special libraries provide technical information-center service.

*Iran*

Modern service is available in several Iranian special libraries and information centers. Two petroleum companies and one trade library provide more than usual library service. The Oil Consortium Geology Library in Tehran uses computer print-outs to keep an index of company reports useful for reference service, as does the consortium's library in Ahwaz. The Tehran library may be the only one in Southwest Asia doing KWIC indexing of technical reports and using links and roles to give added depth and usefulness. Presently, the collection contains only about two thousand volumes, but in a few years it will be large enough to support considerable reference service. The National Iranian Oil Company Library (Lily Arjomand, librarian) has 23,000 volumes plus the American Petroleum Institute computer tapes and abstract services. It offers its engineers and business managers personal reference service and literature searches, and it announces new acquisitions to the entire company each month. The Ministry of Economy Research Center for Trade and Industrial Development library (Mahin Tafazzoli, librarian) answers reference questions and does literature searches for Center staff members.

There are four useful medical libraries in Tehran. The University of Tehran School of Public Health Library publishes a monthly acquisitions list, does literature searches, and obtains photocopies and translations on request. Its collection of index and abstract services is especially comprehensive. The Pasteur Institute Library has a beautiful reading room, a collection of about five thousand bound periodicals, and a good reprint collection. The University of Tehran College of Medicine Library (Nasrin Tajadod, librarian) with about forty thousand volumes, and the University of Tehran Veterinary Medicine Library (Dr. Sohrab, librarian) with large serial holdings, have useful collections, also.

The Parliament and National Libraries in Tehran offer minimal service but contain relatively large book collections—about seventy-five thousand volumes apiece—and receive considerable use. Also Tehran has a good bank library with twenty-five thousand volumes (F. Goharian, librarian) at the Central Bank. It has three professionals, and a major recataloging project is underway. The Malek Library and the Pahlavi Library are major collections of Iranian manuscript and historical material.

Among other Tehran special libraries, the Teachers Training College mathematics library and the Iranian Geological Survey library are small but well organized and distinctive, both having open shelves and large reading rooms. Other University of Tehran branches deserving mention are those serving the Centre for International Affairs, (Shahla Sepehri, librarian) with ten thousand volumes and three professional librarians; the College of Education, (Farangis Omid, librarian) with six thousand volumes and three librarians; and the College of Business and Public Administration, (Mrs. Adagh Sanei, librarian) with ten thousand volumes.

Good special libraries elsewhere in Iran include the Pahlavi University Medical Library in Shiraz, (Lorraine Murphy, librarian) and the Razi Institute Library in Hassarach, (Parviz Nasseri, librarian). Pahlavi has twenty-eight thousand volumes to support an active medical research program, and the Razi Library services the laboratory's researchers and pharmaceutical chemists who are guiding vaccine production. Recently, Pahlavi University has opened a large engineering library with Kenneth Brown as librarian. Karaj's Agricultural College Library is well prepared to give modern reference service also.

There are two documentation centers in Tehran. The French

Documentation Center enables business and professional men to study current copies of French periodicals and utilizes the services of a French industrial consultant. It also presents a lecture series on French life and industry. The national Iranian scientific documentation center, IRANDOC, under the Ministry of Science and Higher Education, was organized only a few months ago, and it is headed by Amir Etemad and Ali Sinai. It now has forty employees and an annual budget of a million dollars. This is the largest library or documentation center budget and staff in Iran. The Center has plans to offer the full range of documentation services in science and social science as well as plans to house a large book collection and national book processing center. It will develop its own computer and facsimile transmission system to bring rapid and comprehensive service to Iranian researchers and professors.

Finally, the Department of Library Science, College of Education, at the University of Tehran offers an English-language master's degree curriculum. There is a required course in Information Science, a course in Special Librarianship, and the opportunity to prepare a research report and do an internship in these areas. Many of the vacancies filled by graduates are in Ministry libraries.

## Iraq

Modern special library service is available to the National Oil Company's petroleum engineers in Baghdad. The Nuclear Research Center Library provides modern service and hopes to add documentation services soon.[2] Baghdad has also an Iraq Museum Library with thirty-eight thousand volumes; a National History Museum Library with sixteen thousand volumes, (Hamid Salaman, librarian); an Institute of Fine Arts Library; an American School of Oriental Research Library; and a National Library with thirty-six thousand volumes. Mosul has a Museum Library and a College of Medicine Library.

The University of Baghdad Central Library (Husham Al-Chawaf, director) is the largest in Iraq, with about eighty thousand volumes.

There are also libraries for the Colleges of Arts (thirty-two thousand volumes); Science, Economics, Political Science, Law, Medicine (sixty thousand volumes); Education (thirty thousand volumes); Agriculture (twelve thousand volumes); Veterinary Medicine; and the Arid Zone Research Institute. The University offered a six month UNESCO library science course in the winter and spring of 1967; it hopes to open a library school to educate librarians for modern government service within the near future.

## Israel

In Haifa, at the Technion, Israel Institute of Technology, Director Gladstein has organized the Library to facilitate literature searching and use. The staff assists with literature searches, but no special documentation service exists. The Library contains ninety thousand volumes and four thousand current periodical titles. The Haifa Public Library keeps a special card file of current Hebrew periodical material, an unusual documentation service.

In Jerusalem the Knesset Library, with its four tiers and fifty thousand volumes, is a showplace for visitors. Parliament members are provided special information service; material pertaining to subjects under debate is collected for their scrutiny by librarian Shmuel Wasserman. The 1.6 million volume Hebrew University and National Library in Jerusalem has one of the largest scientific and technical collections in Southwest Asia, but thus far it offers no documentation service.

The Weizmann Institute of Science Library at Rehovoth is decentralized but totals seventy-five thousand volumes, with part of the collection kept in its attractive central library (Alma Rosenhack, librarian). Its interlibrary loan service is quite active—averaging eighteen volumes per day. Relatively little additional reference service is provided, but the library does publish a list of its one thousand seven hundred periodical subscriptions, and Xerox photocopy service is available. The Wix Library is open seventeen hours per day and houses all material on open shelves.

Other Israeli special libraries worth mentioning can be found in the following cities and institutions.

### Beit Dagan

Israel Meteorological Service
Kimran Veterinary Institute

### Haifa

Israel Ceramic and Silicate Institute
Israel Mining Industries Institute for Research and Development
Sea Fisheries Research Station

### Jerusalem

Atomic Energy Commission
Gulbenkian Library (fifty thousand volumes), a large Armenian research library
Hebrew University Agricultural (fifty-five thousand volumes and two thousand two hundred serial titles) and Medical Schools in Rehovoth and Jerusalem—among the best in all of Asia
Hydrological Service
Institute for Fibres and Forest Products Research
Israel Geological Survey
Supreme Court Library

### Tel Aviv

Central Music Library (forty-two thousand volumes)
Israel Institute of Packaging and Industrial Design
Israel Institute of Petroleum
Israel Institute of Productivity
Israel Standards Institute

### Other locations

Fish Culture Research Station at Dor
Israel Institute for Biological Research, Nesaion
Laboratory for Fish Diseases at Nir Davis
Locust Research Laboratory at Yafo
Neger Institute for Arid Zone Research, Beer Sheva
Soil Erosion Research Station at Emeg Hefer

The leading documentation center is the Center for Scientific and Technological Information, Tel Aviv, established in 1961. Like those in Pakistan, Turkey, and India (PANSDOC, TURDOC, and

INSDOC), this center is a national government agency providing high grade reference service to Ministry and industrial scientists and engineers. Its leaders are Carl Karen and Lydia Vilentchuk, both former engineers. CSTI has a small library and compiles and publishes the following lists and directories:

> Directory of Special Libraries
> List of Scientific and Technical Associations and Institutes
> Directory of Serials Published in Israel
> Union List of Serials in Israel Libraries
> Directory of Current Research in Israel

The Center also publishes the following periodicals:

> Monthly Contents Pages in Data Processing, Ceramics
>   and Silicates, and Electronics
> Semi-annual Calendar of Forthcoming Scientific Events
> Quarterly Desalination Abstracts

Thirty people are employed as literature searchers, abstractors, indexers, and editors. Their literature procurement service will obtain a photocopy in an Israeli or foreign library, absorb the labor cost, and assess the scientist only the photocopy and postal charge. A fee is charged for literature searches and state-of-the-art studies made by canvassing Israeli libraries. The volume of CSTI business in about twenty requests per day, and the total budget is $100,000 per year. The local computer service center is used for experimental purposes.

Courses in special librarianship and information science are given in three Israeli locations. At the Graduate Library School, Hebrew University, two or three courses are given in a diploma program otherwise oriented toward the humanities (Curt Wormann, director). The school's departmental library contains a good collection of material in these fields. CSTI employs an American information scientist, such as Arthur Elias or Isaac Welt, for a six-week series of lectures each year, and it cooperates with the Weizmann Institute and the Ministry of Labor in sponsoring a one-year Diploma program in Information Science. This program aims to provide ten to fifteen educated employees each year for industrial information centers. A course in special librarianship is given each year at the Technion Research and Development Foundation, Tel Aviv. In addition, there is an Israel Society of Special Libraries and Information Centers.[3]

## Jordan

The University of Jordan, in Amman, is improving its library, (twenty-five thousand volumes, Khaled Sakit, director) and offers special library service in its departmental branches. There is also a Ministry of Education Library and a Department of Scientific Research Library in Amman, and the Al-Husseir College of Agriculture Library in Tulkarin.

## Kuwait

Kuwait City has a university library (M.M. Saleh, librarian) with sixty-two thousand volumes (probably including manuscripts), but the only special library there seems to be the Ministry of Health Library.

## Lebanon

The American University in Beirut has forty-four thousand volumes in its medical library, for which new housing is planned. This is one of the largest medical libraries in Southwest Asia. The two hundred seventy thousand volume American University Library intends, when funds permit, to offer documentation service for students and faculty that will cover educational reports and curricular materials. Francis Kent and Ritchie Thomas, the directors, offer a summer workshop in one aspect of librarianship each year, and in cooperation with the World Health Organization, have held short courses in medical librarianship.

The Lebanese Industrial Service in Beirut has recently begun a small scale documentation service for industrial customers. There are also French language medical (twenty thousand volumes) and Law (twenty-five thousand volumes) libraries available at St. Joseph's University. Beirut has several government ministry libraries as well as the national library of one hundred thousand volumes, which is now being reorganized under the leadership of a Swiss UNESCO librarian.

## Pakistan

In Karachi, personal, high-grade reference service is made available to a small clientele from the National Institute for Public Administration Library's collection (Mohammid Arifuddin, librarian). Another small library (fifteen thousand volumes) is in the Jinnah Post-Graduate Medical Centre in Karachi (Zakiuddin Ahmad, librarian). Its collection may not be large, but the library provides modern microfilm service for medical material. Also in Karachi are two excellent bank libraries. The State Bank Library contains twenty-eight thousand volumes, subscribes to five hundred periodicals, does literature searches, and has a commendable book collection. The National Bank Library has many new books and is furnished with private carrels. Both libraries have large budgets, carpeted floors, liberal import licenses, and growing collections open to students, employees, and researchers. Syed Riaauddin and Jameelunnisa Ahmed are the two librarians.

The Pakistan Atomic Energy Centers in Lahore (M. M. Rafique, librarian) and Dacca are providing good library facilities for their researchers. Lahore operates as a technical information center, with numerous bibliographies and union lists compiled. The Pakistan Council for Scientific and Industrial Research Library in Karachi holds chemical research material. The Forestry Institute in Peshawar has a small and attractive library in its field. There are also Irrigation Research and Cotton Research libraries in Pakistan, as well as a Geological Survey Library.

Pansdoc is the largest and oldest documentation center in Southwest Asia, with 125 employees and fourteen years of experience. It also has the greatest amount of business—about seventy-five requests for service per day. It is located in two houses in residential Karachi and will eventually move to new quarters in the capital city, Islamabad. Pansdoc employs two full-time and several part-time specialists translating French and German into English. It uses UDC but has no computer use program at present. Pansdoc procures photocopies or microfilm of material for scientists from libraries in Pakistan and abroad. In some cases it merely finds the material, but in others the material is first obtained and then filmed in Pansdoc's own laboratory. Their studio now has enough film to fill a good percentage of requests. The Pansdoc print shop serves the entire Research Council. Through its offset, VariTyper, and photographic equipment it produces several comprehensive bibliographies, translations, and other reports each year, as well as the necessary art work. To a specialist, Pansdoc can supply a list of organizations working in his field. Union lists of material are maintained for the entire country, and small service branches are located in Dacca and Lahore. A. R. Mohajir, the director, is well known in his field and deserves much credit for Pansdoc's success. The remainder of the staff is made up of library school and science graduates. Bibliographies in English, microfilms, photocopies, translations, and the *Pakistan Science Abstracts* are all supplied for a nominal fee.

The Karachi University Department of Library Science offers one course in information science and two in special librarianship, with both of which Dr. Mohajir cooperates. Special librarianship is also taught at Dacca University's Department of Library Science. And finally, there is a Pakistan Special Librarians Association.

### Saudi Arabia

The University Library at Jeddah is improving, but probably the most modern special library service is offered at the Arabian American Oil Company Central Technical Library in Dhahran. Two other academic libraries exist, at Islamic University in Medina and the University of Riyadh (sixty-five thousand volumes; Mohamed Al-Solai, librarian). Mecca has large and valuable Arabic manuscript libraries, and other special libraries exist at the General Directorate of the Press in Jeddah and the Higher Institute of Technology at Riyadh.

## Syria

Damascus has a university library with sixty thousand volumes, departmental library service, and Yousef Zakkhour as the Librarian. Probably a few government ministry libraries have librarians educated elsewhere who provide modern service. There is also a Center for Study and Documentation in Economics and Political Science at Damascus and a National Library with sixty-five thousand volumes.

## Turkey

One of Ankara's most attractive buildings belongs to the Turkish Historical Society, wherein fifty thousand volumes are available. Researchers and students receive excellent service and literature searches are made frequently by librarian Mahin Ehrin. Through interlibrary loans, authors are given bibliographic assistance. Another Ankara center is the Union Chambers of Commerce Library with its ten thousand volume collection, pleasant setting, and special indexing services for patrons. Gulten Kayaalp is librarian. Two other Ankara special libraries are the National Library (Mujgan Cunbur, librarian) and the Parliament Library (Nazmi Coskuntor, librarian), both large governmental book collections, six hundred thousand and two hundred thousand volumes respectively, but neither has developed its service aspect extensively.

In Istanbul there is a medical school library, a technical university library, a manuscript library (The Suleymaniye), and a state library (The Bayazit). The Suleymaniye is a large manuscript collection, of great interest to Southwest Asian historians, which is housed in a former school (Halit Dener, librarian). The Bayazit is also large and is heavily used by students because of its reading room facilities and copyright deposit collection. There are several good archeological libraries in Turkey, and even the spectacular Topkapi Museum has a library. The Atomic Energy Center in Turkey receives international atomic documentation material and special abstracting and indexing services, thereby serving as an information service center. The Hacettepe University Population Research Information Center provides special indexing, abstracting, and photocopy services, maintains card files, and provides translation service for its subsidized research staff members. It has two full-time staff members and represents modern technical information-center service given in a university setting.

In Ankara, Turkey has its Turdoc as Israel has its CSTI, also a national scientific and technical information center. Turdoc is even younger than CSTI and has only six or seven staff members, including several indexers and abstractors. Turdoc publishes two abstracting journals in English to cover Turkish biological and physical scientific material, a creditable publication program for a young organization. It provides literature searches, photocopy, and microfilm service, and is building up its files in preparation for extensive literature service. Turdoc also has duplication and photographic equipment useful in publication. This Center must expand its physical facilities before it can add enough staff to provide for a large volume of business from researchers. Only one request a day is received now. No work with punched cards was found. This Center was established by A. L. Gardner, UNESCO Documentation Expert. The Research Council Library on the lower floor of Turdoc's building is small but growing rapidly. The collection consists primarily of reference sets and scientific and technical serials. About two hundred periodical titles are received.

There is a small Turkish Special Librarians Association, and library schools exist in Ankara and Istanbul. Both schools graduate undergraduate majors in library science, some of whom enter special librarianship.


*U.A.R.*

The United Arab Republic is one of the richest library countries in the Middle East, with many special libraries in Cairo and Alexandria. Unfortunately no visit could be scheduled there, so all information is second hand.

The following are a few of the larger special libraries:

*Cairo*

Ministry of Education Library (60,000 volumes)
Ministry of Justice Library (50,000 volumes)
Institute of Egypt Library (160,000 volumes)
Entomological Society Library (23,000 volumes)
National Library (700,000 volumes) Addel Moneim Obel, librarian
Bank of Egypt Library (5,000 volumes)
Egyptian Academy of Sciences Library
Geological Survey Library (15,000 volumes)
Ministry of Agriculture Library (25,000 volumes)
University of Cairo Library provides educational documentation service for teachers

*Alexandria*

World Health Organization Library provides modern documentation service.
Institute of Hydrobiology Library (10,000 volumes)

No doubt the leading Egyptian information center is the National Documentation and Information Center (NIDOC) started in Cairo with UNESCO assistance (Ahmad Kabesh, director). This center has a large staff and covers all Arabic-language scientific publications, no matter where published. Its organization resembles that of other UNESCO assisted documentation centers, and it is located in the National Research Center, which has a small library open to the public. Bibliographies are prepared in English and French, while photocopies and microfilm are supplied from any country. Eight languages are translated, and a monthly *Abstracts of Scientific and Technical Papers* is published.

The University of Cairo Department of Library Science, the only library school in an Arab country, teaches some undergraduate courses useful to special librarians and in recent years has given a course in documentation. Three- and four-week courses on documentation, in French and English, are offered by the Documentation Center in Cairo to university graduates.

*Conclusion*

Special libraries and information centers are well represented in an area of the world generally considered to be underdeveloped. There are several examples of modern reference service, and every possible current method of providing service is represented in either the practice or the plans of some library or center. Four examples of the most up-to-date and intensive reference service are shown in the large documentation centers, and at least one of them is internationally famous for its services. The future looks promising, for undoubtedly special libraries and information centers will increase and improve as industry expands, government ministries demand better service, and publication programs enlarge. More formal instruction is needed, but several countries have made a start toward a special library or information science curriculum, with Israel leading the way.

Although the commercial indexing and abstracting services published in these countries may not be comparable with those of the United States, they are improving, too. It should be noted that modern service has not been restricted to the scientific and technical fields, but has been incorporated into banking and historical libraries. The extension of the modern information service philosophy, which seeks maximum benefits from a collection of materials, is more important than the mere spread of libraries.

Since many agencies in this geographic area are now giving good service, it can be suggested that they cooperate more closely and coordinate their activities. If the documentation centers in Ankara, Karachi, Tel Aviv, Tehran, and Cairo could work closely together in extending their service, each would save money by using the data store accumulated by the others. Improved telephone and telex service between these centers would be required, and, eventually, facsimile transmission and on-line computer service to each other and to European centers. With such cooperation, subject concentration for each center and frequent exchange of abstracted material could follow.

In the entire area, five countries lead the way: Israel, Turkey, Pakistan, UAR, and Iran. The documentation centers give the best service, with Pansdoc, Nidoc, and Tel Aviv ahead of Turdoc and Irandoc. Strong libraries include the Pahlavi University Medical Library, and the Centre for International Affairs in Iran, the Knesset in Jerusalem, the Turkish Historical Society and the Union Chambers of Commerce in Ankara, and the Suleymaniye in Istanbul. Other excellent special libraries are the Central Banks in both Karachi and Tehran, the State Bank in Karachi, and the Atomic Energy Center Library in Lahore. The librarians of these libraries are among the best in the area with the addition of Arifuddin and Ahmad in Pakistan, Tafazzoli, Arjomand, Vartany, Sinai, and Brown in Iran.

## NOTES

1.  Other papers containing information on this subject: "Iranian Library Perspective," *Library Journal* 93 (15 November 1968): 4239-4445; "The Iranian Library Scene," *International Library Review* (March 1969); "Pakistan and Afghan Librarianship," *Pakistan Library Review* (March 1969); "Librarianship in Six Southwest Asian Countries," *Turkish Library Association Bulletin* (to be published); Francis Kent, "Training of Librarians and Documentalists in Arabic Speaking Countries," *UNESCO Library Bulletin* 21 (November-December 1967):301-310. Additionally, written reports have been prepared to guide the development of several Iranian special libraries and information centers. Other sources include *American Library Directory* (New York: R. R. Bowker Co., 1966) and *World of Learning* (London: Europa Publications, 1967).
2.  Personal communication from G. W. Derwish, Director, Nuclear Research Centre, Baghdad, 16 September 1968.
3.  National Council for Research and Development, *Scientific Research in Israel,* (Tel Aviv: 1968).

# Appendix / Books in the National Libraries of the U.S.S.R., Latin America, Africa*

### U.S.S.R.

| Republic | Founded | Book Stock Size (Volumes) |
|---|---|---|
| Lenin Library (Moscow)[a] | 1862 | 25,000,000 |
| Armenian S.S.R. (Erevan) | 1921 | 5,000,000 |
| Azerbaijan S.S.R. (Baku) | n. d. | 2,184,116 |
| Belorussian S.S.R. (Minsk) | n. d. | 3,300,000 |
| Estonian S.S.R. (Tallin) | 1940 | 2,000,000 |
| Georgian S.S.R. (Tbilisi) | n. d. | 8,000,000 |
| Kazakh S.S.R. (Alma-Ata) | 1931 | 2,000,000 |
| Kirghiz S.S.R. (Frunze) | n. d. | 2,374,134 |
| Latvian S.S.R. (Riga) | n. d. | 3,214,000 |
| Lithuanian S.S.R. (Vilnius) | n. d. | 3,000,000 |
| Moldavian S.S.R. (Kishinev) | n. d. | 2,000,000 |
| Tajik S.S.R. (Dushanbe) | n. d. | 1,500,000 |
| Turkmen S.S.R. (Ashkhabad) | n. d. | 2,000,000 |
| Ukrainian S.S.R. (Kiev) | n. d. | 1,000,000 |
| Uzbek S.S.R. (Tashkent) | n. d. | 3,000,000 |

[a] The Lenin Library serves as the central library specializing in bibliographical and reference services for the entire nation.

* The dates and figures given in these tables are for the national libraries as defined in Part 4 of this book. In some countries the central public library, government archives, or some other similar institution has been designated to serve as the national library. Figures are from *The World of Learning, 1968–1969* (London: Europa Publishing Ltd., 1969).

## LATIN AMERICA

| Country | Founded | Book Stock Size (Volumes) |
|---|---|---|
| Argentinia (Buenos Aires) | 1810 | 682,794 |
| Bolivia (Sucre) | 1836 | 26,000 |
| Brazil (Rio de Janeiro) | 1810 | 2,000,000 |
| Chile (Santiago) | 1813 | 950,000 |
| Colombia (Bogotá) | 1939 | 350,000 |
| Costa Rica (San José) | 1888 | 175,000 |
| Cuba (Havana) | 1901 | 800,000 |
| Ecuador (Quito) | 1792 | 55,000 |
| El Salvador (San Salvador) | 1870 | 95,000 |
| Guatemala (Guatemala City) | 1879 | 75,000 |
| Haiti (Port-au-Prince) | 1940 | 19,000 |
| Honduras (Tegucigalpa) | 1880 | 55,000 |
| Mexico (Mexico City) | 1833 | 800,000 |
| Nicaragua (Managua) | 1882 | 70,000 |
| Panama (Panama City) | 1892 | 156,000 |
| Paraguay (Asunción) | 1869 | 44,000 |
| Peru (Lima) | 1821 | 500,000 |
| Uruguay (Montevideo) | 1816 | 500,000 |
| Venezuela (Caracas) | 1833 | 400,000 |

## AFRICA

| Country | Founded | Book Stock Size (Volumes) |
|---------|---------|---------------------------|
| Algeria (Algiers) | n. d. | 600,000 |
| Cameroon (Yaoundé) | n. d. | 10,000 |
| Dahomey (Porto Novo) | 1914 | 7,500 |
| Egypt (United Arab Republic) (Cairo) | 1870 | 1,000,000 |
| Ethiopia (Addis Ababa) | 1944 | 63,000 |
| Ghana (Accra) | 1950 | 400,000[a] |
| Guinea (Conakry) | 1960 | 10,000 |
| Liberia (Monrovia) | 1959 | 15,000[b] |
| Malawi (Zomba) | 1967 | No figures available |
| Malagasy Republic (Tananarive) | 1961 | 84,000 |
| Mali (Bamako) | 1913 | 5,000 |
| Morocco (Rabat) | 1920 | 200,000 |
| Nigeria (Lagos) | 1962 | 40,000 |
| Rhodesia (Salisbury) | 1936 | 60,000 |
| Sierra Leone (Freetown) | 1961 | 250,000[c] |
| Somali Republic (Mogadishu) | 1934 | 18,000 |
| South Africa (Pretoria) | 1887 | 551,000 |
| Togo (Lomé) | 1949 | 5,500 |
| Tunisia (Tunis) | 1883 | 500,000 |

[a] The Ghana Library Board.
[b] The National Public Library of Liberia.
[c] The Sierra Leone Library Board.

# *Index*

AASL-DAVI, 5. *See also* American Association of School Libraries.

Abstracts, presenting of, 264-266.

Academic library: automation in, 139-162. *See also* Library; Public Library; University library.

Accessions: number of, 6.

Accounting: computer in, 139.

Accra Central Library, 116.

Acquisitions, 6-10; automation and, 141-142, 156; in Latin American national libraries, 201-202; in West Africa university libraries, 129-130.

ACRL standards, 5.

Adams, Walter, 117.

Afghanistan: libraries and information centers in, 275-276.

Africa: libraries and number of volumes in (table), 293; national libraries and bibliographies in, 229-248. *See also* West Africa.

Africana: bibliographic work pertaining to, 245.

*African Abstracts*, 246.

*African Experience*, 247.

Ahmad, Zakiuddin, 289.

Ahmadu Bello University Library, 124, 127.

Ahmed, Jameelunnisa, 283.

ALA Intellectual Freedom Committee, 7.

ALA Library Education Division, 16.

ALA-NCATE, 16.

ALA Reference Service Division, 15.

*See also* American Library Association.

Albee, Edward F., 21.

Al-Chawaf, Husham, 278.

Alden Company, 153.

Alexandria, Egypt: special libraries and information centers in, 287.

Al-Husseir College of Agriculture Library, Jordan, 282.

Alisher Navoi State Library, Uzbek, S.S.R., 183.

Allen, James, 65.

Allen, Joan, 238.

All-Russian Conference in Adult Education, 174.

All-Union Book Chamber, Soviet Union, xii, 175, 179, 180, 184-186.

All-Unions Standards and Specifications Reference Library, 260.

Al-Solai, Mohamed, 284.

American Association of School Libraries, 5, 63, 70.

*American Documentation*, 15, 143.

American Library Association (ALA), 5, 7, 13-16, 127, 221, 232.

American School of Oriental Research Library, 278.

American University, Beirut, 282.

Ankara, Turkey: special libraries in, 285-286.

Anthropology, African, 245-246.

Arabian American Oil Company Central Technical Library, 284.